SINGAPORE

SINGAPORE

Irene Hoe

Photography by R. Ian Lloyd

Hong Kong

©The Guidebook Company Ltd 1991, 1989
Revised edition 1991

British Library Cataloguing-in-Publication Data
A catalogue record for this book is held by the British Library

Distribution in the UK, Ireland, Europe and certain Commonwealth countries by
Hodder & Stoughton, Mill Road, Dunton Green, Sevenoaks, Kent TN13 2YA

Grateful acknowledgement is made to the following authors and publishers for permissions
granted:

Curtis Brown Ltd for
Saint Jack © Paul Theroux 1973

Times Editions Ptd Ltd for
When Singapore was Syonan-to © N I Low

Editors: Peter Fredenburg, Ralph Kiggell and Robyn Fleming
Series Editor: Claire Banham
Illustrations Editors: Carolyn Watts and Caroline Robertson
Map Design: Bai Yiliang
Design: Unity Design Studio

Additional photography: Singapore Tourist Information Bureau, Hong Kong p.17

Production by Twin Age Limited, Hong Kong
Printed in Hong Kong by Sing Cheong Printing Co.

Contents

Introduction

Singapore has had many beginnings, but the date uppermost in local memory (and celebrated in the name of one upmarket eatery, Restaurant 1819) is January of that year, which saw the founding of modern Singapore by Englishman Stamford Raffles, who claimed the island as a trading settlement for the East India Company. Singapore's strategic location on the vital Straits of Malacca helped the city to become one of the world's busiest ports.

The rest may be history, but as historian Carl A. Trocki asserts in *Prince of Pirates*, his study of old Johor and Singapore between 1784 and 1885, 'No country's history is so well documented yet so poorly understood as that of a former colony.' Trocki adds that this is particularly true of Malaya, the historical name for the Malayan Peninsula and the islands of Singapore and Penang, where the world knows more about what the Europeans did or wanted to do than about what actually happened in the colonized region. The indigenous peoples and institutions of the day got short shrift, and Malaya's history itself became colonized, because the colonizers wrote the history.

Western scribes are still plentiful, and visitors should not be surprised to find many works of local history by foreigners — generally British — many of whom have chosen World War II and the Japanese occupation of Singapore as the subject of their published catharses. As the country operates increasingly in English, a natural tendency is to look to English or colonial roots. In fact, it is even more natural for Singaporeans, many of whom are the descendants of immigrants, not to look back at all, but to be consumed by the future, in which McDonald's, Macintosh and Matsushita already play a big part.

Make no mistake: despite the colour of its recent and ancient past, Singapore is a determinedly modern city, almost too modern for some. It is also a geographical and political curiosity, because, against all logic, it is a thriving nation of some 2.6 million where telephones, even public telephones, work, where most streets appear so squeaky clean as to invite — no, demand — comment, where the rubbish is collected promptly and mail delivered with equal dispatch (with some post offices operating every day of the year), and where it is possible to walk the streets free of fear at night.

Private real estate prices provoke raised eyebrows and usually prompt comparison with New York or London. Amazingly, however, some 90 percent of the population own their homes, an overwhelming number of which are affordable public housing apartments built during the 30 years since the city-state became self-governing. Another fact of Singaporean life that raises eyebrows is the durable Prime Minister Lee Kuan Yew, who headed the government from 1959 to November 1990 and now continues in the Cabinet as Senior Minister. On November 28th 1990, Goh Chok Tong became the new Prime Minister for Singapore.

History

Early Singapore

The old story goes that there were only 150 sea gypsies, known locally as *Orang Laut* (sea people), on the island when Raffles landed. In fact, the number and make-up of the population in January 1819 is not known exactly. Historian C M Turnbull, for example, estimates that the island could have had about a thousand inhabitants, mainly *Orang Laut*, but including as many as 20 or 30 Chinese settlers.

For documentary proof of a settled Singapore, we have to look to the 14th century. Temasek, the ancient name for Singapore, was given in Vietnamese historical annals of that time as *Sach-ma-tich*. The ancient settlement was also mentioned in a Javanese court poem, the *Nagarakretagama*, and in an eye-witness account by a Chinese trader, Wang Ta Yuan. Wang was none too complimentary. He wrote of 'Tan Ma-Hsi' as a land where piracy was a way of life and where the inhabitants lived off plunder from passing junks. He noted that the Chinese inhabitants of this barbaric place lived and dressed like the natives.

From the 17th century the *Malay Annals*, or *Sejarah Melayu*, offer a colourful account of Temasek's past, though where history ends and myth begins is hard to tell. The *Annals* tell how the emperor of China tricked the Indian warrior king, Raja Chulan, a descendant of Alexander the Great. Raja Chulan sought to conquer China and camped at Temasek on his way there. The Chinese emperor sent to Temasek a boat loaded with rusty needles and mature fruit trees and manned by a senile, toothless crew, who convinced Raja Chulan that they had set out from China as youths, when the needles were iron bars and the trees mere seeds. Believing China too far away, the would-be invader gave up his plan of conquest.

Many visited Singapore or knew of it through hearsay. In the 13th century, Marco Polo mentioned a *Chiamassie* that could have been Temasek. Much earlier, a third-century Chinese account makes mention of *P'u Luo Chung*, a transliteration of the Malay name Pulau Ujong, which means 'island at the end of the peninsula'. As early as the second century, Ptolemy recorded a place called *Sabara* in an area that matches Singapore's location.

Raffles himself had more than an inkling of the island's fascinating past. Some time before his expedition to look for a trading post, the founder of modern Singapore wrote to a friend, 'You must not be surprised if my next letter to you is dated from the site of the ancient city of Singapura.'

Raffles was spurred to found a trading station in the Malayan region because he was alarmed at the broad reach of Dutch influence in the area. When an exploratory expedition found the Karimon Islands unsuitable for development as a trading base, the fleet headed for Singapore.

There was no state as we know it for Raffles to negotiate with when he landed in Singapore. The sea lord or *temenggong*, Abdul Rahman, lived on the island, but the sultan held court at Lingga, south of Singapore. This sultan was recognized by the Dutch and implicitly by the English through an earlier treaty. This did not stop Raffles, who made a deal with the temenggong and installed a rival claimant to the throne, the sultan's elder brother Hussein. Raffles then signed an agreement with the temenggong and the newly created Sultan Hussein on 6 February 1819, under which the East India Company was allowed to set up a trading station at Singapore.

Life in the Colony

When Raffles first arrived, the island was so cloaked in jungle that there was only a small plot by the Singapore River where his party could camp. Raffles quickly raised the Union Jack, landed soldiers and set about making an encampment that could be defended. Then he left Singapore in the hands of his friend, Colonel William Farquhar, not returning until three years later to check on the progress of the island he had once called 'my almost only child'.

Business was good from the start, despite the protests of the Dutch, who called the British acquisition illegal. Raffles' enterprising new colony handled eight million Spanish dollars worth of trade in its first two and a half years, a period that saw nearly 3,000 ships calling at Singapore. By 1820, Farquhar was able to report that merchants were gathering so fast that they needed more ground for building.

Rats also gathered in the town, according to Abdullah bin Kadir, a linguist proficient in Arabic, Malay and Tamil who was at one time employed in Raffles' office. 'There were thousands of rats all over the district, some almost as large as cats. They were so big they used to attack us if we went out walking at night and many people were knocked over,' he wrote in his autobiographical account, *Hikayat Abdullah*, which provides much of the spice of our knowledge of the time. To get rid of the rats, Farquhar launched what has become a Singaporean tradition — a campaign. He offered a reward for each rat caught, a tactic that harvested thousands of rodents each morning and which Farquhar next employed against the centipedes plaguing the town.

None of these nuisances deterred immigration. The country's ethnic diversity was assured from the earliest days of the colony by an influx that included Arabs, Armenians, Indians and Europeans. By 1821, the population had grown to about 5,000, with many Chinese and Malay immigrants from Riau and Malacca — also Balinese, Bugis and Javanese who came to trade and find work and decided to settle and intermarry with the indigenous Malays. Five years after Raffles' arrival, island Malays made up some 60 percent of the population.

Indians were among the first migrants to the new settlement. A trader from

Penang, Naraina Pillay, actually arrived with Raffles, as did some 120 Indian soldiers. News of jobs in Singapore drew more migrants from Malaya, India and Ceylon (now Sri Lanka), who settled into business or took up administrative jobs at the new trading post.

Frontier territory that it was, Singapore earned a reputation for lawlessness. The sultan's and temenggong's men constantly quarrelled and fought with the Malays from Malacca. At sea, piracy grew apace with trade, and Temenggong Abdul Rahman, whose followers were suspected of being in league with the pirates, was forced to move out of Singapore town.

The temenggong looked on the arrival of the English as a chance to revive his own empire under their protection. Unhappily for him, his aspirations were not shared by the colonizers. He soon found that he needed more money, so in 1824 the treaty was rewritten. In effect, he signed away to the East India Company all rights to Singapore and islands within ten miles of its shores. He moved west to Telok Blangah, and a scant 16 months later he was dead.

Raffles had said his farewells to Singapore for the last time in 1823, and he died in 1826, the year Singapore became part of the Straits Settlements, together with the older settled areas of Penang and Malacca.

Only five years earlier, the first junk carrying *sin khek* or 'new men', as the migrants from China were called, had made landfall in Singapore, but by 1830 the Chinese were its largest community. They still are today. Chinatown flourished and developed quickly, but it was not till the 1870s that women arrived from southern China in significant numbers. A Manchu official, Li Chung Chu, spent a month in Singapore around that time and, according to *Chinatown: An Album of a Singapore Community*, published by the Archives and Oral History Department of Singapore, came away with these impressions:

> As far as prosperity is concerned, no area in Singapore can compare with 'Greater Town'. All the foreign firms [and] banks, [the] post office and [the] customs office are found along the seaside there. Although there are also bazaars in Lesser Town they are set up by the natives to sell local products and various foodstuffs. Not a single big market is found there. There is a place known as Kereta Ayer in 'Greater Town' where restaurants, theatres and brothels are concentrated. It is the most populated area where filth and dirt are hidden.

The coming of the steamship and the opening of the Suez Canal in the 1860s allowed Singapore to make the most of its strategic position and natural harbour. Chinese immigration to Singapore continued apace. Some of it was undoubtedly spurred by the success story of rubber, which began in Singapore and spread to Malaya. In 1912 as many as a quarter of a million Chinese arrived in Singapore. Trade ballooned. But even before the end of the 19th century, Singapore had put the older settlements of Penang and Malacca quite in the shade.

At War and After

The combat, air raids and general horror of World War II made less of an impression on the people of Singapore than the spectacle of the Western colonizer humbled by an Asian power and the Japanese occupation itself. Singapore fell on 15 February 1942, the eve of Chinese New Year, a surrender that Winston Churchill, Britain's wartime prime minister, called 'the worst disaster and the largest capitulation in British history'.

Rubbing salt into the wound, the Japanese conqueror, Tomoyuki Yamashita, who became known as the Tiger of Malaya, later acknowledged he had in fact pulled off a magnificent bluff and that British troops then on the island outnumbered the Japanese invading force three to one. For the next three and a half years, Singapore, dubbed by the Japanese *Syonan* or 'Light of the South', faced a reign of terror under the *Kempeitai*, or secret police, who tortured and killed many civilians and military personnel. Young people were taught Japanese in school and began their day singing the Japanese national anthem. Those traumatic years are among the most written about in Singapore's history, and photographs of the suffering endured by prisoners of war and civilians are still on permanent display in Singapore.

The Japanese surrendered to the Allied forces on 21 August 1945, and once again Britannia ruled. A British military administration was set up that year and ruled about seven months before Singapore became a separate Crown colony on 1 April 1946 under a British governor.

The governor worked with an advisory council, six of whose nine members were to be elected. Singapore held its first-ever full-scale election on 20 March 1948. Three more elected members were added in 1950. The candidates were largely English-educated professionals suffering no quarrel with life under the colonial yoke and therefore content with their token voice in government. Not so the Chinese-educated, though, who still felt the influence of China and were inclined towards union with Malaya; their sentiments were well exploited by the Communist Party of Malaya.

Singapore lurched towards independence by fits and starts. Changes wrought by a new constitution resulted in fresh elections in 1955 to choose a chief minister and the 32-member Legislative Assembly. The pro-British Progressive Party won a mere four seats, the Democratic Party, essentially a group of Chinese businessmen, secured two, and the Labour Front, with ten seats, supplied Singapore's first chief minister, David Marshall. Marshall, a brilliant criminal lawyer (and currently Singapore's ambassador to France), led a coalition government for over a year, resigning in June 1956 when the British would not agree to full internal self-government.

Eyes on the Horizon

I shall say nothing of the importance which I attach to the permanence of the position I have taken up at Singapore; it is a child of my own. But for my Malay studies I should hardly have known that such a place existed; not only the European but the Indian world also was ignorant of it. It is impossible to conceive a place combining more advantages; it is within a week's sail of China, still closer to Siam, Cochin-China, &c. in the very heart of the Archipelago, or as the Malays call it, "the Navel of the Malay countries"; already a population of above five thousand souls has collected under our flag, the number is daily increasing, the harbour, in every way superior, is filled with Shipping from all quarters; and although our Settlement has not been established more than four months every one is comfortably housed, provisions are in abundance, the Troops healthy, and every thing bears the appearance of content and abundance. I am sure you will wish me success, and I will therefore only add that if my plans are confirmed at home, it is my intention to make this my principal residence, and to devote the remaining years of my residence in the East to the advancement of a Colony which in every way in which it can be viewed bids fair to be one of the most important, and at the same time one of the least expensive and troublesome, that we possess. Our object is not territory but trade, a great commercial Emporium, and a fulcrum *whence we may extend our influence politically, as circumstances may hereafter require. By taking immediate possession we put a negative to the Dutch claim of exclusion, and at the same time revive the drooping confidence of our allies and friends; one Free Port in these Seas must eventually destroy the spell of Dutch monopoly; and what Malta is in the West, that may Singapore become in the East.*

Stamford Raffles (later Sir Stamford Raffles)
letter to Colonel Addenbrooke, *10 June 1819*

His deputy, Lim Yew Hock, then took over for the next three years. Lim's tenure was marked by violent communist-inspired riots. Massive arrests of communists and leftists all but destroyed front organizations of the Communist Party of Malaya, but they also branded Lim and his party anti-Chinese and ruined all hope of their re-election. Ironically, though Lim successfully negotiated the 1958 Constitutional Agreement under which the British agreed to self-government for Singapore, it was the People's Action Party (PAP) that won Singapore's first general election in May 1959, thus starting one of the longest winning streaks in modern political history.

Of the 51 who represented Singapore in its first fully elected·Legislative Assembly, 43 belonged to the PAP, which won more than 53 percent of the votes cast. Renamed the Singapore People's Alliance, the Labour Front, which had dominated government in the preceding four years, did abysmally, winning just four seats in this general election, though an independent candidate it supported did win his seat. Three other seats were won by an alliance of the United Malays National Organization (UMNO) and the Malayan Chinese Association (MCA).

The new government was sworn in on 5 June with Lee Kuan Yew as prime minister and Sir William Goode, the last British governor of colonial Singapore, as acting *yang di-pertuan negara* (head of state) until Yusof bin Ishak was installed at year's end.

The Treasury was bare and the party's victory, viewed as a triumph of the Left, had frightened investors away. They had to be wooed back to nurture the newly industrializing economy. Convinced that Singapore could not make it alone, Lee Kuan Yew advocated merger into a new Federation of Malaysia with Singapore's northern neighbour, Malaya, and the states of Brunei, Sabah and Sarawak to the east. The marriage came about in 1963, over the protests of Indonesia's President Sukarno and Philippines' President Macapagal — and without Brunei, which opted out at the eleventh hour.

Singapore on its Own

A new start came on 9 August 1965, when Singapore found itself suddenly single again, unceremoniously divorced from a turbulent two-year relationship so scarred by violent racial riots and dissension between the central government and Singapore leaders that Malaysian Prime Minister Tengku Abdul Rahman decided that separation was the only answer.

After advocating scant years earlier that Singapore had to be part of a larger entity to survive, its leaders now found they were arguing the reverse. It became necessary to assemble a military force through National Service (conscription of males over 17 for a two-year term), tackle severe unemployment and a continuing housing problem, and provide basic education for the whole population. Then the British dropped their bombshell, announcing in mid-1967 that they intended to pull back their forces from Singapore. Up to that time, the post-colonial military establishment had generated about 15 percent of a struggling economy and employed some 40,000 people, who would now have to be retrained for industrial jobs.

Economic success came quickly, even miraculously. In the first decade after independence, Singapore's gross national product (GNP) trebled to more than $6 billion. And by the 1970s, when the worst of the housing shortage had been overcome, when double-digit economic growth seemed almost inescapable and labour shortages had forced the import of workers from Malaysia, it was easy to think that prosperity had been inevitable from the word 'go'.

However, the tide turned suddenly in a brief but nonetheless severe recession in the mid-1980s. A calamitous and unprecedented downturn in the tourism industry left Tourist Row awash with empty luxury rooms. This problem has receded somewhat, but the collapse of the property market is taking longer to mend. Anticipating the stock crash of 1987 by nearly two years — though not providing any immunity from it — the local stock market, which is still tied to Malaysia's, took investors to the cleaners in 1985 and again in the wake of Wall Street's free-fall in 1987. The country now seems past the recession and is looking forward to a sustained period of prosperity. The new national target is to achieve for Singaporeans the standard of living enjoyed by the Swiss in the mid-1980s.

Since the turbulent '60s, political stability has been the rule, with the People's Action Party winning every seat in the 1968, 1972, 1976 and 1980 elections and conceding only four in 1991, when there was a significant swing to the opposition. (The PAP had already lost two seats in the 1984 election.) The party's clean sweep in four elections had in fact been helped by an opposition boycott of Parliament in the 1960s, which effectively shut the dozen or so opposition parties out of the chamber until 1981. Singapore's government is now largely in the hands of a younger generation of leaders, most of whom are technocrats in their 40s. Few veterans of Singapore's first Parliament in 1965—and still fewer pioneers of the 1959 Legislative Assembly—remain. Mr Lee Kuan Yew, Prime Minister for 32 years, and now Senior Minister, Prime Minister's Office without portfolio, remains an often awe-inspiring father figure approaching mythical proportions in the national consciousness. In or out of the Prime Minister's seat, he casts a long shadow over Singapore.

Geography

The main island of Singapore and some 57 islets lie at the foot of the Malayan Peninsula, about 137 kilometres (85 miles) north of the Equator. The diamond-shaped main island is 42 kilometres (26 miles) long and measures nearly 23 kilometres (14 miles) at its widest, making for a coastline of nearly 136 kilometres (85 miles) and a total area of just over 570 square kilometres (220 square miles). If one includes the offshore islands, the land area is nearly 622 square kilometres (240 square miles) and growing, due to extensive reclamation.

Geologically, Singapore divides into three areas. While most of the island is no more than 15 metres (50 feet) above sea level, the hilly centre is made up of igneous rock (like granite) and rises to its highest point at Bukit Timah, which is 163 metres (535 feet) high. Hills and valleys of sedimentary rock dominate the northwest, and the sandy, gravelly eastern region is much flatter in comparison.

Agriculture occupies a diminishing role in increasingly urban Singapore, and farmland currently occupies less than 40 square kilometres (15 square miles) of the land. Much of the lush tropical rainforest that almost completely covered Singapore 170 years ago is gone. Even the 2,000 hectares (5,000 acres) of forest managed by the Nature Reserves Board is chiefly secondary forest. Mangroves, which lined the coasts and tidal creeks when Raffles arrived, now cover only 15 square kilometres (six square miles) along stretches of the northern coast and parts of several offshore islands.

Botanically as well as demographically, Singapore is a nation of immigrants. So many foreign plants have been introduced to what the slogans like to call the Garden City that most people would be hard put to identify a native among the imports. Some 80 percent of the shade and ornamental plants here were imported, including the bougainvillea that line the roadway between the airport and the city.

Truly native plants can be found in the 75-hectare (185-acre) Bukit Timah Nature Reserve, one of the last remnants of tropical forest in Singapore. Some species are not found at all outside this special area. Tiger, wild boar and deer once roamed the forest. They have long since been killed off, but squirrel, civet cat, long-tailed macaque and other small mammals survive, along with reptiles like the water monitor (a type of lizard) and 40 types of snakes, hundreds of species of butterfly and a large variety of insects.

Here, nature has been forced to adapt to the concrete jungle. More than 300 square kilometres (115 square miles) of Singapore is built-up with concrete apartment blocks of massive public housing estates, office buildings, shopping centres and industrial parks. The government and its agencies are the largest landlords in the country. The Housing and Development Board plans, builds and oversees all public housing estates. Much of the city falls under the sway of the Urban Redevelopment Authority, and prime industrial land is largely under the control of the Jurong Town Corporation. All are statutory arms of the Ministry of National Development, which has played the largest role in shaping modern Singapore.

People

Singapore's population, estimated in 1988 at about 2.6 million, is more than three-quarters ethnic Chinese. Malays are the largest minority. Indians, a census group that also embraces Pakistanis, Bangladeshis and Sri Lankans, are the next largest, and other ethnic groups include Eurasians, Jews and people of European origin. This variety explains why Singapore has four official languages — Malay, English, Mandarin and Tamil.

Malay is the national language, though most business, including government business, is conducted in English. Mandarin, which all Chinese Singaporeans must study in school, is used increasingly, mainly because of a continuing 'Speak Mandarin' campaign. Tamil is the language of the south Indians, who represent the majority of the early Indian immigrants.

The various communities once lived, by design, separately in their own ethnic enclaves, but in recent years the concentrations of single ethnic groups have been deliberately dispersed by public housing policy. The over-whelming majority of people, 85 percent in 1987, own or rent apartments in ethnically balanced estates built by the Housing and Development Board.

Singapore, once touted as the shining example of third world population control, has been altogether too successful in this. The growth rate (one percent in 1986) has fallen below replacement level, and the old slogan, 'Two is enough' has given way to 'Have three or more, if you can afford it'. Most people work in manufacturing, commerce and services. Except during a recession in the mid-1980s, labour demand has been so heavy that local industries rely greatly on workers from Malaysia and now increasingly from Indonesia, Thailand, the Philippines and Sri Lanka.

Religion

Buddhism, Taoism, Islam, Christianity and Hinduism are Singapore's major religions. Smaller religious groups include Sikhs, Jews, Jains and Zoroastrians. The Constitution of the Republic of Singapore guarantees freedom of worship.

More than half of the people (56 percent of those over ten years old in the 1980 Census) profess to be Buddhists or Taoists. Virtually all Taoists, who practise ancestor worship and follow the teachings of Chinese sages (Confucius, Lao She, Mencius), are Chinese. Most Buddhists are also Chinese, and many actually practise a syncretic blend of Buddhism, Confucianism and Taoism, as shown by the wide variety of deities worshipped in Chinese temples. Many temples established by the earliest Chinese sojourners and settlers, like the Thian Hock Keng in Telok Ayer Street, still survive in modern Singapore.

Muslims are ethnically more diverse, though the overwhelming majority are Malays. Arab and Indian merchants are believed to have brought Islam to this part of the world; Muslims from south India built some of Singapore's earliest mosques, and still today many of Singapore's Muslims are Indian in origin. However, more than 1,000 are ethnic Chinese. The Muslim Religious Council of Singapore, the highest Islamic authority in the country, advises the government on Muslim affairs, coordinates the annual pilgrimage to Mecca and administers the mosque building programme, among other duties.

Christians are only two-thirds as numerous as Muslims but constitute a significant minority in the economic and political life of the country. Catholics and the Protestants founded many of the best schools in the country and thus exerted a great influence on the educated elite from the earliest times.

Though more than 80 percent are Chinese, the Christians are easily the most ethnically and linguistically diverse religious group in the country. The four largest Protestant groups are Anglican, Methodist, Brethren and Presbyterian, though the charismatic movement is gaining strength. Large-scale and big-budget Christian rallies and evangelical events are not unusual, though 'televangelism' has yet to make an appearance, if only because broadcasting is state controlled and determinedly secular.

With few exceptions Singapore Hindus are of Indian ethnic origin, mostly from south India. Early immigrants also built and rebuilt their temples here, and the oldest is the Sri Mariamman Temple on South Bridge Road in Chinatown. Many of the well-known temples were built by *chettiars*, or moneylenders. The Sri Thandayupathani Temple in Tank Road, which is the hub of many Hindu festivals, including the annual Thaipusam procession, is also known as the Chettiars' Temple. The Hindu Advisory Board advises the government on Hindu customs, religion and related concerns.

The Singapore Swing

Life has been good to Singapore in the 1980s. Its people enjoy the highest standard of living in Asia after Japan. Its per capita Gross National Product is more than $15,000 (about US$7,500). Some complain that, barring the brief recession in mid-decade (which sent the unemployment rate up to 6.5 percent for a time in 1986) times have been almost too good.

Employers bemoan choosy Singaporeans, who disdain workplaces without air-conditioning, and workers who hop from job to job without a qualm. At the same time, the working day at many offices and other workplaces stretches to such lengths that almost anyone would call those within workaholics.

This is a nation that is driven to excel, especially in its education system. Education is not compulsory, and registration for entry into schools taxes the

nerves of parents keen to place their child in the 'right' school. Many of those who can afford to do so hire tutors for their children to improve their chances of achieving eye-catching academic records. Increasingly, however, there are worries about the long-term effects of 'hot-housing' young people — worries that parallel fears that they will not be as hard-working as their forebears.

To many visitors, Singapore appears very Westernized. To experience the place in all its complexity, one must abandon air-conditioning and Orchard Road and be prepared to tour Chinatown, Little India and Geylang Serai at a walking pace. To understand it even better, it is helpful to meander through one of Singapore's ubiquitous housing estates and perhaps visit a family in their apartment. To delve a little into the national psyche, have a meal with Singaporeans. You can do this quite simply by visiting a food centre at supper time.

A night spent watching one of three local television channels (5, 8 and 12) can be instructive and sometimes entertaining. Why watch TV? Because most of Singapore switches on too. More than half a million licences for TV sets were issued in 1986, or roughly one for every five people. Many of the programmes are American or British imports, but a growing number are locally produced, the most popular being Mandarin soap operas with local themes, some of which are dubbed into English and rerun.

Here as anywhere, TV and video have nurtured many a couch potato, but Singaporeans are also becoming increasingly fitness conscious. This is as much a result of compulsory military service for men as of a long-standing 'Sports for All' policy pushed chiefly by the Singapore Sports Council, which manages the National Stadium, athletic centres, sports fields, sports halls, swimming pools, fitness parks and courts for netball, squash, tennis and badminton, among other facilities. The ultra-fit punish themselves in the Singapore Marathon and, since 1988, a triathlon.

Ruling Singapore

Singapore is a parliamentary republic with a president as head of state and a prime minister as head of government. Though one parliament may serve a maximum of five years, it has been the custom to hold a general election every four years, usually in December. Parliament elects the president every four years, and the president appoints the prime minister, the member of Parliament who has the confidence of the parliamentary majority. The prime minister and the Cabinet are responsible to Parliament.

Under the Constitution, Parliament is the supreme legislative body, its members elected by secret ballot. Its numbers have grown steadily, rising to 81 seats in the 1991 election.

Until the 1988 election, all constituencies were held by single members, but now there are 13 Group Representation Constituencies, or GRCs, each a cluster of three electoral districts. In GRCs, political candidates stand for election in teams of three. One of the three candidates in a GRC must be non-Chinese. The aim is to ensure that minority groups do not go unrepresented, as can happen easily in a first-past-the-post election, which tends to favour the majority ethnic group, the Chinese. Voting is compulsory and ballot papers are numbered to prevent fraud.

Singapore had 21 political parties in 1992, but only one, the People's Action Party (PAP), has governed since 1959. The only opposition parties to make a dent in PAP's armour in recent times have been the Worker's Party and the Singapore Democratic Party, although the PAP still controlled 77 of the 81 seats in the 1991 Parliament.

Since the mid-1970s, the government has presided over a transition from the first-generation politicians led by former Prime Minister Lee Kuan Yew, who fought for the country's independence, to a second generation of technocrats led by current Prime Minister Goh Chok Tong, formerly a civil servant and head of the national shipping line.

Brigadier-General Lee Hsien Loong, son of Lee Kuan Yew, is now one of two Deputy Prime Ministers. The Brigadier-General or "BG" as he is known, entered Parliament in 1984 and was Minister for Trade and Industry and Second Minister for Defence when he was named Deputy Prime Minister.

Art and Culture — Mixing Bowl and Melting Pot

The arts scene in Singapore is unusual in that, until the mid-1980s, most of its performing groups were amateur. The national cultural diary consisted chiefly of performances by visiting professionals and local amateur groups, the latter sustaining a lively vernacular theatre in the four major languages. The only major groups of full-time professional performers were the People's Association Chinese Orchestra and the Singapore Symphony Orchestra. The SSO, as locals call it, was formed in 1979 under government auspices and includes a large number of foreign musicians, though its musical director, Choo Huey, is Singaporean.

In the 1980s, two English-language professional theatre companies were established. Act 3 has made a name for itself in children's theatre, while TheatreWorks produces a mix of plays by foreign and Singaporean playwrights. More recently a third drama group, Practice Theatre Ensemble, which performs primarily in Mandarin, has gone semi-professional. Then, in 1988, Singapore Dance Theatre, the country's first full-time professional dance company, gave its debut performance during the biennial Festival of Arts, and in the same year TheatreWorks presented the country's first musical. The principal event of the cultural diary, the Festival of Arts, is organized by the Ministry of Community Development.

The label 'cultural desert' — often applied to Singapore in the past — is now rarely used in the present tense. The ministry's Cultural Affairs Division, which has a finger in virtually every artistic pie in the country, has been going flat out in the latter half of the 1980s.

To nurture professionalism in the performing arts, the ministry, which directly or indirectly controls the principal performance venues, offers their use rent-free to established performing groups. A major condition is that performing companies must stage at least four productions a year, of which two must be new productions, preferably of Singaporean works.

All this does not mean that the earlier cultural scene was lifeless, only that few people, if any, had attempted to make a full-time living in the arts other than as teachers. At grassroots level, a large network of community centres has long supported a host of performing groups, such as Singapore's well-know lion and dragon dancers, as have clan associations and pugilistic groups. Also, the National Dance Company has been in existence for years, but most of its erstwhile members are employed full-time elsewhere.

In the past, those who chose to make a career in the performing arts generally trained overseas, returning to Singapore only for an occasional performance. This is still generally true, though two schools of fine art provide an avenue for would-be artists.

Practitioners of the visual arts have been able to find a supportive clientèle in corporations and private collectors, and have also enjoyed a higher profile overseas. Spurred in part by more visible and vocal government support for the visual arts, a new generation of young full-time artists is emerging.

The works of the better-known Singaporean artists are displayed in the permanent collection of the National Museum Art Gallery. Some names to look for are Cheong Soo Pieng, Lee Man Fong, Georgette Chen, Liu Kang, Tan Swie Hian, Thomas Yeo, Eng Tow and Lin Hsin Hsin. Art students and others exhibit their work for sale on the Orchard Mall on the first Sunday of the month.

Important venues for theatre and dance are the Drama Centre, Victoria Theatre, World Trade Centre, the Substation and Fort Canning where the Singapore Dance Theatre and TheatreWorks, both professional performing arts groups, are based. Musical performances usually take place at the Victoria Concert Hall, home of the symphony orchestra, and the Singapore Conference Hall. Chinese opera is generally performed at the Victoria Theatre, Kallang Theatre or Kreta Ayer People's Theatre. Touring troupes also perform in the street during festivals, especially in the seventh lunar month, which falls around August. The Singapore Indoor Stadium is a popular venue for large, scale events.

Tickets for most events can be bought at the Victoria Theatre, Tangs and Centrepoint. Previews and reviews are carried daily in Section Two of the national daily, *The Straits Times,* and in its weekly city supplement, *Timeszone Central*, which appears on Thursday.

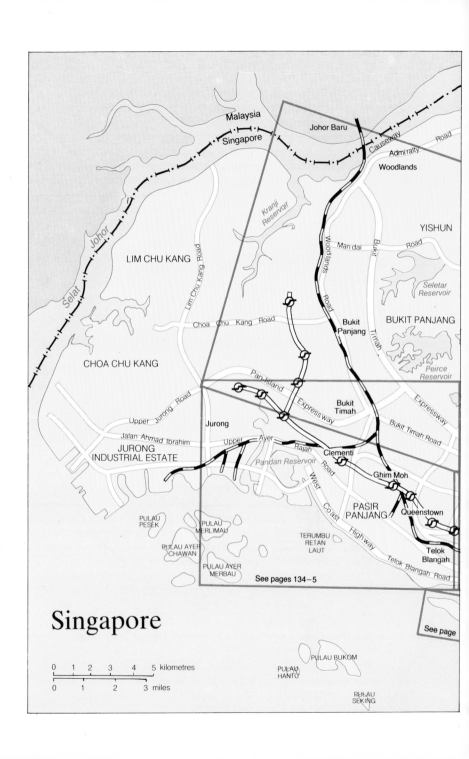

Malaysia

Johor Baru

Singapore

Causeway

Admiralty Road

Woodlands

YISHUN

Johor

Selat

Kranji Reservoir

LIM CHU KANG

Mandai

Bukit

Seletar Reservoir

Woodlands Road

Road

Lim Chu Kang Road

Choa Chu Kang Road

BUKIT PANJANG

Bukit Panjang

Bukit Timah

Peirce Reservoir

CHOA CHU KANG

Pan-Island

Upper Jurong Road

Expressway

Bukit Timah

Expressway

Jurong

Bukit Timah Road

Jalan Ahmad Ibrahim

Upper Ayer

Clementi

Rajah

JURONG INDUSTRIAL ESTATE

Pandan Reservoir

Road

Ghim Moh

West

Queenstown

PULAU PESEK

PULAU MERLIMAU

TERUMBU RETAN LAUT

PASIR PANJANG

RULAU AYER CHAWAN

Coast

Highway

Telok Blangah

PULAU AYER MERBAU

See pages 134–5

Telok Blangah Road

See page

Singapore

0 1 2 3 4 5 kilometres

0 1 2 3 miles

PULAU BUKOM

PULAU HANTU

PULAU SEKING

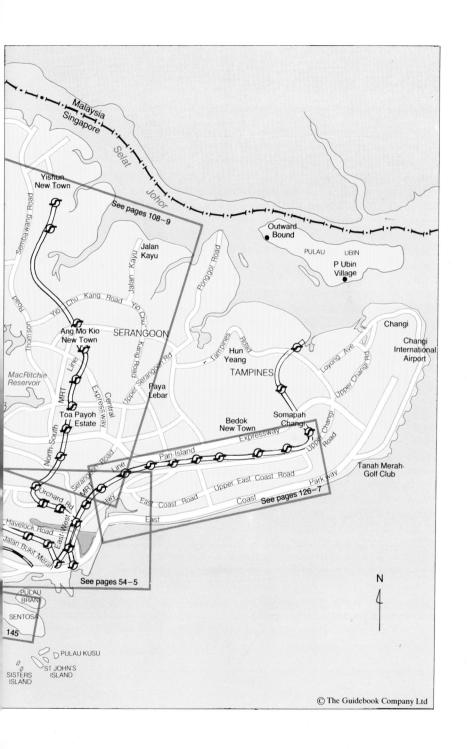

Malaysia
Singapore

Selat Johor

Yishun
New Town

See pages 108-9

Sembawang Road

Jalan
Kayu

Ponggol Road

Outward
Bound

PULAU   UBIN

P Ubin
Village

Yio Chu Kang Road

Jalan Kayu

Yio Chu Kang Road

Thomson Road

Ang Mo Kio
New Town

SERANGOON

Upper Serangoon Rd

Tampines Road

Hun
Yeang

TAMPINES

Changi

Changi
International
Airport

Loyong Ave

Upper Changi Rd

MacRitchie
Reservoir

MRT

Line

North-South

Central Expressway

Paya
Lebar

Toa Payoh
Estate

Bedok
New Town

Expressway

Somapah
Changi

Upper Changi Road

Tanah Merah
Golf Club

Pan-Island

Line

MRT

Orchard Rd

Serangoon Road

Ewy

Upper East Coast Road

Park way

See pages 126-7

East Coast Road

East Coast Road

Coast

Havelock Road

East-West

East

Jalan Bukit Merah

See pages 54-5

N

PULAU
BRANI

SENTOSA

145

PULAU KUSU

SISTERS
ISLAND

ST JOHN'S
ISLAND

© The Guidebook Company Ltd

Facts for the Traveller

Getting There

By air Singapore's Changi Airport is linked to 91 cities in 51 countries by 47 international airlines. Together they offer 620 services a week to and from Singapore. Direct non-stop flights from Asian cities are the rule. There are also direct flights from the West Coast of the United States and from the major cities of Europe and Australia. Singapore Airlines, the flag carrier, serves 55 cities in 36 countries, including China, France, Japan and the United States. Approximate flying times to selected destinations are as follows: Hong Kong 3.30, Perth 4.30, Tokyo 6.30, Sydney 7.30, London, Paris, Frankfurt or Zurich 15.00, San Francisco 17.00, and Chicago or New York 23.00.

By sea Singapore is a regular port of call for cruise liners, including the cream of the Cunard, Holland-America and Royal Viking fleets. Some liners berth conveniently at the World Trade Centre, from which it is quite easy to get around. Cruise-fly alternatives are popular on Asia-Pacific packages, which usually take in destinations like Bali, Bangkok, Hong Kong, Jakarta and Manila, and provide quicker and less expensive itineraries on round-the-world routes.

By road The causeway linking West Malaysia and Singapore is a popular gateway in both directions. Malaysian trunk roads are generally good and adequately mapped, though drivers must contend with a disconcerting number of trucks and logging trailers. Road works may make for unexpected detours, often with little warning. But if you are game to explore the peninsula, it is easy to hire a car from Penang or Kuala Lumpur, the two most common entry points in Malaysia, and head south for Singapore.

It is probably easier to take in the scenery by sharing a taxi to Singapore or taking the bus. There are express services from Kuala Lumpur (7–8 hours), Kuantan (7–8 hours), Malacca (5 hours), Penang (14 hours) and other towns.

By rail The train from Bangkok to Singapore traverses Malaysia by way of Butterworth (near Penang) and Kuala Lumpur. Expect to spend two days travelling if you board the train in Bangkok. The express takes about seven hours from Kuala Lumpur and about double that from Penang.

Rail travel is cheap, but be warned that the toilets in second- and third-class cars can be enough to put off the most devout fan of train travel. The excellent air-conditioned sleeperette cars are good value if you can secure a seat. All trains go to Tanjong Pagar Railway Station, just outside Singapore's Central Business District.

Visas

Most visitors do not need visas for stays as long as two weeks if they have onward or return tickets as well as sufficient funds for their stay. However, entry visas are required of citizens of Afghanistan, Cambodia, India, Laos, the People's Republic of China, the Soviet Union and Vietnam. Those travelling on Hong Kong Certificates of Identity, or refugee travel papers such as the Document Voyage Pour les Refugies Palestinian, also must have entry visas.

Customs

Singapore is a virtual free port, but cigarettes and other tobacco products, alcoholic beverages, furniture and clothing are dutiable. Visitors may bring in duty-free a reasonable amount of personal effects and up to $50 worth of prepared foods such as biscuits, cakes or chocolates for their own consumption.

Visitors over 18 years old and entering Singapore from any country other than Malaysia may also bring in one litre of wine or port and one litre of hard liquor. From 1 January 1991, Singapore ceased to allow visitors to bring in duty-free cigarettes.

Magazines such as *Playboy* and *Penthouse* are considered pornography and can be confiscated. Import permits are needed for all arms, including ornamental knives and ceremonial swords. The same goes for videotapes and films, which have to be passed by the Board of Film Censors. Visitors without import permits are required to hand such items to Customs on entry, and they may be collected on departure.

The death sentence is mandatory for anyone convicted of trafficking in or transporting into or out of Singapore more than 15 grams (half an ounce) of heroin or more than 30 grams (an ounce) of morphine. This is strictly enforced and there are stringent checks at all entry points.

Health

Visitors must be vaccinated against yellow fever if they come from or have within the preceding six days passed through any infected country. Malaria is not common here, but recently there have been cases of dengue haemorrhagic fever, which is mosquito-borne like malaria and can be fatal. A gamma globulin inoculation (against hepatitis A) is recommended. A cholera vaccination is unnecessary. As health regulations can change, you should check before departure with any Singapore Tourist Promotion Board office or Republic of Singapore embassy or consul, or your travel agent.

It is quite safe to drink water from the tap. If you come from a temperate climate, you should drink more fluids than usual, as you will find yourself

Survival of the Fittest

A t that time there were few animals, wild or tame on the Island of Singapore, except rats. There were thousands of rats all over the district, some almost as large as cats. They were so big that they used to attack us if we went out walking at night and many people were knocked over. In the house where I was living we used to keep a cat. One night at about midnight we heard the cat mewing, and my friend went out carrying a light to see why the cat was making such a noise. He saw six or seven rats crowding round and biting the cat; some bit its ears, some its paws, some its nose so that it could no longer move but only utter cry after cry. When my companion saw what was happening he shouted to me and I ran out at the back to have a look. Six or seven men came pressing round to watch but did nothing to release the cat, which only cried the louder at the sight of so many men, like a person beseeching help. Then someone fetched a stick and struck at the rats, killing the two which were biting the cat's ears. Its ears freed, the cat then pounced on another rat and killed it.

This was the state of affairs in all the houses, which were full of rats. They could hardly be kept under control, and the time had come when they took notice of people. Colonel Farquhar's place was also in the same state and he made an order saying 'To anyone who kills a rat I will give one wang'. When people heard of this they devised all manner of instruments for killing rats. Some made spring-traps, some pincer-traps, some cage-traps, some traps with running nooses, some traps with closing doors, others laid poison or put down lime. Some searched for rat-holes, some speared the rats or killed them in various other ways. Every day crowds of people brought the dead bodies to Colonel Farquhar's place, some having fifty or sixty, others only six or seven. At first the rats brought in every morning were counted almost in thousands, and Colonel Farquhar paid out according to his promise. After six or seven days a multitude of rats were still to be seen, and he promised five duit for each rat caught. They were still brought in in thousands and Colonel Farquhar ordered a very deep trench to be dug and the dead bodies to be buried. So the numbers began to dwindle, until people were bringing in only some ten or twenty a day. Finally the uproar and the campaign against the rats in Singapore came to an end, the infestation having completely subsided.

The Autobiography of Abdullah bin Kadir *(1797-1854)*

sweating it off in the heat. At the beach or on the water especially, it is wise to keep fairly well covered up till about mid-afternoon.

Money

The Singapore dollar is one of Asia's more stable currencies. Over the years, it has steadily appreciated against sterling and the US dollar. In the 1960s, the exchange rate held at about US$1 to $3 and one pound sterling to $8.50. It has since risen to about US$1 to $1.70, one pound sterling to $3.30, Australian $1 to $1.40, and 100 Japanese yen is equivalent to about $1.30. Unless otherwise stated all prices in this book are given in Singapore dollars. Local shops are required to give prices in Singapore dollars.

Banknote denominations in circulation are 1, 5, 10, 50, 100, 500, 1,000 and 10,000. Coin values are 5, 10, 20 and 50 cents and $1, with 1 cent coins rarely seen except in some supermarkets. Silver and gold coins in higher denominations are minted for collectors.

Brunei has the only currency completely interchangeable with Singapore's. The Malaysian currency, the ringgit, used to be interchangeable, but it has dropped in value and you should not accept it in change.

Foreign and local currency may be brought in and out of Singapore freely. Bureaux de change are open at the airport whenever there are flights arriving or departing, and rates are fair though perhaps marginally lower than you might get in the city.

Travellers cheques are widely accepted in hotels and stores, even in fairly small shops. You should have your passport handy when presenting a travellers cheque. It is more advantageous to cash them at a bank or money changer where, for most currencies, travellers cheques secure a better rate than hard cash. You will generally get a better rate at a money changer in Orchard Road because of the proliferation of money changers' booths there. Some banks may impose a small charge if you wish to cash the cheque in the same currency in which it is made out.

Major international credit cards are generally accepted in Singapore, but some shops may refuse credit on sale items or impose a surcharge, and cash will almost always secure you a better price in shops other than department stores.

Banks are normally open for business 10 am – 3 pm Monday to Friday and 9.30 – 11.30 am Saturday. DBS Bank is open until 3 pm on Saturday at the following branches: Bukit Timah, Katong, Orchard, Thomson and Toa Payoh. Some banks may refuse or limit foreign currency transactions on Saturday.

Where to Stay

In 1987, there were more than 24,000 hotel rooms in 60 gazetted hotels and nearly 90 non-gazetted establishments.

A high percentage boasts five stars, though you will find all grades of room available, from spartan accommodations without a private bathroom to plush suites with several bathrooms (see page 208 for listing). Many of the top hotels have executive floors for business travellers which offer breakfast, high tea, valet services and personalized stationery, among other comforts, as part of the service. For travellers not on a liberal expense account, it pays to shop around, and a few telephone calls from the airport can yield dividends.

Getting Around

By bus This is the cheapest way to sightsee and a good way to rub shoulders with the locals. The first buses start running from about 6 am and the last sets off around 11.30 pm. Generally, fares start at 50 cents.

You need exact change for most buses, so visitors may be better off buying one-day ($5) or three-day ($12) **Singapore Explorer bus tickets**, which allow unlimited travel anywhere on either service. A bus map showing stops and major points of interest comes with the ticket. Signboards listing nearby attractions are located at bus stops along six special routes — Historic Singapore, the Chinese Touch, the Temple Route, the Food Trail, the Flora and Fauna Route and Island of Contrasts — designed for exploring on your own.

The Singapore Bus Service produces a pocket-sized guide to its own routes, which is usually available from newsagents and bookshops. Be warned that parts of the guide get outdated fairly quickly because of rapid changes in transportation patterns and that it is wise to check it against the bus stop 'flags' that list bus numbers and route information at each city stop. Don't hesitate to ask around.

By Taxi All of Singapore's 11,500 or so taxis are metered and can carry up to four passengers. The largest fleet belongs to the taxi cooperative Comfort (light and dark blue livery). Other taxi companies are Singapore Commuter (all yellow livery), SABS (green, cream and yellow), and SBS (white and red, white top). The black and yellow taxis (also called yellow tops) are independent operators. Most taxis are air-conditioned, indicated by a blue 'Taxi' sign on the roof. At night, you can spot an empty taxi by the lighted sign on its roof—but this does not necessarily mean he will stop for you!

Within the city area, taxis are required to stop at marked taxi stops, but experience shows that they will stop almost anywhere — even right in front of a 'No Stopping' sign. On the streets, it is generally every man for himself, so visitors may find it less stressful to wait at a hotel entrance or at a marked taxi stop.

Local taxis are affordable. Flag-fall is $2.20 for the first 1.5 kilometres (almost a mile) plus ten cents every 250 metres for the first 5 kilometres (3 miles) and ten cents for every 225 metres thereafter. Every 45 seconds of waiting time is ten cents. While most taxi drivers speak some English, they may not always understand your instructions. Because of the proliferation of new buildings, residential areas and the rapid creation of and changes to roads in Singapore, even locals can have trouble figuring out what is where.

On the other hand, some taxi drivers are so adept at finding their way around that they also offer to double (illegally) as tourist guides. Free maps are available from most hotels. If you are planning an extended stay and intend to visit outlying areas, you may want to buy a street directory.

Make sure the meter is flagged down only after you get into the taxi and ensure before starting off that the driver knows your destination as exactly as possible. If not, he could zoom off, only to turn around minutes later to ask you to point him in the right direction. Tipping is not customary, so you need pay only the amount on the meter, provided none of the following applies:

— Between 12 midnight and 6 am, there is a 50 percent surcharge on the metered fare.

— If you board the taxi at Singapore Changi Airport, a $3 surcharge is payable. (There is no surcharge on taxi rides *to* the airport.) With the surcharge, your taxi fare from Changi to the Orchard Road area should come to about $20.

— If you order a taxi by telephone, you pay $1 above the metered fare. If the taxi is booked at least half an hour in advance, you pay $3 above the metered fare.

— Passengers pay a $1 surcharge on all trips leaving the Central Business District at peak times, which are between 4 and 7 pm weekdays and between noon and 3 pm Saturdays. There is no surcharge on Sunday.

— If the taxi has to enter the Central Business District between 7.30 and 10.15 am Monday to Saturday and 4.40 and 6.30 pm Monday to Friday, the passenger must buy an area licence for $5 at kiosks just outside the restricted zone. There is no extra charge if the taxi is already displaying an area licence or if it is hailed within the CBD.

Round the clock, radio-taxis may be ordered from these kiosks:
Singapore Radio Taxi Service: 466–9809, 468–6188, 468–6189
Clementi Taxi Service: 467–2363, 466–8386
Singapore Commuter: 474–7707
Comfort: 452–5555

If you have complaints or commendations about the taxi service, please send them with the taxi number, time and date of the incident to the Registrar of Vehicles, Sin Ming Drive, Singapore 2057 or to the Singapore Tourist Promotion Board, Raffles City Tower, 36-04, 250 North Bridge Road, Singapore 0617.

By MRT Though it was launched late in 1987, the MRT has already become a habit, especially for Singaporeans living near its suburban stops. Those who work or shop in the city area find it convenient for commuting from point to point within the city, especially in rain or at peak times, when taxis are scarce and buses crowded.

The minimum fare is 60 cents. Train tickets may be bought for a single trip, but you can avoid having to queue up at ticket machines each time — which can be a real nuisance during peak travel times — by purchasing a stored-value ticket (blue) for $10 from the booth. Concession stored-value tickets (red) are available for children. Senior citizens enjoy concessionary off-peak travel (orange tickets). Stored-value tickets are valid for four months.

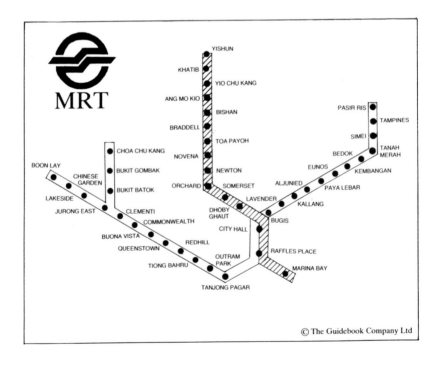

© The Guidebook Company Ltd

MRT

The newest ticket to ride is the MRT, which almost everybody, whatever language he speaks, refers to as 'Em Ar Tee'. It is an expensive ticket that will cost the country some $5 billion, which is the amount of capital the government has sunk into the country's largest single development project to date.

MRT, which stands for Mass Rapid Transit, was launched on 7 November 1987 with a north–south line. By 12 December the line had been extended to Orchard Road and other stations, a boon to retailers already enjoying the annual Christmas shopping frenzy. Part of the western arm of the second line, which runs east–west, opened early 1988.

The 67-kilometre (42-mile) network, which looks on the map like a distorted 'W', now has 42 stations—the majority of them elevated—and an ambitious expansion programme is scheduled. Transport officials believe the system will be carrying 800,000 passengers per day by the year 2000.

The MRT's 15 stations in the city are undergound, and some of them have been reinforced to double as bomb shelters. No bureaucratic whimsy this; the country's Civil Defence Force has already run much-publicized disaster drills in some stations. With surfaces of granite and polished stainless steel, however, the stations are far from the grim, grey bomb shelters of the popular imagination.

Some of the city stations are showcases from Singaporean art, with the lion's share of commissioned pieces going to the Orchard Station. There, a mosaic mural depicting Singapore's sightseeing attractions and a curved wall of enamel make popular backdrops for photographic souvenirs. Some of the art is frightfully pretty, but some of it is pretty frightful.

In the MRT's first months of operation, the novelty of Singapore's subway attracted hordes of eager commuters. They included Malaysian visitors, students on holiday and whole families who would ride the trains for hours, getting off frequently to admire station interiors and making a thorough picnic of it all. Now there is a time limit on the tickets, and those who dally beyond it can face a fine.

Though the companies that run the MRT and the bus services are separate corporate entities, the Transitlink Farecard common stored value ticket allows commuters to use just one ticket for both.

About 40 percent of Singapore's business and industrial areas are located near MRT lines, and about one in three Singaporeans live within walking distance of a station. The question is: will they walk?

From Monday to Saturday the first trains start running between 6 and 6.40
am, the last between 11 pm and midnight. Last trains arrive at depots at 12.15
am. On Sundays and public holidays, the first trains are between 6.45 and
7.25 am and the last between 10.45 and 11.45 pm, arriving at depots at
midnight.

Trains run at three- to six-minute intervals at peak periods, which are 7.30
– 9 am and 5 – 6.30 pm (Monday to Friday). On Saturday, the second peak is
between noon and 2 pm. Off peak, they are scheduled to run at intervals of
five to eight minutes. However, Friday and Saturday nights are natural peaks
(without the trains to match) and a wait of 15 to 20 minutes is not unheard of.
At such times, crowding makes nonsense of the air-conditioning, so it is
every bit as warm and muggy underground as above, and you might be better
off walking.

By hired car Chauffeur-driven limousines or self-drive hire cars are
easily rented, but public transport is so well developed there is really no need
to drive yourself unless you want to. The rule in Singapore is right-hand drive
cars, though you will occasionally see a left-hand drive vehicle. Avis,
Budget, Hertz, National and Thrifty are all represented here, along with a
host of local rental companies. Check under 'Motorcar Renting and Leasing'
in the Yellow Pages of the Singapore Telephone Book.

If you plan to drive yourself, technically you need a valid international

driving licence, though a valid driver's licence issued in your home country will usually suffice. You should remember that Singapore drives on the left-hand side of the road and gives way to traffic on the right at a circus or roundabout intersection. On divided roads, U-turns can be made only where there is a U-turn sign. The speed limit is 50 kilometres (30 miles) per hour on all roads except where indicated with a sign with the maximum shown in a circle. On expressways, the maximum speed rises to 80 kilometres (50 miles) per hour.

A unique feature of driving in Singapore is the Area Licensing Scheme (ALS), which was implemented in June 1975 to minimize jams in the city at peak hours. Under the ALS, motor cars and taxis carrying fewer than four persons (including the driver) cannot enter the Central Business District between 7.30 am and 10.15 am, Monday to Saturday and 4.30 am and 6.30 pm Monday to Friday, without an area licence displayed on the windscreen. This costs $6 a day for company-registered cars and $3 for other vehicles. Hefty fines await transgressors. The ALS is suspended on Sundays and public holidays.

Another good reason not to drive yourself is Singapore's coupon parking system, which is of such Byzantine complexity that it trips up even the locals. For street parking, you need to buy coupons, at the time of writing 80 cents and up. The appropriate numbers (year, month, day, hour, minute) must be torn out and the coupons displayed prominently. Simple enough. The difficulty especially for a visitor, lies in knowing how the system operates from area to area. In some places, the 80-cent coupon will give you an hour of parking — in others, only a half hour. If you overstay, or forget to use a coupon, you pay a fine. In some areas parking is free after 5 pm, in others after 10 pm, and in public housing estates all day Sunday. Moreover, some lots are only for those with season parking permits.

Getting to and from Changi Airport

The easiest way to the city is by taxi. Again, a $3 surcharge applies for trips originating from the airport, and the fare will be in the region of $20 (inclusive of the surcharge) if you are going to Orchard Road. The taxi queue is right outside the Passenger Terminal Building, on the same floor as the arrival hall.

If you are backpacking or carrying very little luggage, the bus is a cheap alternative from Changi to the city or vice versa. For 90 cents, you can ride all the way to the Orchard Road area. Look for the Number 390 bus queue on the lowest level of the Passenger Terminal Building. It should take about 50 minutes or more if the bus driver is keeping within the speed limit (some actually do), but usually the bus positively flies.

There is no airport limousine service, nor is there a city air terminal. In off-peak traffic the airport is seldom more than half an hour away from most parts of Singapore, and the East Coast Parkway, which leads directly from the city to the airport, is a relatively easy ride. However there are occasions when some roads may be completely or partly closed. Most of Orchard Road is closed for several hours on the morning of the Chingay Parade, Christmas Eve, New Year's Eve and some Sundays. Traffic may also be held up when the Singapore Marathon is run or on National Day (9 August), when some roads are closed.

For departing passengers, clearing Customs and Immigration is even more of a breeze than arriving. All baggage must be security-checked and tagged before it will be accepted for check-in. This is generally efficient even at peak periods. Hand-luggage is X-rayed at the departure gate. Though the machines are said to be film safe, it is advisable to use a leadlined bag to protect your film.

There is a departure tax of $5 for passengers headed for Malaysia or Brunei. For all other departures, the tax is $12, payable only in Singapore dollars.

Shopping does not have to stop just because you are leaving. Changi's duty-free emporium offers fairly competitive prices for perfumes (which are duty-free in Singapore in any event), cigarettes and cigars. Prices at shops selling watches, camera equipment, electronics and other goods are much the same as those elsewhere in Singapore. A popular buy here are chocolates shaped like the Merlion, Singapore's tourism emblem.

What to Pack

Pack light summer wear at all times of the year, since the temperature rarely varies from 28°C (82°F). Because of the heat, dressing is a fairly relaxed affair in Singapore, with the accent on comfort. Some restaurants draw the line at shorts and slippers, though, and most discos insist that their 'smart casual' dress code does not include blue jeans and tee-shirts. Some require a jacket and tie for men for dinner. If you expect to be invited to a country club, you may need to dress up. But even if you left the lot at home (or the airline lost it), virtually anything can be bought in Singapore. And a custom-made suit or dress can be run up in a day. Avoid wearing shorts, short skirts or sleeveless tops to mosques and temples.

Though the temperature seldom drops below 25°C (77°F), do bring a jacket, shawl or sweater. Aggressive air-conditioning in some hotels makes for quite a wintry atmosphere, especially at night, and the constant toing and froing between hot and freezing encourages chills.

Natural fibres such as linen, cotton or silk are the most comfortable to wear in Singapore, where it is quite humid even during the drier months from

May to July. Most hotels offer same-day laundry services. There are some inexpensive laundry shops on Orchard Road, though even this can be a rather expensive alternative to a wash-and-wear travel wardrobe.

If you come from a temperate climate, you may find that shoes which were comfortable at home become tight in Singapore. You should have at least one pair of comfortable and fairly loose walking shoes. Outdoors in the day, a hat and sunglasses are advisable. In rainier months, an umbrella comes in handy, but this can be bought locally for as little as $5.

Pharmacies in Singapore are well stocked and generally able to fill any prescription, but it is still simpler to bring a full supply.

Some hotels have 110-volt outlets for shavers in the bathrooms, but the standard voltage in Singapore is 230–250 volts AC. Dual-voltage appliances like hair dryers are handy. Most hotel housekeepers have transformers and adaptors (the three-pin square plug is the standard here), and the better hotels all have hairdryers.

Rules and Regulations

Local comics observe wryly that Singapore is a fine city — there is a fine for littering, a fine for jaywalking, a fine for smoking in no-smoking areas (which now include all cinemas, government buildings, theatres, taxis and lifts, among other places, leaving smokers with virtually no place to light up but the great outdoors).

While foreigners might consider these regulations to be intolerable restrictions on self-expression and individual liberty, most Singaporeans accept them as unavoidable inconveniences necessary to keep life on an even and pleasant keel. Without that $1,000 anti-littering fine (it used to be $500) backed by an energetic army of street cleaners, it is unlikely that Singapore would be as clean as it is.

If you are walking, remember that you can be fined for crossing a road against the lights, or within 50 metres (yards) of a zebra crossing, traffic light or overhead pedestrian bridge.

Drug abuse carries the heaviest penalties. In Singapore the death penalty is mandatory for trafficking in 15 grams (half an ounce) of heroin or 30 grams (an ounce) of morphine. Abuse of so-called 'soft' drugs like marijuana is also a punishable offence.

Singapore Time

Singapore is eight hours ahead of GMT, two and a half hours ahead of New Delhi, one hour ahead of Bangkok and Jakarta, the same time as Kuala Lumpur, Taipei and Hong Kong, one hour behind Tokyo, two hours behind Sydney, 15 hours ahead of Los Angeles and 12 hours ahead of New York.

Employers are moving to five-day work weeks, but government and many

city offices generally work Saturday mornings as well. Most open 9 – 9.30 am and close for the day anytime from 5 pm Monday to Friday. Many workplaces, including most government offices, start at 8.30 am. Many factories, especially those in the electronics industry, work on three shifts around the clock.

Though shopping times vary, everything — but everything! — is open between 11 am and 5 pm on weekdays. Most department stores stay open until at least 9 pm, and some until 10 pm, and most are open every day of the week, as are many shops. Some smaller shops close on Sundays, but their weekday hours can be flexible, depending on whether there are still customers to be served. Tangs, at the junction of Orchard and Scotts roads, is the only department store that closes on Sundays, which it does resolutely even during the Christmas rush.

If you attend musical or theatrical performances, you will notice that Singaporean audiences have a rather elastic view of time. It is not uncommon to see stragglers entering even half an hour after a performance has commenced. That same elasticity extends to lunch, dinner and other appointments. If invited to a Chinese wedding, with the time announced as 7 pm sharp, be warned that you may not sit down to eat till 8.30 pm or later.

Security

Singapore is one city in which one can safely take a midnight stroll on the streets. But here, as anywhere, you should use your common sense and, for example, avoid walking alone through deserted areas or parks at night. Travellers cheques are a better bet than cash (remember to keep a record of cheque numbers separately in case you lose the cheques), and you should use safe-deposit boxes (usually provided free in hotels) to keep cash and other valuables.

Snatch thefts are rare but not unheard of. Pickpockets do operate, especially in crowded places and shopping centres. Open or unattended bags and wallets in back pockets are easy pickings. Report lost or stolen property to the police at once.

While hotels do take precautions such as asking callers for guests' names, male guests may be approached on the telephone by unscrupulous people offering the services of call girls, among other delights. You may also be propositioned (usually quite discreetly) on the streets or find a business card slipped under your hotel door. Do yourself and your fellow hotel guests a favour and make a complaint to the hotel management. Do not under any circumstances take up the offer. Doped drinks and rigged card games are some of the milder tricks that can be played on you.

Also bad news are the shopping touts who hang around outside the larger shopping complexes — Orchard Towers and Lucky Plaza are two prime spots on Orchard Road — to persuade you to visit certain shops. You can be certain that whatever seemingly incredible bargain you strike will include profit enough to pay the tout's commission.

Tipping

Tipping is discouraged in Singapore. Airport porters are not supposed to be tipped, nor are most hotel staff. However, you usually tip the hotel bellboy who brings your luggage to your room — $1 is enough. A table service charge of ten percent is added to the bill at virtually all hotels and most restaurants — where it is not, a ten percent tip is sufficient. It is not customary to tip taxi drivers.

Telephones

In Singapore you are never far from a telephone. Apart from the booths set up by the local telephone authority, Telecoms, every hotel has several pay phones in its lobby. The same bright orange phones are also found in many shops, all supermarkets and almost all restaurants. Even many newsagents and stallholders at food centres have a pay phone handy for the convenience of their customers. The local telephone directory is published every year in July. For directory enquiries, call 103.

Local calls on public telephones cost ten cents, but there is a time limit of three minutes and a maximum call time of nine minutes. There is no charge for local calls made from a subscriber's telephone and from most hotel rooms. International direct dial (IDD) calls to most countries can be made from your hotel room, but you should check on surcharges beforehand.

Far cheaper than making IDD calls from your hotel room is to use a booth at the General Post Office at Collyer Quay or from Telecoms' customer service centre at its headquarters in Exeter Road, which is open around the clock. They also provide 24-hour telex, telefax and other services.

IDD calls can also be made at any time from booths at Changi Airport. Arriving or departing passengers can make free local calls within the airport's restricted area. When arriving, look for the red telephones before the baggage claim. On departure, you can see the telephones almost immediately after clearing Immigration.

Phone cards are now widely used and there are plans to convert all coin phones to card phones. Card phones can be used to make international calls and phone cards in denominations of $2 and up can be bought at many outlets as well as all post offices. Credit-card phones are becoming more widely used.

Mail

Post offices are numerous (88 at last count) and conveniently located. The Customer Service Centre at Comcentre in Exeter Road and the post office at Changi Airport never close. All offer ordinary, registered and parcel post services, and some also offer a local urgent mail (more popularly known as LUM) facility. Many offer Speedpost services to certain foreign countries as well as Surface Air Lifted service. The majority of post offices are open 8.30 am–5 pm weekdays with one late closing. The staff are helpful and generally speak English well.

Popular Entertainment

If Singapore seems serious and straight-laced, it is so only on the surface. The country and its people are quite capable of relaxing and having fun — in moderation. Check *Timeszone Central* (see immediately above) for current shows.

Don't expect to find girlie bars, strip shows or topless waitresses; Singapore is not Bangkok, though even people who have never set foot here know about the drag queens of Bugis Street. Dressed to thrill, these bewigged beauties played nightly, the audience mostly foreigners prepared to pay for Singapore's highest-priced beer and soft drinks. The original Bugis Street is no more. Demolished for the construction of the Mass Rapid Transit railway, it is slated for reconstruction on the opposite side of Victoria Street. Whether its 'girls' will be allowed back is uncertain, given officialdom's general disapproval.

When you say 'nightlife', most Singaporeans will point you to Orchard Road. The night scene here is civilized and enjoyable, but it is not exactly inexpensive. In the upper reaches of Orchard Road, head for Orchard Towers, which has a collection of popular nightspots with live music, principally Top Ten, Celebrities and Caesar's.

On the opposite side of Orchard Road, look for the Music Room in the Singapore Hilton; and, next door to the Hilton, in the Far East Shopping Centre, Hime Karaoke Lounge, where the audience sings along in English, Cantonese, Hokkien, Japanese and Mandarin. Further down the road is Brannigan's with live music and exotic drinks, and the Chinoiserie, an upscale disco, at the Hyatt Regency; the Kasbah, where the house band plays amid neo-Arabian decor; and the Library, a classy disco at the Mandarin.

The largest discotheque is the Warehouse, on the Singapore River next to the River View Hotel. It also has a daytime disco (locals call it a 'teadance') and is much favoured by young people—from 2–6 pm.

Floor shows, tastefully presented (when topless, the dancers actually do dance, not just jiggle), can be found at a theatre restaurant, the Neptune, at Collyer Quay. For raunchier entertainment, head across the causeway to Johor Baru, in West Malaysia, to a well-known nightspot called Mechinta.

If you are a movie buff, you can now catch most new releases here. Cinemas operate seven days a week, and most of those in the Orchard Road area (Orchard and Cathay) generally show movies in English. On weekdays the first shows start at about 11 am and the last at about 9 pm. Check the daily cinema ads in *The Straits Times* . Tickets for most shows cost $3.50 but blockbusters can cost more. The Picturehouse, a small cinema for quality movies, opened in 1991.

In 1988, the street party came into being. Swing Singapore is held once a year in August. Orchard Road is closed for what must be one of the world's largest block parties—but arguably its safest as the streets swarm with police to keep order. People still manage to have a whale of a time with music provided by popular entertainers from strategic spots on the shopping strip. The MRT runs till later than usual so people can get home, but many stay on to breakfast at Orchard Road. On the last Sunday of the month, the street is also closed and many organisations take this opportunity to organise fairs and other mass events.

A fad which took off in the late 1980's is the karaoke lounge. There are lounges which cater mainly to a Chinese-speaking crowd and play Mandarin and Hokkien songs (Hokkien is a southern Chinese dialect). Some cater exclusively to Japanese tastes — principally Japanese businessmen's tastes and their musical menu is tailored accordingly. Karaoke, means "empty orchestra" in Japanese. The audience provides the entertainment. Some lounges are pretty slick, with music and videos supplied on video-discs. You don't even have to know the lyrics—the newer places have a TV monitor on which you can read the lyrics as you perform.

Europa in Changi Village started as a diner called Europe. It changed hands in 1979 and was renamed Europa by Dennis Foo, its new owner. Drinks are reasonable or downright cheap if you compare the prices with what the pubs and bars charge on Orchard Road. It still serves lunch and dinner too.

Memories at Marine Parade Central is another East Coast delight. Decorated with record sleeves featuring the local musical pioneers of the 1950s and 1960s, it opens at 5 pm but showtime is 9 pm. Just off Orchard Road is Ridley's at the Century Park Sheraton where the young and trendy hang out. On Scotts Road, the upscale head for Brannigan's.

The City

From the start, Singapore was a planned development. Sir Stamford Raffles, Singapore's founder, drew up an initial plan during his second visit to Singapore in mid-1819. In the four weeks he spent here, he directed, among other things, that separate areas be set aside for the various ethnic communities. All Chinese, for instance, were to settle on the right bank of the river, while the European quarter was to be east of the cantonment. Farquhar apparently did not carry out these instructions to Raffles' satisfaction, so when Raffles returned in 1822, after a break of three years, he appointed a town committee to draw up detailed plans for development.

The committee's new plan called for the north bank of the Singapore River to be reserved for government buildings. First the swampy area on the southwest bank was filled in — the first of many land reclamation projects. A hillock was levelled to provide the necessary landfill, and Commercial Square was created; even then it was the business hub of the country. It has since been rechristened Raffles Place, and most of the major banks now have their headquarters on the square or near it.

City Sights

Raffles Square has been closed to traffic for many years. Below the mall, Mass Rapid Transit trains rumble through a major underground station. Above ground, the square has been completely rebuilt to the dictates of business. Not so the government quarters of the colonial regime, though some of the 19th-century buildings have fallen prey to a national obsession to pull down and rebuild. That urge has now been tempered by a growing appreciation of Singapore's architectural heritage, and the authorities are trying to preserve a limited number of historic areas as a whole, not just individual buildings of note.

The Padang

Considering how newly independent countries have generally done their utmost to erase all trace of their colonial past, the feeling of empire remains surprisingly intact in Singapore. One senses it especially in and around the historic green space in front of City Hall called the Padang, which is Malay for 'field'. That the Padang still exists today is no thanks to Raffles. After claiming the island on behalf of the British East India Company in 1819, his plan was to keep the Padang for the use of the European merchants. The traders thought it unsuitable, so in 1822 Raffles agreed that it should remain an open field.

Today, few objects evoke colonial nostalgia as much as the Padang, which was once almost a synonym for cricket. The game is still played here as it has been since the 1820s, when the tradition was begun by British merchants. Since there were only 74 Europeans in Singapore in 1824, according to a census taken that year, practically the whole community must have been down on the Padang either as a player or spectator in those days. Cricket exercised such sway then that in 1852 *The Straits Times* was moved to declare, 'Cricket is beyond all doubt a powerful agent in keeping away that dreadful disease, cholera.' Cricket's heyday was in the 1890s, when teams from Hong Kong, Ceylon (now Sri Lanka) and Shanghai would compete in Singapore.

Some years ago *The Straits Times* carried a report that revealed ambitious development plans for this open space, which was about to be transformed into a dazzling new hub for the city. Readers who failed to note that this momentous news was being delivered on April Fools' Day were outraged to think that this historic patch of turf, the city's most prominent green lung, was going the way of much of the old city. In land-starved Singapore, the property market was then at its most buoyant, so it was not surprising that so many fell for the tale. The resultant wave of protests from readers was a revealing demonstration of popular feeling about the country's colonial heritage.

Actually, there have been plans in the past — all scotched — to transform the Padang. Three decades ago, the newly elected government threatened to turn it into a recreation ground. Prime Minister Lee Kuan Yew said at a mass rally in 1959, 'Do you know that we wanted to use this padang for our election rallies at night? But a small group of Europeans who were given this field by the former colonial government refused, although they only use it in the day time for a few people to play games.'

If cricket matches on the Padang were not such a sweaty business, spectator and player alike might well imagine themselves in England, especially when sipping tea at 4 pm on the verandahs of the **Singapore Cricket Club**. Renovated and repainted but in essence unchanged, the club commands the western end of the Padang, as it has for more than 140 years. The Eurasian community's playground was at the opposite end of the field — at the **Singapore Recreation Club**. The SRC, as it is commonly called, was founded in 1883 by a group of 30 Eurasian men. Both Padang clubs are still favourite watering-holes of the city's professionals and civil servants.

Cricket season is March until September, when games generally start at 1.30 pm Saturdays and Sundays. (Check with the Singapore Cricket Club, at 338-9271.) There is no charge for watching from the Padang, but the clubhouse is a 'members only' sanctum.

From September until March, the game on the Padang is rugby. Kick-off is at 5.30 pm. Field hockey and lawn tennis are also played on the Padang, and at night it is becoming an increasingly popular venue for open-air and televised entertainment, including pop song contests.

Since independence, the Padang has become a focus for national pride, as it divides the honour of hosting the 9 August National Day Parade with the National Stadium in Kallang.

Queen Elizabeth Walk

Landfill took away the Padang's sea frontage long ago. More reclamation has filled in the sea in front of the paved seafront promenade variously called the Esplanade or Queen Elizabeth Walk. Now the walk is linked to newly reclaimed acreage dominated by a huge hotel and shopping development, Marina Square. This landscaped area is popular with joggers, walkers and anglers, and Marina Park is set to become a major city recreation area and performance venue. The biggest show so far was the launch of the Festival of Arts, a biennial event, in 1988. Some 80,000 people gathered to watch a two-hour spectacle complete with sky-divers performing precision jumps, commandos rappelling down walls in time to music and fireworks exploding from hotel roofs.

The open-air stalls of the nearby Satay Club serve up sizzling skewers of beef, mutton and chicken grilled over flaming charcoal, an evening treat that still draws crowds, especially on fine nights.

Monuments

Some of Singapore's monuments have shifty habits. Take the century-old bronze statue of **Sir Stamford Raffles**, which now stands in the plaza in front of the Victoria Concert Hall and Victoria Theatre. This prominent position has not always belonged to Raffles. The space was once occupied by a bronze elephant on a rectangular pedestal, which had been presented by King Chulalongkorn of Siam, the monarch of the musical *The King and I*, when he visited Singapore in 1871. (Since 1919 or so, the Siamese tusker has stood guard in front of Parliament House.) After the elephant came the **Dalhousie Obelisk**, which was erected in 1850 to commemorate the visit of the Marquis of Dalhousie, who was then governor-general of India. In 1911 (when there was no danger of Dalhousie making a return visit), the obelisk was moved to its present site closer to the Singapore River.

The bronze Raffles figure was officially unveiled on 27 June 1887 in the middle of the Padang. The occasion was Queen Victoria's Golden Jubilee celebrations. Thirty-two years later, to mark Singapore's centenary on 6 February 1919, Raffles was moved to his present position.

As long as most can remember, **Tan Kim Seng's Fountain** has been on the Esplanade in front of the Padang, surrounded by a steel enclosure. The pretty cast-iron fountain was unveiled in 1882 in Battery Road near Fullerton Square, just outside the business hub, Commercial Square. It commemorated

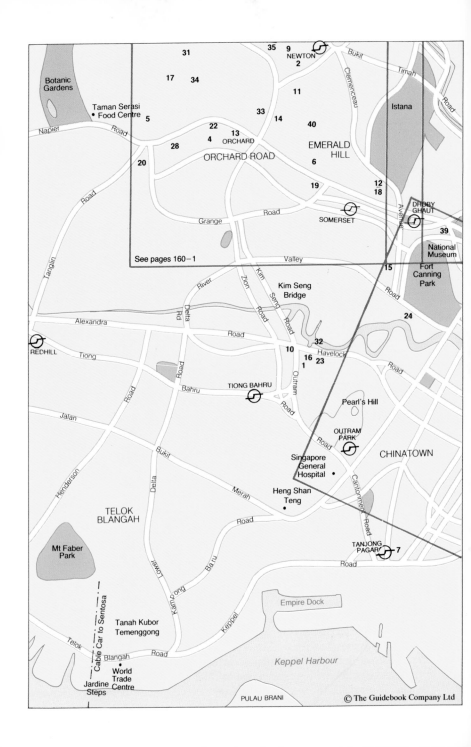

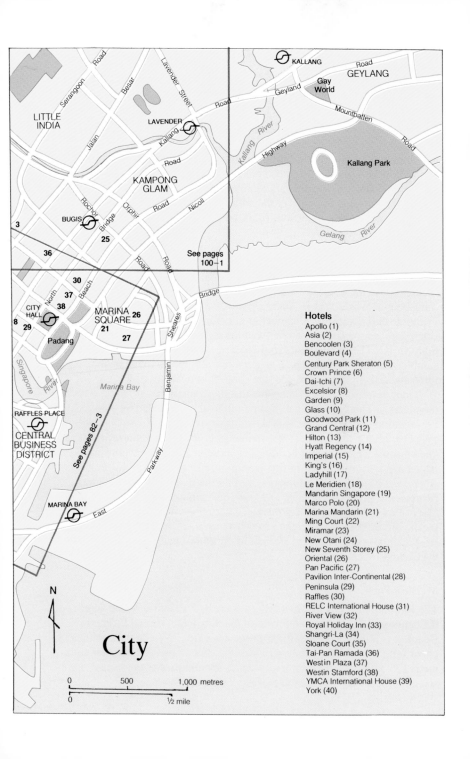

City

Hotels
Apollo (1)
Asia (2)
Bencoolen (3)
Boulevard (4)
Century Park Sheraton (5)
Crown Prince (6)
Dai-Ichi (7)
Excelsior (8)
Garden (9)
Glass (10)
Goodwood Park (11)
Grand Central (12)
Hilton (13)
Hyatt Regency (14)
Imperial (15)
King's (16)
Ladyhill (17)
Le Meridien (18)
Mandarin Singapore (19)
Marco Polo (20)
Marina Mandarin (21)
Ming Court (22)
Miramar (23)
New Otani (24)
New Seventh Storey (25)
Oriental (26)
Pan Pacific (27)
Pavilion Inter-Continental (28)
Peninsula (29)
Raffles (30)
RELC International House (31)
River View (32)
Royal Holiday Inn (33)
Shangri-La (34)
Sloane Court (35)
Tai-Pan Ramada (36)
Westin Plaza (37)
Westin Stamford (38)
YMCA International House (39)
York (40)

See pages 100-1

See pages 82-3

Tan Kim Seng's gift of $13,000 to the government for a better town water supply. It took almost 20 years to finish the waterworks, and its benefactor did not live to see its opening.

On the same promenade is the pagoda-like **Lim Bo Seng Memorial**, dedicated to the Hokkien businessman who was prominent in anti-Japanese activities and active in Singapore's defence against the Japanese invasion in World War II. Though he escaped before Singapore surrendered, Lim lost most of his family to the dreaded *Kempeitai*, the Japanese secret police. He recruited volunteers in India for the underground resistance in Malaya, but when he returned to join the guerrillas, he was captured by the Japanese and died after being tortured.

The dominant memorial on the Esplanade is the sombre **Cenotaph**, which commemorates the dead of both world wars. The country's tallest monument, however, is farther north in Memorial Park, on Beach Road. This is the **war memorial** for the civilians who died during the Japanese occupation of Singapore in World War II. Once a year, the Japanese ambassador and members of the Japanese Chamber of Commerce and Industry gather with war veterans for a simple ceremony at the foot of this 70-metre (230-foot) high edifice. The monument's four tapering white columns are designed to symbolize Singapore's main cultural groups, but locals have taken to referring to them irreverently as 'the chopsticks'.

It may confuse visitors somewhat that these structures are not gazetted monuments. There are 19 'national monuments' designated by the Preservation of Monuments Board, but most are places of worship built in the 19th century. Of the three secular buildings gazetted as monuments, the best known is the **Telok Ayer Market**, Singapore's newest attraction. An octagonal, cast-iron structure first put up in 1825 as a market for immigrant workers, it needed frequent repairs even during its earliest years. A more permanent market dating from 1894 was dismantled to make way for the MRT. Now a food centre, flea market, entertainment centre and cultural theatre are all housed under the recently renovated Victorian shell. Hawkers, strolling players and buskers create a lively atmosphere right in the heart of the Central Business District.

Merlion Park

The Merlion, half lion and half fish, was created as a promotable symbol of the country. As the official emblem of the Singapore Tourist Promotion Board, it is found on souvenir tee-shirts, postcards, key-chains, bookmarks, paper weights and also as bite-size Merlion chocolates. The original eight-metre (26-foot) tall white sculpture stands spouting water in postage stamp-sized Merlion Park, at the mouth of the Singapore River.

General Post Office/Fullerton Building

One of the first modern conservation experiments was the General Post Office, also known as the Fullerton Building. Perhaps the only survivor from the colonial era that still serves its original charter, it is usually referred to simply as 'Gee Pee Oh'. There were several earlier buildings on the site, the first of which was Fort Fullerton. The present building dates from 1928 and remains one of the most distinctive waterfront landmarks, though it is now dwarfed by neighbouring skyscrapers. It reopened in August 1985 following two years of renovations, an elaborate makeover in which the building was stripped of excessive wooden panelling and false ceilings, revealing its original barrel vault ceilings with their delicate mouldings. Today the interior looks more like a reception area in a fairly plush hotel than a functioning post office. The GPO is a popular meeting place for backpacking travellers who use Singapore as a base for exploring Southeast Asia and for similarly budget-inclined visitors who find its poste restante and international telephone facilities convenient to use.

Empress Place

Across the Singapore River from the GPO is the Empress Place Building, which once housed the Immigration Department and National Registration Office, among other government offices. It has been remade into a museum for Asian art and cultural exhibits. This completes the cultural rebirth of Empress Place, which is presided over by the Victoria Concert Hall and Victoria Theatre. They stand on a site where the Singapore Town Hall was built. For decades the town hall served as ballroom, public meeting room, theatre and concert hall — the hub of the Europeans' social and cultural life.

When Queen Victoria's Diamond Jubilee approached in the 1890s, the government felt the need to erect a new town hall and assembly rooms to mark the occasion. This was not a popular decision at the time, and for a while it looked as though both hall and theatre might become white elephants. Chinese residents christened the twin buildings Tai Chung Lau (Big Clock Tower), and most taxi drivers even now recognize the colloquial name even if they are completely ignorant of the location of 'Victoria Theatre'. The theatre is a popular venue for dance and drama, while its next-door neighbour, Victoria Concert Hall, is now the home of the Singapore Symphony Orchestra.

Parliament House

Parliament House is immediately behind the two Victorias. Its distinguished white-washed exterior elicits little recognition from taxi-drivers, but since the local TV station began broadcasting extended summaries of House proceedings some years ago, most Singaporeans have become intimately

How the Other Half Lives

The Chinese girl's life in the Straits Settlements, though freer and less irksome than that of her sister in China, is not an enviable one. Its monotony is intolerable. . . She is apparently well contented with her lot, for she makes no complaint whatever. So accustomed is she to her surroundings that were she placed in the English girl's shoes, she would feel quite out of her element.

The happiest and merriest period of her life is that spent during her childhood, when no restraint whatever is put upon her actions. She is permitted to associate with boys and romp about the house and streets (there being no nursery) to her heart's content, which accounts for the dirty and unkempt appearance she sometimes presents. Her seclusion dates from the time when she arrives at the age of 13 or 14, and everything considered unladylike is forbidden her. The parents here do not look upon their daughters as being altogether worthless. No girl is ever sold into slavery. When unwanted, she is usually given away to be adopted into some family, and is there treated as a daughter of the house.

As soon as she is 13 or 14, she has to undergo a course of training in cooking and sewing. These two are essential accomplishments to achieve, without which she has scant hope of securing a good match. Education is not yet considered necessary, but her value would be very much enhanced were she able to read and write a little English. The only books ever perused are printed in Romanised Malay, the mother tongue here being Malay, and the Chinese language practically unknown. Her sewing comprises the embroidery of slippers, pouches, belts, etc., which form features of a Chinese girl's trousseau.

The attire of a Chinese girl consists of a long dress called a 'kabayah' which extends far below the knees, a 'sarong' and a short jacket. Slippers are worn without any stockings, and the dress, which opens in front, is fastened by means of three brooches or 'krosangs' of three different shapes. This costume is almost an exact replica of the Malay woman's, the only difference being the mode of dressing the hair, into which, in the case of the former, are stuck three hairpins. Some of the girls have adopted the Chinese costume on a modified scale, as being more suitable to their nationality.

The life is indeed lonely and dull . . . She is never permitted to venture outside the doors of her abode, unless to pay occasional visits to her closest relations. When she does go out it is in conveyances which are entirely covered up, and either her mother or an aged relative acts as her chaperone. She lives in a sphere of her own, quite out of touch with the society of men.

The Chinese girl is seldom provided with an adequate education, the passing of the third and fourth standard being deemed sufficient. Consequently, she possesses but very vague notions concerning English etiquette and customs. Parents regard it as a waste of money to educate their daughters, who are supposed to be incapable of maintaining the family in time of need, seeing that, according to Chinese customs, it is indecent and disgraceful for girls to work for their living, which must of necessity entail their going out incessantly and thus exposing themselves to the public gaze.

The age at which the Chinese girl is married is either 18 or 19, sometimes two or three years earlier, as is common among the wealthier classes. It is the parents who bring about the matches and make all the arrangements. In most cases the marriage takes place between people who are total strangers to one another. The girl is so completely under the control of her parents that her wishes are not consulted at all: in fact, she is entirely ignorant of the proceedings which are being carried out until the matter is quite settled. Even then, she is not informed of the identity, position, age, appearance, etc., of her future husband.

The wedding costume is typically Chinese, and a great deal of jewellery is worn with it, which is of such dreadful weight that no wonder a delicate girl often succumbs in a fainting fit when going through the ceremony of making her obeisance to her parents and other people of importance. The life of the newly made wife would be rendered far happier if there were no mother-in-law, who makes her lead a wretched existence by behaving tyrannically in the house. The poor wife becomes the drudge of the household, and must be ready to wait on her mother-in-law at all hours. Of course there are exceptions, but these are few indeed.

Miss Lee Choo Neo, writing in the London Queen, September 1913 acquainted with Parliament's interior decor — as well as with the cut and thrust of political debate. It was also apparent that the chamber was getting quite squeezed for space; the number of parliamentarians had grown by more than half since 1959, making it necessary to carry out renovations and add more seats in late 1988.

The architect cannot be blamed for poor planning. George Dromgold Coleman (see page 72), who was responsible for much of the country's colonial architecture, had no idea that the building he began in 1826 as a private home for a Java merchant, John Argyle Maxwell, would eventually house Parliament. In fact, the merchant never lived in his splendid home by the Singapore River. He leased it to the government, which has used it by turns as a court house, government offices, the recorder's office, the legislative assembly and, now, parliament.

It is possible to visit Parliament and see the House in session, though there are no tours for the public. One can watch the debate from the vantage point of the Strangers' Gallery, but only if there is room. A good part of the gallery is reserved for the press and civil servants, and student groups take up most of the other rows. The House debates the budget in March and sits for its longest sessions then, other sessions being scheduled irregularly. Identification is needed, and those intending to visit should call ahead (tel. 336-8811).

City Hall

The building most associated with governmental power is City Hall, which has been home at various times to the City Council, Prime Minister's Office, Ministry of Foreign Affairs, Ministry of Culture and others. The site was once occupied by two large colonial houses that were taken over and used as the Municipal Office. The existing building was considered the most important architectural work of the former Municipal Architects Department. City Hall took three years to build and was completed in 1929. Until 1951, it was known as the Municipal Building, and it has been witness to such milestones of Singaporean history as the surrender of the Japanese forces to the Allies on 12 September 1945. The name City Hall is something of a misnomer, for Singapore has neither a municipal council nor a mayor.

Supreme Court

City Hall has now been annexed by its next-door neighbour, the Supreme Court, which had been suffering a space shortage. Around 1830 the architect G D Coleman (also the designer of Parliament House) built a private house on the site. The house then became part of the London Hotel, which was subsequently renamed the Hotel de l'Esperance and then the Hotel de l'Europe. The original hotel buildings were pulled down in 1900, and a new building costing $1 million opened in 1905 with 120 rooms and a roof garden. This was pulled down to make way for the Supreme Court building now standing. Designed by the government architect, F Dorrington-Ward, the Supreme Court was begun in 1927 and completed only two years later. Its façade, however, owes much to an Italian who came to Singapore later in 1931. According to Marjorie Doggett, who photographed and documented Singapore's early buildings in her excellent book, *Characters of Light*, the Corinthian columns, facing and sculpture were the work of Cavaliere Rodolfo Nolli, who ventured out East with a group of Italians commissioned by the King of Siam to build a new Throne Room in Bangkok.

Raffles Hotel

As a hotel, the Raffles is dwarfed by its neighbours just across the road, the Westins Plaza and Stamford. But none of Singapore's many-splendoured, many-starred hostelries can hold a candle to the venerable Raffles when it comes to sheer reputation. In this, the Raffles is unique.

Names — and name dropping — are all at the Raffles. Which other hotel can truthfully claim to have hosted a collection of heads of government and state that includes Ethiopian Emperor Haile Selassie, Canadian Premier Pierre Trudeau, Australian Prime Minister Malcolm Fraser, Austrian Chancellor Dr Bruno Kreisky, French President Valéry Giscard d'Estaing, Chinese Premier Zhou Enlai, Cambodian Prince Norodom Sihanouk and Indian Premier Jawaharlal Nehru?

Indira Gandhi also slept here — though not while prime minister of India. So did the beautiful Princess Soraya. In *Meet You At Raffles*, a history of the hotel by Raymond Flower (who has also been known to stay at the Raffles), we learn that when the king of Saudi Arabia (which one, he does not say) stayed at Raffles, three suites had to be knocked into one just for this royal occasion.

Adlai Stevenson, the distinguished American presidential advisor, and Henry Ford II, of the automobile dynasty, have signed the hotel register, as have a long line of British luminaries, including Lord Louis Mountbatten, James Callaghan, Harold Wilson and Anthony Eden. Ugandan leader Milton Obote actually lost his job while having lunch at the Raffles with other Commonwealth prime ministers, says Flower.

Filmdom has sent its own delegation, which includes Charlie Chaplin, Douglas Fairbanks, Mary Pickford, Jean Harlow, Jeanette MacDonald, Grace Kelly, Linda Christian, Tyrone Power, Elizabeth Taylor, Orson Welles, Peter Bogdanovich, Richard Burton, William Holden, Marlon Brando, Hayley Mills, Trevor Howard, Maurice Chevalier, Jean Simmons, Claudia Cardinale and Ingrid Bergman. Flower tells us that Ava Gardner and Robert Kennedy slept in Suite 222 — at different times of course.

But it is the literati, not the glitterati, that the hotel is most proud of having bedded down, and it has named many of its suites after them. The list includes W Somerset Maugham, Noel Barber, Arthur Hailey, Robert Elegant, Maxine Hong Kingston, André Malraux, Günter Grass and James Michener. The hotel believes (though it has no proof) that Joseph Conrad, who worked for the Scottish firm McAllister's in Singapore, was one of the Raffles's first guests, so a suite has been named after him, too.

Certainly no other hotel in Singapore can claim to have been endorsed by Rudyard Kipling, who made the Raffles famous when he wrote, 'Providence conducted me along a beach in full view of five miles of shipping — five solid miles of masts and funnels — to a place called Raffles Hotel, where the food is as excellent as the rooms are bad. Let the traveller take note. Feed at Raffles and sleep at the Hotel de l'Europe.'

Succeeding owners and managers at Raffles have made full use of 'Feed at Raffles . . . where the food is excellent' while conveniently ignoring the rest of Kipling's advice, which in any case was rendered irrelevant by the demolition of the Hotel de l'Europe and its replacement by the Supreme Court.

Luckily there is no more talk of razing Raffles to the ground and building some megabuck multi-storey monstrosity in its place. Restoration plans mooted during the 1980's have resulted in a much-need facelift, upgrading the hotel to an all-suites establishment. A new wing has been opened, known simply as Raffles, housing a Victorian-style theatre playhouse, The Jubilee Hall and Raffles Hotel Museum.

Despite these renovations, the hotel remains largely as it has been for years. It is not unlike a *grande dame* who has fallen on somewhat hard times but still manages to keep up a good front—especially for the tourists who flock there by the busload to quaff a Singapore Sling or three at the Long Bar. It was barman Ngiam Tong Boon who started it all when he concocted the first Singapore Sling in 1915, and his nephew Robert Ngiam still slings a mean drink at the Long Bar. There is no secret to the recipe (Beefeater gin, cherry brandy, fruit juice, Angostura, Cointreau and Benedictine), but the hotel is justly proud that it serves some 1,200 slings a day!

Many prefer to have their drinks in the garden, where the nostalgic still reminisce about the tea dances of old. These started well after the Armenian Sarkies brothers, Martin and Tigran, took over from Captain George Mildray Dare, who had fallen on hard times and turned his billiard room into a tiffin room providing some of the best lunches in Singapore.

The Sarkies leased the property in the summer of 1886 and opened the hotel on 1 December the following year. The hotel, which had 48 bedrooms, each with a private bathroom and verandah, a billiard room large enough to hold four tables, and European-made furniture, soon gained a fine reputation. In 1890 the adjoining building, the American Consulate, was acquired, and

two wings were added to the central block of the hotel. Until land reclamation took away its beach frontage in this century, the Raffles had a panoramic view of the harbour and the islands off Singapore.

Tigran Sarkies did not invent name dropping, but he elevated it to new heights in Singapore, listing all the crowned heads — and the merely famous or powerful — who slept at the Raffles. The hotel was rebuilt during Queen Victoria's Diamond Jubilee and was then able to boast that it had the largest dining room in the East. In 1905, a London newspaper described it as the 'Savoy of Singapore'.

A vintage advertisement describes the old Raffles thus, 'The only private enterprise possessing its own Electric Lights and Fan Installation, Ice Plant and Cold Storage Room, Electric Lights and Fans in every room, telephone in every room with outside connections, Motor Cars garaged, repaired and painted, Motor Cars and Lorries for hire, Motor Workshop for repairing cars, Bakery, Confectionery and Restaurant; Post, Telegraph and Telephone Office on the premises.' Apparently the rest of Singapore town was electrified only in 1906.

When the British surrendered to the Japanese invaders in World War II, many Europeans sought refuge at the Raffles, and the hotel staff buried the silver roast beef trolley and treasures. The hotel was then commandeered for the use of ranking Japanese officers and renamed Syonan Ryokan — Light of the South Hotel. It was at this time that the entrance of the hotel was moved from Bras Basah Road to Beach Road, which was thought to be more secure. Clocks all over the islands were set to Tokyo time and a Hungarian orchestra played Japanese songs. General Tojo himself stayed at the hotel for a few days, but his name is not often dropped.

After the war, the Overseas-Chinese Banking Corporation (OCBC) bought control of the Raffles in the 1950s and DBS Bank also owns a chunk of it. In 1988, the Minstry of National Development announced plans to preserve and extend it. At the time of writing the grand dame of hotels in Singapore was being restored and upgraded. The project aims to create a 1930s ambience.

House of Tan Yeok Nee

This house at 207 Clemenceau Avenue, north of Fort Canning, has been the Salvation Army's Headquarters since 1940, but it was built for a wealthy 19th-century Teochew trader, Tan Yeok Nee. His is literally a rags to riches story, for he began his career as a cloth pedlar. It is said that he visited Telok Blangah, where he made friends with royalty. He became successful as a pepper and gambier trader. Through his royal connections, he came to own considerable property in Johore and Singapore.

Tan had his house built in the style popular at the time in southern China. It is one of only four such homes to be built in a purely Chinese style and is the only one that survives to this day. Early this century, a railway line was laid through Tank Road, which leads on from Clemenceau Avenue. Tan's property was apparently acquired for the railway, whose main terminus was at Tank Road until 1932, when the present railway station was built at Tanjong Pagar. The railway station master lived in the merchant's home for a while. Then it was used as an Anglican school and home for girls until the Salvation Army took it over. Tan Yeok Nee died at the age of 75 in his home village in China.

The Istana

This building, the official residence of the president of Singapore, is not generally on public display, though the well-kept grounds are open on public holidays. The changing of the guard on the first Sunday of the month is always a public and much-photographed event. The land on which the Istana stands was once part of the extensive nutmeg plantation of Mount Sophia. It was bought for the government's use in 1867. Indian convicts completed this graceful mansion in 1869. Until 1959, when Singapore became self-governing, it was the official home of the British governor and known then as Government House. Its grounds are often used for official functions, including informal gatherings of civic leaders, and has the country's most exclusive golf course. The prime minister has his office in the Istana Annexe.

Fort Canning

The English once called this mound Singapore Hill. When Raffles established his residence here in the early 1820s, it became known as Government Hill. Then it became Fort Canning. Now all that remains of the fort are its old gateway and the barrels of two 18th-century cannon. The old fortification walls can be partly traced, though the site was rebuilt subsequently. Archivists and researchers have tried without success to find the fort's original plans, which are thought to be in Calcutta.

Actually, Fort Canning's history predates the arrival of the English, though there are few pointers to an exalted ancient past. Archaeological excavations have convinced historians that Fort Canning is the earliest known seat of government in Singapore, with finds indicating that there were people living on or near Fort Canning about 600 years ago, though too little remains to detail how they lived. In 1925, workers excavating a reservoir literally struck gold when digging at the roots of a tree, their find a small cache of gold ornaments lying five or six feet below the surface. Some pieces were lost during World War II, but the rest, along with some fragments of Chinese celadon ware found on Fort Canning in 1940, are in the National Museum.

The King's Chinese

The Straits Chinese may not have originated the saying, 'The way to a man's heart is through his stomach', but they most certainly believe it. In days gone by, this was almost a religious tenet of the Straits Chinese, or Peranakan (meaning 'local-born'), community. Their well-rooted tradition of home cooking has nurtured taste buds as refined as any oenologist's nose. To have one's food pronounced *chayer* (watered-down) or, worse still, *tak alus* (not refined) was the kiss of death for a would-be wife, whose ability to cook was once a significant determinant in making a marriage.

In the past, some of the best guardians of the cuisine were the matchmakers. The late grande dame of Peranakan cooking, Mrs Lee Chin Koon, noted that the matchmakers would usually call on a prospective bride's home at 10 am, when the young women of the house would be pounding the *rempah*, the spices and condiments essential to Straits Chinese cuisine. 'They [the matchmakers] could tell by the sound of the mortar and pestle if there were good cooks in the house. There should be a rhythm to the pounding. From the sound of the pounding, we can tell which ingredient is being pounded and also whether the person who is pounding is an experienced cook,' she wrote in 1974.

But now *Babas* and *Nonyas*, as Straits Chinese men and women are called, can dine out — and dine well — every day without having to pound a single *buah keras, a* candlenut commonly used in Nonya cuisine. In recent years there have been new books, a rash of new plays for newly nostalgic audiences, and a premium put on Straits Chinese antiques, whose appeal is limited mainly to Singapore and Malaysia.

The community's artefacts and lifestyle are on display at Peranakan Place, a complex housing a museum, souvenir shops and restaurants in reconstructed shophouses at the intersection of Emerald Hill Road and Orchard Road. In Bibi's Restaurant one can taste the food and theatre of the Peranakans and even attend a staged wedding. The museum is a recreated Peranakan home displaying the community's heritage, an attractive marriage of Chinese and Malay elements.

The Peranakan community evolved from the early Chinese traders who settled in Penang, Malacca and Singapore (the Straits Settlements of Malaya) and took Malay wives. Male children were sent to China for their education, but the girls stayed put. As they were not allowed to marry Malay men, the growing pool of locally born Chinese women had to look for husbands within their own community or among new arrivals. Until early in the nineteenth century, local Chinese families took a keen, even proprietary, interest in the arrival of the junks from China, which brought fresh cargoes of potential husbands.

Sir Song Ong Siang describes the life of a Straits Chinese girl in his history of the Chinese in Singapore. Song quotes Dr Lee Choo Neo, a Peranakan woman doctor, thus, 'The happiest and merriest period of her life is that spent during her childhood when no restraint whatever is put upon her actions. She is permitted to associate with boys and romp around the house and streets to her heart's content . . . . She is well aware that all these harmless games must cease when she arrives at the age of 13 or 14. Her seclusion dates from this time and everything considered unladylike is forbidden her . . . . As soon as she is 13 or 14, she has to make herself useful in the household and to undergo a course of training in cooking and sewing . . . . She is never permitted to venture outside the doors of her abode unless it be to pay occasional visits to her closest connections.'

What really sets the Straits Chinese apart is the language they use, a pithy and often pungent Chinese-flavoured Malay called Baba Malay, which came about after several centuries of settlement in Malaya. The women almost gave up using Chinese altogether, though the men still used Hokkien, the dialect of Fujian province, as the language of trade. Though most Straits Chinese today still sprinkle their speech with Baba Malay, and many Singaporeans who are not of Baba ancestry borrow from its vocabulary, few young Babas or Nonyas are really at home with the idiom.

J D Vaughan, a colonial administrator and lawyer in 19th-century Singapore, was intrigued by the Straits Chinese. He observed even then that most Babas were switching from studying Chinese to learning English. 'Few of the rising generation are taught Chinese and doubtless in a decade or two English will supersede the Chinese language altogether. With reference to the spoken language, the Babas, especially those of Malacca, so interlard their conversation with Malay words and sentences that, it is difficult sometimes to say whether they are speaking Chinese or Malay,' he wrote in his *Manners and Customs of the Chinese of the Straits Settlements* (1879).

Vaughan observed that 'they have social clubs of their own to which they will admit no native of China' and claimed to have seen Babas bridle and say they were 'British subjects' when asked if they were Chinese. At their clubs the Babas imbibed brandy and soda, and played billiards, bowls and other European games. 'Yet they adhere strictly to the Chinese costume — the queue, thick-soled shoes, mandarin dresses, and conical hats on state occasions, and the manners and the customs of those people who otherwise they have no sympathies with,' noted Vaughan.

As if to emphasize how different they were from the China-born, the Peranakan men formed an association in 1900 named the Straits Chinese British Association. One of its objectives was 'to promote among the members an intelligent interest in the affairs of the British Empire, and to encourage and maintain their loyalty as subjects of the Queen.' So gung-ho British were the Straits Chinese that they came to be known as the King's Chinese. G E Raine, a lawyer, public speaker and writer, said of them, 'The Chinese are passionately loyal to the King and country of their adoption. They obey the laws which they have a voice in making: they have a corps in the Volunteers, and a very smart corps too: they subscribe most generously to every public movement. The Chinese in the Straits are essential to us, and we are indispensable to them.' In fact, the advent of the Boxer Rebellion in China inspired several of its members to declare themselves ready to fight — for the British.

The most recent excavations were in 1988.

The Malays long regarded the hill as sacred, and some still bear offerings to a hill-top tomb known as **Keramat Iskandar Syah**. In Arabic, *keramat* means a shrine or a place invested with supernatural power. The *Sejarah Melayu*, or *Malay Annals*, tell that Sri Sultan Iskandar Syah, the first ruler of Malacca, now part of Malaysia, was a fifth-generation descendant of Sri Tri Buana, who was a 14th-century prince from Palembang, in what is now south Sumatra, and founder of Temasek, an early name for Singapore. There is no documentary proof that this keramat is indeed the grave of Iskandar Syah.

The keramat looked much more picturesque in earlier times. Photographs taken as recently as the 1950s show a low-roofed brick-and-plaster structure, which was torn down apparently because drug addicts were using it for shelter. A low cement and mosaic wall with a painted steel gate now surrounds the keramat, but it is open to the elements. The current caretaker's family has been looking after the place for generations.

The nexus between fact and folklore tends to fog when one goes back a few hundred years, but ancient kings are said to have built their palaces there, and it was forbidden for any man to go up the hill except when summoned by royalty. Behind flowed the 'Forbidden Stream' where the ruler's wife and consorts used to bathe, and none was allowed to approach this place.

So strong was the grip of belief on the local population that when the first British resident of Singapore, Major William Farquhar, wanted to ascend the hill, the locals would not go with him for fear of offending the spirits. Eventually, he went up with Malays from Malacca. They pulled a cannon with them, and on reaching the summit Major Farquhar ordered the gun loaded and fired 12 rounds over the top of the hill. He then had a flagpole erected and hoisted up the English flag. Once the jungle had been cleared and a dirt road to the summit made, Raffles had a large wooden bungalow built as his residence. This, the first Government House, lasted some 40 years, until the fort was built.

The fort that gives the hill its name is something of a historical joke. Construction began in 1858, when the Madras Engineers arrived in Singapore to build simple defence works that could serve as a refuge for the European population in case of a local uprising. The task was left to a certain Captain Collyer. He lopped off the top of the hill to build Fort Canning, which was named after the governor-general of India at the time. It was rather useless as a fort, according to historian C M Turnbull, who holds that it might have been more appropriate to call it Collyer's Folly. 'It could not provide refuge for the European population during internal riots because it had no independent water supply, he wrote. 'Its guns could not protect the town against external attack because they were out of range of enemy ships and would merely destroy the town and shipping in the harbour.' During World War II, when it was the British military headquarters, it became known as 'Confusion Castle'.

Downhill of the fort is an old **Christian cemetery** consecrated in 1834 and containing many interesting old gravestones. The architect G D Coleman is among those buried here, his grave on the upper slopes of the cemetery in front of the old military barracks, which are now squash courts. It is thought that Coleman may have designed the Gothic gateways to the cemetery, as well as two of the surviving monuments over unidentified graves.

The Armenian **Church of St Gregory the Illuminator**, at the foot of Fort Canning, is the earliest surviving Christian church in Singapore. The interior is circular, and the original building came with a dome and bell-turret, which were later demolished for safety reasons. The Armenians were a small community when in 1827 they started a collection to build a church of their own. The building was completed in 1835 and its spire added in 1850. It continues to be maintained by the small Armenian community in Singapore though it has been used by other Christians for church services.

Across the street from the church is the **Masonic Hall**, which was built in 1879. The Masonic Brotherhood was set up much earlier, however, and established its first lodge in December 1845. Zetland Lodge was in a house in Armenian Street. A lawyer, William Napier, was the first Mason to be initiated locally. Singapore's first Masons laid the foundation stone of Horsburgh Lighthouse at the eastern end of the Straits of Singapore in 1850. The Scotsman James Horsburgh, as the East India Company's hydrographer, prepared many of the navigational charts in the seas of this region, and the lighthouse at Pedra Branca was a memorial to him. The Masons also laid the foundations for Raffles Lighthouse in 1854.

Development plans of one sort or another over the years have obliterated much of the history of the hill without greatly changing its appearance. It has been at various times home to a girls' hostel, the Syariah Court (which administers Islamic law), the National Archives and the headquarters of Toto, a state-run lottery. The hill is still home to the Registry of Marriages, where many local people exchange wedding vows. It also holds the Drama Centre, where many of Singapore's amateur and professional theatre groups perform.

Singapore Dance Theatre, the country's first professional ballet company; and TheatreWorks are arguably the most successful of the home-grown professional groups, which staged the David Hwang hit play Madame Butterfly.

The Substation
One of the latest additions to the arts scene, this former electrical sub-station is now home to a dance studio, theatre, art gallery and other performing and display spaces for the arts. There is always something going on at the Substation whose prime mover is well-known Singapore dramatist,

Kuo Pao Kun. This is one place to catch made-in-Singapore drama (English and Mandarin), exhibitions by up-and-coming artists, and lectures on theatre and other performing arts.

National Museum

This elegant, domed museum building on Stamford Road, at the foot of historic Fort Canning, dates from 1887. It was once famed for the anthropological and natural history collection begun by Raffles in 1849 and, consequently, was called the Raffles Library and Museum. The insect, fish, mammal, bird and other natural history exhibits, dubbed the Raffles Collection, were moved out of the museum in the 1970s; some of the preserved fauna are now displayed at the Singapore Science Centre (see page 133). The 10,000 volumes of journals, books and natural history publications are now known as the Zoological Reference Collection.

The museum now houses a collection that showcases the ethnology, history and art of Singapore and Southeast Asia. Bronzes, stone sculptures and traditional textiles from India and Southeast Asia, ancient ceramics from different parts of Indochina and Thailand, and Chinese ceramics dating from the Neolithic period to the Qing Dynasty are some of the museum's most interesting artefacts. The museum is presently closed for major repairs, and is not scheduled to re-open until late 1990.

But it is to the ground-floor **History of Singapore Gallery** that visitors should go first for its speedy, visual introduction to Singapore. History is compressed here into a series of 20 miniature dioramas depicting scenes from the founding of Singapore to the meeting of the first parliament of independent Singapore in December 1965.

One of the most interesting tableaux is an imaginative reconstruction of Fort Canning as it might have been in February 1822, when an inquisitive Englishman, Dr John Crawfurd, who was later to become the second British resident of Singapore, took a walk up Forbidden Hill and stumbled across a brick platform and sandstone blocks there, the ruins of ancient buildings. He also found shards of Chinese and local pottery and several Chinese copper coins that dated from as far back as the first century. No trace of Crawfurd's finds remains today, but he recorded in his journal, 'Among these ruins, the most distinguished are those seated on a square terrace, of about forty feet [12 metres] to a side near the summit of the hill. On the edge of this terrace, we find fourteen large blocks of sandstone; which [I deduce] from the hole in each, had probably been the pedestals of as many wooden posts which supported the building.'

Other dioramas show the Serangoon Road area as it was in the 19th century, when horse-drawn gharries were a popular mode of transport; the cramped and dingy dormitories where new immigrants from China lived; and Raffles signing an agreement with the local chief, or *temenggong*, to set up a trading post on the island.

A favourite room is the **Straits Chinese Gallery**, which is opposite the History of Singapore Gallery. This shows the unique syncretic blend of Malay and Chinese elements from which arose the *Peranakan* (meaning 'local-born') or *nonya* culture. Many exhibits are donations or on loan from private collections. Permanent exhibits include a household ancestral altar, heavily carved, clothed and laden with offerings as it would have been in the traditional home. Dressed in the elaborate layers of a bride's wedding clothes, a life-sized mannequin stands beside a wedding bed, its carved and gilded supports draped with embroidered wedding silks. The Straits Chinese were so gung-ho for Empire that they were sometimes known as the King's Chinese, and their furniture and gewgaws tended to reflect European influence as well. Revolving exhibitions within the gallery show the colourful porcelain (imported from China), delicately hammered silver and beadwork favoured by the community.

Upstairs, Southeast Asia's love affair with ceramics is recorded in the museum's **Trade Ceramics Gallery**, so called because the porcelain was shipped to or through Singapore. The ceramic trade was at its height from the tenth to the 13th century and the gallery displays mainly Chinese, Thai and Vietnamese ceramics. A collection of jade carvings and other art works in precious and semi-precious stone is also popular. Downstairs, a small theatre screens a half-hour audio-visual show on Singapore's multi-cultural history four times a day.

Just as ancient treasures were buried on top of Fort Canning, modern treasures have been interred at its foot. In 1984, a two-metre (six-foot) long time capsule was lowered into the ground. Its contents include a microwave oven and a radio watch, and it is scheduled for recovery in the year 2009.

A large part of the museum is now devoted to the **National Museum Art Gallery**, a collection built up around a gift of 115 early works of Singaporean and Malaysian artists from a Singaporean philanthropist in the 1960s. Many Singaporean artists have donated their own work to the permanent collection of paintings, calligraphy and sculpture, and other benefactors include the American investment firm of Goldman-Sachs, which recently presented three paintings by Singaporean artists.

The gallery's permanent collection includes works by well-known Singaporean artists like Georgette Chen, Liu Kang, Chen Wen-Hsi, Eng Tow, Thomas Yeo and Tan Swie Hian, as well as by a new generation of young full-time artists such as Goh Ee Choo. The art gallery, which opened only in 1976, also presents temporary exhibitions of artists of Singapore and

the region, as well as international artists like Paul Klee and contemporary French and British painters. Individual artists and art societies rent gallery space for their own exhibitions. A Painting of the Year exhibition run by the United Overseas Bank is one of the highlights of the exhibition programme. Frequent changes of exhibition are necessitated by the lack of display space, so it is sometimes possible to see two or three different shows within a week.

In the National Museum's **Discovery Room**, at the opposite end of the corridor from the Art Gallery, two education officers and a small army of enthusiastic volunteers teach children how to create their own puppet theatre, lion dances and *gamelan* (traditional Indonesian) orchestras.

The activity sessions are usually for organized groups of schoolchildren, but walk-in visitors are always welcome if there is space. Places are limited, and the room is open only at certain times. Call ahead (tel. 337-7355) to find out when.

The National Museum is open 9 am – 4.30 pm (the Art Gallery until 5.30 pm) Tuesday to Sunday (closed Monday). Admission to the museum is $1 (50 cents for children), but free to the Art Gallery.

Emerald Hill

Nutmeg trees once crowned Emerald Hill, before the distinctive row houses were built in the first quarter of the century. These houses were ornamented with elaborate plaster mouldings, European tiles and wood carvings in keeping with the style and taste of their largely Straits Chinese owners, though their designers included Indian, Malay, Eurasian, British and Chinese architects. In 1981, part of Emerald Hill was declared a conservation area, Singapore's first. Since then, prices for the irreplaceable homes have gone through the roof.

The new owners of Singapore's answer to San Francisco's painted ladies (those wonderful Victorian Gothic gingerbread houses painted in all colours) are often architects, for they were the first to see the area's possibilities and take a chance that the old houses would not fall victim to demolition and redevelopment. New owners, architects or not, have restored, redecorated and often rented out their new acquisitions to others keen to live in what has become a very chic part of town. A bonus is that Emerald Hill is just off the main shopping and hotel strip of Orchard Road — two minutes away from 'everything', as a former resident described it.

The story of the hill began in the 1830s with William Cuppage, a former postal clerk who rose to become acting postmaster-general. Cuppage aspired to be a nutmeg farmer, according to architect Lee Kip Lin, the author of *Emerald Hill: The Story of a Street in Words and Pictures*. But by the time his crop was ready for market, nutmeg prices had suffered a drastic decline.

His venture did eventually become profitable, but this was cut short in the
mid-1800s by beetles that wiped out Cuppage's plantation, along with all
other nutmeg plantations on the island.

If Cuppage, who died in 1827, could only have guessed then what a
goldmine his plantation property would become! Before the turn of the
century, there were just three houses on the property, two built by Cuppage
and a third by his son-in-law, Edwin Koek, who sold out in 1891. The
property was sold again in 1900, this time to two Chinese who subdivided
and resold it. By 1918, there were 67 homes here, and another 37 were put up
between 1924 and 1925. Dr Lim Boon Keng, a leader of the Straits Chinese
community, bought the house called 'Claregrove', which had been built for
Koek. But the house was pulled down in 1924 so that the Singapore Chinese
Girls School, which still functions here, could be built on the site.

As the town advanced and the hill was developed, Emerald Hill underwent
an inescapable metamorphosis from country to suburb and finally to city.
Emerald Hill Road is now closed to traffic at its lower end, which has
become a lively mall — sometimes too lively for the taste of the neighbours
— where one can down a few beers, listen to music and have a meal. The
mall is part of **Peranakan Place**, a corner dedicated to the Straits Chinese
who made Emerald Hill their own. Peranakan Place is one of the earliest
'restoration' projects of the Urban Redevelopment Authority, which tore
down and rebuilt the entire corner into a complex of restaurants, shops and
entertainment space. Purists moan about the lack of authenticity in the food
(Straits Chinese are particularly discriminating about authenticity in their
cuisine) and entertainment (anything from ballads of the 1940s and 1950s to
hard rock and mime), but blissfully uninformed patrons simply enjoy the
food and the chance to down a long drink outdoors in the evening, a
surprisingly uncommon opportunity in Singapore. What undoubtedly is
authentic is the Peranakan Museum, a house set up as if for newly-weds,
complete with a lavishly carved and decorated bridal bed. Guided tours
through the house can be joined for a small charge during the daytime. Ask at
Keday Kopi, Peranakan Place's coffee shop. Bibi's Restaurant upstairs is
almost a museum unto itself, decorated with vintage photographs and carved
panels.

The original Emerald Hill Road dates back to 1901, though it was then
nothing like today's asphalted, paved and tiled walkway. A walk through is
well worth your time. The grand old bungalows that once graced the hill are
history, but the terraced houses give Emerald Hill a distinctive look. Many of
the houses have now been refinished to varying degrees of authenticity. A
couple of them are whitewashed with the wooden doors and windows lightly
stained or unstained to appear natural. While the simple, stripped-down look
may be aesthetically pleasing, a Peranakan house that is a riot of colours is
more likely to be true to its origins. Look for the *pintu pagar* — half-doors

set on hinges, usually with elaborately carved panels — which keep out prying eyes while allowing a degree of ventilation. House No. 127, built about 60 years ago, has a marvellous pair of carved doors, though the window grills are modern. At some other windows, though, one may sometimes find modesty panels — carved wood, tinted glass or basketweave panels — which perform the same function and allow the occupants to see out without being seen. The row of houses from Nos. 39 to 45 still has tiled gateways opening on to neat courtyards. Motifs that recur in house after house include dragons and fu dogs, crabs, deer, roses and other flowers. These are not merely decorative flourishes; many have considerable symbolic meaning — usually to do with luck, longevity and happiness.

Botanic Gardens

The *Hevea brasiliensis* takes some finding, though they are the most eminent residents of the Botanic Gardens. *Hevea* is of course the para-rubber plant brought to Malaya from England's famed Kew Gardens. First planted in 1877 in the gardens' Palm Valley, these historic seedlings were the parents of Southeast Asia's rubber plantations.

Palm Valley, which has one of the most varied collections of palms in the world, is not short of eminent residents. Part of its living collection is the double coconut, or sea coconut, of the Seychelles. Its unusual fruit, measuring up to half a metre (20 inches) long, is the largest and heaviest seed known to man.

These are only two of the many reasons to visit the Botanic Gardens. Planned as a park, the gardens developed into a research centre for Malayan and regional flora. In recent years they have become a regular venue for open-air symphonic and jazz concerts and theatrical performances. The gardens come to life at dawn, with an uninhibited invasion of joggers and small armies of *tai chi* enthusiasts. In their wake come occasional groups of students on field trips — and tourists by the busload.

The chequered history of the Botanics, as locals call the gardens, goes back to 1822, when Sir Stamford Raffles set up an experimental garden on Fort Canning to grow nutmeg, cloves and cocoa. It was not a roaring success. The present gardens date from 1859 when the government was persuaded to set aside some 25 tiger-infested hectares (60 acres) in then-rural Tanglin for a park. Part of the area was an abandoned plantation, the rest, virgin jungle.

Some four hectares (ten acres) of that jungle remain — a manageable, unthreatening and now tiger-less territory to traipse through. It is the only piece of virgin tropical forest left in Singapore, apart from the nature reserve at Bukit Timah, a hill to the north of the gardens. The jungle contains Singapore's original 'skyscrapers' —a bower of *Dipterocarps* and other arboreal giants towering 30 metres (100 feet) or more above the ferns, seedlings and shrubs of the forest floor. One tree stands 50 metres (160 feet) tall, its top wired with a lightning rod.

The gardens' oldest resident, a cotton plant, actually predates the founding of modern Singapore, as it was collected in India in 1763 and sent to the gardens here in an exchange of flora. The famous para-rubber plant owes its success to Dr Henry Ridley (branded 'Mad' Ridley by his detractors), who was director from 1888 to 1912. Ridley planted rubber seedlings wherever he could find space in the gardens, and it was he who convinced sceptical planters to try out this new crop. By 1917, the gardens had distributed millions of seeds to avid Malayan planters.

Ridley was also an ardent orchid fancier, and it was to him that, in 1893, an excited Armenian resident, Agnes Joaquim, brought the purple orchid hybrid she had discovered growing in a stand of bamboo in her garden. To her joy, Ridley confirmed that this scion of *Vanda hookerana* and *Vanda teres* was indeed a new orchid. A naturally occurring hybrid, *Vanda Miss Joaquim* is now Singapore's national flower.

The highest point in the gardens is the octagonal bandstand atop the circular knoll rather grandiosely named Bandstand Hill. Built in 1860, the green-and-white shelter sits all of 33 metres (110 feet) above sea level. The gardens also contain a temperate house, a bonsai exhibit and two ornamental lakes. A third lake is in a fairly new extension to the rear of the gardens proper. The extension connects to the main gardens via a tunnel under Cluny Road.

A ten-minute walk from Orchard Road takes you to the gardens' newly rebuilt front gate. Admission is free. The gates are open 5 am – 11 pm weekdays and until midnight on Saturday, Sunday and public holidays.

The Singapore River

The Singapore River is like an old friend caught between careers. A commercial lifeline yesterday, it is trying to make a new life for itself as a place for culture, recreation and entertainment. As with many urban dockland areas, the city is looking for new avenues of business and exploring a whole new way of living, hoping that a different and moneyed breed of home-owner and entrepreneur will want to move in.

When Singapore was founded the river quickly became an important conduit of trade. Ships arrived bearing coffee and spices from the East Indies, gold dust and opium from India, and porcelain and silks from China. These commodities were sometimes traded right in the middle of the river for cotton goods, ironware and steel. The river trade slowed with the opening of the Suez Canal and the arrival of the steamship, then picked up again, but the bumboats (floating vendors) and lighters that plied the river always had to contend with the vagaries of the tides — low water meant it was nearly

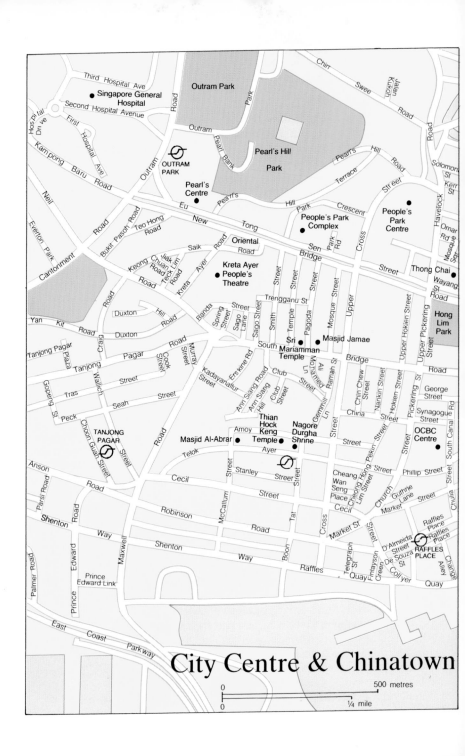

City Centre & Chinatown

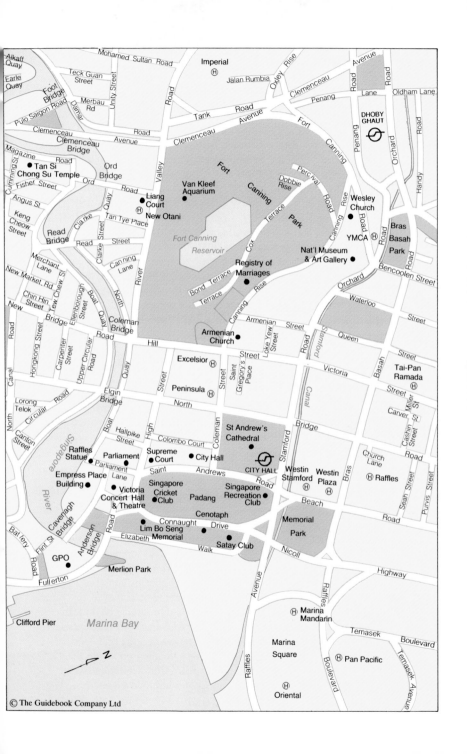

impossible to tie up at the quayside, while low bridges contrived to prevent boats from moving upstream at high water.

The Singapore River does not reach far inland. Beyond Kim Seng Bridge, it narrows into little more than a monsoon drain. (The bridge is named after the wealthy, philanthropic Straits Chinese trader and civic leader Tan Kim Seng, who left a fortune of some two million dollars when he died in the mid-19th century. Until the early 1980s, his sprawling family home, Panglima Prang, stood near the bridge and road that bear his name. The site is now occupied by an upscale condominium development.) In the river's upper reaches, the water is only paddle-deep — even shallower at low tide. The People's Association, a national umbrella organization that oversees a network of community and sports centres, plans to set up a boating and watersports centre in a disused warehouse here.

As with everything on the river, the future is never too far from the past. The graceful Tan Si Chong Temple on Magazine Road, which has stood by the river since 1876, may soon be a prime vantage point for watching canoes splash up and down the river and squads of kayaks execute acrobatic flips on hitherto calm waters, just as it is now for the boisterous Dragon Boat Races regularly held here. Beautiful in its own way but less imposing than Thian Hock Keng, the Hokkien temple on Hokkien Street, Tan Si Chong Su, is also a national monument. It belongs to the Hokkien Tan Clan and was funded by Tan Kim Ching and Tan Beng Swee, sons of wealthy Singapore pioneers. The temple they built was chiefly intended as a gathering place for the clan. Built in 1876, it faces a quiet portion of the Singapore River, an area of old warehouses that does not see much traffic these days. Dragons slither around the temple's carved granite pillars and guard the roof. Richly gilded 'door gods' adorn its side entrances.

In recent years, the part of the river between Cavenagh Bridge and Read Bridge has been the focus of several national celebrations and is used increasingly as an outdoor venue for other festivities. The Chinese New Year, for example, is the occasion for pop shows on river barges, carnival stalls and outdoor theatre. Boat Quay remains among the river's most photographed sights. Around the widest curve of the river, towering skyscrapers emblazoned with the corporate insignia of the country's major banks positively reek of money. They stand with windows glinting in the sun, staring down at the century-old shophouses clustered at their feet.

Many of the fortunes assembled by Singapore's immigrants have been made on the river. Tan Tock Seng, a settler from Malacca who became one of Singapore's richest traders, started as a humble hawker on the quayside. Other millionaires started as coolies loading and unloading goods on the river, or as the tallymen overseeing them. Upstream from Coleman Bridge, the river was the preserve of fish dealers, most of whom were Teochew. The wholesale business at Ellenborough Market started as early as 2 am, when boats arrived from *kelongs* (offshore fishing platforms on stilts) to unload their cargo.

The smell of fish lingered throughout the day and into the night. No doubt more than the smell found its way into the river waters. One writer in the 1930s was moved to remark, 'There is no sweetness in that river! It insists on making its presence known through the agency of an original and abominable stench at low tide; and at high tide, though somewhat less offensive and overpowering, is yet not all violets.' The fish trade moved in the 1970s to the Jurong Central Fish Market. More visibly missed are the old bumboats which ferried rubber, rice and other commodities up and down the waterway. They were also a major source of pollution.

On the plus side, the river is most certainly cleaner now and less odoriferous — even at low tide. Some of Singapore's more intrepid swimmers — out to prove a point — took the plunge *en masse* some years ago to demonstrate that one could swim the river and survive. They made history of sorts, but no one seems keen to follow where they led. Weekend anglers with their fishing lines, and prawn and crab nets are now a common sight on Anderson and Cavenagh bridges near the river mouth, and one assumes they do eat their catch.

The river's historical place in Singapore was set when Raffles sailed up the estuary in 1819. No one knows for sure where it was he first stepped ashore, but his likely landing place, just behind Parliament House, is now marked with a copy, in white polymarble, of the century-old bronze statue of him that stands a short distance away in front of the Victoria Theatre and Victoria Concert Hall. A floating village of Malay homes inhabited the river mouth, and about 30 families of *Orang Laut* (sea gypsies) lived upriver. They made daily offerings at a pointed rock shaped like the snout of a Long Tom or garfish. The Orang Laut believed this rock to be home to spirits that had to be propitiated daily lest they slay them on their way through the estuary.

Another rock found nearby provides an important clue to Singapore's ancient past. This huge piece of sandstone was inscribed in what is believed to be the ancient writing of the once-powerful Javanese empire of Majapahit. The Singapore Stone, as historians call it, was found when the area was being cleared. In 1843, it was blown up so that quarters for the commander of Fort Fullerton could be built on the site. Some fragments were rescued by a colonel who sent three slabs to Calcutta to have the inscription analysed. Another fragment, which had been serving as a seat, was also rescued — only to be hacked into gravel for road-making on Fort Canning. A small fragment of the Singapore Stone survives in the National Museum.

Like the stone, much of the old river life has been done away with in the name of development. When Linda Barry, an American then living in Singapore, took camera and notebook to the river to capture a way of life, she found herself, quite unexpectedly, documenting its passing. 'Nearly three

quays have disappeared since I started photographing the river with the result that when I was unhappy with pictures, I found on my return to the scene, even days later, it was too late; my subject was gone,' she wrote. In her book, *Singapore River: A Living Legacy* (1982), she looked ahead and saw what has since come to pass, 'The hard truth is that the river scenery will change beyond all recognition and a way of life will be lost in the next few years.' A year later the bumboats were moved out of the river and westwards to Pasir Panjang. The boatmen do come back to their old social haunts. Some pop in for a drink and a natter with old comrades at the wine shops they frequented as river workers, where you are unlikely to find names like Christian Brothers or Gallo. Ask instead for Snake or Tiger Bone wine, which taste as strong as they sound.

The men and their boats were once central to trade on the river, a business that more often than not was the preserve of Hokkiens and Teochews from southern China. Most of them bore the surnames Tan or Lim. North Boat Quay between Coleman Bridge (New Bridge Road) and Read Bridge (Merchant Bridge) was practically owned by the Teochew Lim clan and the Tan clan. The big wholesalers set up their offices by the river and established godowns (warehouses) some distance away, while the small wholesalers operated from shophouses by the river. They dominated the commodity trade then, and Hokkien merchants in Telok Ayer and Market streets are still major players in the rice import business. The Hokkiens also dealt in beans, copra, coffee, sugar and animal feed from Indonesia. Teochew rice merchants set up their shops at Boat Quay near Elgin Bridge and were chiefly wholesalers. The Teochew traders led the dry seafood trade, providing products like dried shrimp, salted fish, sharks' fin and sea cucumber. Some shops still do business in the North Canal Road area.

The river and its traditions are best experienced on foot, but there are also boat cruises for those who would rather cruise the waterway and imagine what it was like. Two organizations offer river cruises by bumboat:

Lian Hup Choon's half-hour boat ride takes you from Raffles Landing on North Boat Quay behind Parliament House, upriver past godowns, the Empress Place Building (which last housed the Immigration Department and is now being converted into an exhibition hall) and historic bridges and quays, then back downriver and out to Marina Bay, the venue for two annual international events, the mid-year Dragon Boat Races and the Powerboat Grand Prix held in November. Tours leave every half hour, tides and weather permitting, between 9 am and 7 pm daily. The cost is $6 per person ($3 for children under 12). Tel. 222–2528/224–6383.

Eastwind Organization starts it tours from Clifford Pier. Cruises leave at two-hourly intervals between 10 am and 4 pm daily, with passengers embarking 15 minutes before departure. The cost is $20 per person ($10 for children under 12). Tel. 533-3432/534-3848.

Chinatown

It may seem surprising to visitors that there should be a Chinatown at all in a
place in which three-quarters of the people are Chinese. But there is. Young
people call it Chinatown. Older folk know it as Gu Chia Chwi (literally
'buffalo cart water') after the buffalo-drawn water carts that supplied the
dwellings before the advent of running water. Today the place is also known
as Kreta Ayer (Malay for 'water cart'). Locals are quite accustomed to using
the names interchangeably, and it may well be that only in Singapore would
Malay and English names be applied in this way to a historic Chinese
settlement.

The old city might have looked quite different had Raffles not decided
very early on that the Chinese should live in the area southwest of the
Singapore River. He even laid down where the various dialect groups should
set up home. Historically, the Hokkiens, the largest Chinese group, settled
around Amoy, China, Telok Ayer and Hokien streets. The industrious
Hokkiens, from China's Fujian (Fukien) Province, were mainly merchants,
carpenters and odd-job labourers, so these areas came to be identified with
their trades for years. On the other hand, the Cantonese, traditionally
goldsmiths and tailors, also owned teahouses and restaurants, with which the
areas around Temple, Pagoda and Mosque streets are still associated. The
distinctive flavour they have given to the streets still remains.

Parts of Chinatown are spectacularly dilapidated. Old paint peels off many
of its shophouses like decaying bark. (The row houses are called 'shophouses'
because it was common for the family to live above the shop.) Many
shophouses do get spruced up for the Lunar New Year season, which is,
incidentally, the best time to visit as there is more street life at night than at
other times of year.

Up to the 1830s, wrote Charles Burton Buckley in his *Anecdotal History
of Old Times in Singapore*, no woman from China had ever settled in
Singapore. The newspapers of the time reported that the only Chinese women
to ever set (dainty) foot on the island were two ladies with bound feet en
route to London to be exhibited.

Chinatown's most visible residents are the aged, many of them marginal
entrepreneurs who make a living rescuing and selling fruit and vegetables
discarded by wholesalers, or by collecting old newspapers and cardboard
cartons for resale. There is no museum, no multi-screen audio-visual show,
no visitor centre or structured attraction here — not yet, at any rate.
Chinatown's charm is in its past and its present. It continues to be a refuge
for craftsmen like Wong Yu Pui, a carpenter for 30 years, whose stack of
hand-made wooden stools is a sidewalk landmark in Mosque Street. Another
craftsman, most often to be found outside the Sri Mariamman Temple on
South Bridge Road, is mask maker Ban Kok, whose bicycle cart bears the

likenesses of Mickey Mouse and Donald Duck as well as the Chinese opera figurines and masks which have made him something of a minor celebrity, much photographed by visitors.

The presence of craftsmen and aged poor, bypassed by the world of silicon chips and rising expectations in a generally clean, orderly and upwardly mobile society, make Chinatown irresistible to tourist, architect and sociologist alike. The dusty ochres, pale greens, cobalt blues and vivid reds of its streetscape reflect the rich history and social colour that have become rare in a cityscape dominated by the greys of glass-walled skyscrapers.

Though not all of Chinatown is safe from urban renewal, much of it is to be saved, with no new highrises allowed within the preservation area. Redevelopment also has to follow strict design guidelines in keeping with the spirit of the original architecture. Conservation efforts will now form an integral part of the Urban Redevelopment Authority's Central Area Structure Plan. Since most of the property is privately owned, the authority now faces the task of convincing owners, including absentee landlords, to restore and renovate their properties properly.

Some of these buildings are more than a century old, as Chinatown's development began in earnest in the early 1840s. A census shows that by 1871 immigration had swelled Singapore's Chinese population to 54,572. Along with immigrants came the slave trade, secret societies and prostitution, and these social problems grew so acute that the Chinese Protectorate was set up in 1877 to deal with them. Most of the early immigrants were indentured to a *gongsi* (company), which paid their passage from China. They then had to work off what they owed. Common jobs were in rubber tapping, unloading goods or transporting cargo to godowns under the command of a coolie agent or headman known as a *khektow*. Many later became hawkers who plied the streets selling anything from clogs to cooked food.

When the wealthier immigrants took the first leases in Chinatown in the 1840s, they built their homes in neat rows in the simple style of homes in southern China. When the pioneers moved on, elaboration set in. Later immigrants transformed the dwellings to shophouses, favouring facades with arched windows, pilasters and Greco-Roman columns. As Chinatown grew more crowded, ground floors became shops and families moved upstairs, often to a single floor partitioned and re-partitioned to accommodate growing numbers. Whole families lived in a single sunless cubicle and shared toilets and charcoal-fired clay stoves with scores of other people.

Chinese Temples

A favourite stop on Telok Ayer Street is Singapore's oldest Hokkien temple, **Thian Hock Keng,** or the Temple of Heavenly Bliss. One of the most graceful temples in Singapore, Thian Hock Keng started out as a joss house (incense shrine) in the early 1820s. The temple is one of several on what used

to be the coastline of Singapore before the 1880s, when the bay was reclaimed. When sailors and settlers landed, their first stop was this joss house dedicated to Ma Chu Po, the Mother of Heavenly Sages, to offer thanks for a safe journey. Thian Hock Keng was completed around 1841 at a cost of some 30,000 Spanish dollars.

Like many of the temple's early worshippers, who had just stepped off the boat, most modern visitors to the temple are also recent arrivals, but, unlike them, they are tourists. Immediately inside the portal are huge beams and elaborately carved pillars supporting the roof, which were shipped from south China. Most of the building material and many of the statues that adorn the altars also come from China, and a marble tablet at the entrance records the names of its principal benefactors.

The temple comprises a series of squares, the main square dominated by a shrine to Ma Chu Po, with a smaller altar to Guan Yin in a rear courtyard. Ma Chu Po's statue arrived before the existing temple was ready. She came by junk in 1840 from Amoy (Xiamen), Fujian Province, and was borne in procession from the waterfront to the temple.

There have been few attempts to pretty up Thian Hock Keng, though more than a decade ago, when the temple was in a very bad state, parts of the roof were plastered, and damaged roof tiles were replaced. The work was designed to leave the temple sound but looking its age. Restoration, which took four years to complete, cost $500,000, or twice what the owners had estimated. Thian Hock Keng, unlike Heng Shan Teng Temple or the now-defunct Soon Theng Keong Temple, is a national monument and thereby protected from demolition.

Fuk Tak Chi, another of the seafront temples, was constructed by the Cantonese and Hakkas (both south Chinese communities) in 1825 on Telok Ayer Street. It is one of Singapore's oldest Chinese temples. The profusion of deities would take a week of Sundays to explain, as this temple blends Buddhist, Taoist and Confucianist practices and appears to have acquired all the requisite deities as well.

On nearby Phillip Street which was also on the seafront, is **Wak Hai Cheng Bio**, the Temple of the Calm Sea, which was built between 1852 and 1855. As early as 1826, early Teochew immigrants from Guangdong Province in southern China started it off as a joss house where they gave thanks for a safe journey. On feast days you may see traditional Chinese street theatre troupes performing on a stage set up in the temple's large courtyard.

Hong San See was first built in 1829 south of Chinatown in Tras Street but was relocated north of the Singapore River when the colonial government took over the land. Finished in 1913, the 'new' building in Mohamed Sultan Road stands on 4,000 square metres (an acre) of land once owned by an Englishman named Tomlinson. He sold it to men from Nam An in Fujian Province, and the Nam An community still owns the temple, but worshippers represent many other dialect groups. The street on which it stands is quiet, a haven just off bustling River Valley Road. Though the builders set their house of worship atop a long flight of stairs, the long haul up is worth the effort, if only to admire the round columns decorated with fine calligraphy and the dragons that run riot on its granite pillars.

Mosques and Hindu Temples

Chinatown is not exclusively a Chinese enclave, containing as it does a number of historic mosques and Hindu temples along with Chinese temples.

Masjid Jamae, a modest structure in South Bridge Road, which is best known for its goldsmiths, was built by Muslims from southern India. The mosque stands on the site of an earlier building erected in 1826 or 1827. The existing mosque, with its distinctive square, tiered pagodas, was built between 1830 and 1835 and is an official national monument. It is still used for worship.

The **Nagore Durgha Shrine**, also built by Muslims from southern India, is on Telok Ayer Street, on the fringes of Chinatown. Once known as Shahul Hamid Durgha, it was built between 1828 and 1830, when the waves all but lapped the street. The sea has been pushed back by reclamation, but Nagore Durgha, which has the same squared-off pagodas as Masjid Jamae, still stands as a marker of the old pre-1880s shoreline. Nagore Durgha is a national monument.

Masjid Al-Abrar, further up Telok Ayer Street, is a more modest-looking mosque, but also a national monument. It is also known as Masjid Chulia after the Chulias, or south Indian Muslims, who built it in 1827 and rebuilt it between 1850 and 1855. Tamils also call it Kuchu Palli (*kuchu* being Tamil for 'hut' and *palli* meaning 'mosque'). Between the two Islamic monuments is **Thian Hock Keng**, or Temple of Heavenly Bliss (see page 89), one of the oldest and best-known temples in Singapore.

In the very heart of Chinatown is the country's oldest surviving Hindu shrine, **Sri Mariamman**. Its gateway is crowned with a *gopuram*, a many-tiered tower of deities. The gopuram has had several facelifts, most recently in 1984 when craftsmen from India spent months rebuilding it. Named a national monument in 1973, it was originally a wood and attap (palm thatch) building put up in the early 1820s by Naraina Pillai, an Indian merchant from Penang who is believed to be Singapore's first Indian immigrant. The building that survives today is thought to have been built by Indian and Chinese workers sometime in the early 1860s. Though it is officially a monument, it remains very much an active place of worship and a focus of every major Hindu festival, including the fire-walking festival of Thimithi, when barefoot devotees keep the faith by walking over a bed of hot coals.

The Market

At most times, a walk through Chinatown tends to be rather a hot and sticky affair, so the best time to see it is early in the morning or in the evening. Though market stalls no longer pack the streets each morning, the morning bustle at the 'wet market' (so called because of its wet floors) in the highrise Chinatown Complex is still an experience. Many residents in this area still do not own refrigerators and consequently need to do their food shopping every day. Non-residents also head here because of the variety of Chinese foodstuffs, especially dried food, available in the shops. One can snack one's way through Eu Tong Sen Street and New Bridge Road, which run parallel to each other.

Pagoda Street

Nearby Pagoda Street was once known for its opium dens. This was also the street where many of the coolies or manual labourers had their lodgings. There are still about 1,000 opium addicts in Singapore. Some say it is still possible to visit an opium den in Chinatown, though none exists legally since opium and utensils for smoking the drug were outlawed in 1946. In the old days, this street was the centre of the slave trade. One of the firms involved was known as Kwong Hup Yuen, at 37 Pagoda Street, the ground floor of which is now a bicycle shop. Old-timers still refer to this street as Kwong Hup Yuen Kai (*kai* meaning street).

Temple Street to Sago Lane

Lots around Temple Street, Smith Street, and Sago Lane were granted or leased to the public from 1843. At the clog shop in Temple Street, one of a handful that still sell the traditional wooden footwear, a sign informs you brusquely that photographers are not welcome. But there is no charge for looking on as the clogmaker deftly nails colourful plastic strips to the wooden soles. The clogs, usually lacquered in red, are often purchased as souvenirs.

At Sago Street's funerary paper works, there is always something new to see. The shop at 14 Sago Street can sometimes look like a Mercedes-Benz dealership, except that the paper cars sold here are made to be burnt as offerings to propitiate the spirits of the dead. One can order a scaled-down *Ben-zee* complete with smartly uniformed chauffeur, tape deck and auspiciously numbered licence plate. If style is what you are after, how about a scaled-down cruise liner (captain and crew included). Next door at No. 16, they make all sorts of paper figures, from the traditional offerings (horses, houses, servants and chests full of paper clothes) to such modern necessities as video recorders, jumbo jets, computers and even credit cards — all to comfort departed souls on their final journey. These shops are especially busy just before the festival of Qing Ming in the third lunar month, the Chinese

Chinese Temples

According to historians, the rebuilding of Chinese temples in Singapore has never been seriously encumbered by sentiment. As early temples and shrines in Singapore and neighbouring Malaya were not much more than thatched-roof structures, they inevitably needed replacing by more permanent buildings.

Not surprisingly, the magnificence of a temple is relative to the size of the community and wealth of its patrons. It also helps if the deity to which the temple is dedicated is a popular one. That there are so many temples dedicated to Tua Pek Kong, the god of wealth, tells one a great deal about the pragmatic nature of temple founders and devotees.

The most photographed feature of a temple is its roof, with its grand ridges terminating in an upward sweep of swallow or fish tails. A dragon pearl, dragon bead or blazing pearl (which also represents the sun) often dominates the ridge of the roof.

The pagoda, carp, phoenix, gourd, dragon and dragon horse are other popular ornaments. While the pagoda is generally associated with the Chinese, this feature was originally borrowed from India. It symbolizes cosmic Mt Meru, where the gods are thought to reside. This being the case, a pagoda is one sure way to keep evil spirits at bay, or so the thinking goes. Another ornament able to trap spirits (and thereby prevent their coming near in the first place) is the gourd, or *hu lu*, which symbolizes longevity. Inside the gourd is a place in which souls exist in a state of bliss, according to a scholar of Chinese architecture in the Straits Settlements, David G Kohl, in his study of the subject. Carp symbolize success because they swim upstream against the current. If the carp wishes to be reborn as a dragon — a being of intellect and power — it must successfully leap the Dragon Gate rapids of the Yellow River. Thus the dragon, another common temple ornament, symbolizes both success and life.

Temples are also for entertainment. Periodically, temporary stages materialize in front of a temple, and a full Chinese opera or a puppet opera brings the street to life for many nights. The occasion might be a feast of the chief deity or any of his lesser deities. The spectacle is free, and the show goes on rain or shine, with or without a human audience, for the most important spectators are the gods.

Some of the earliest places of worship are sited on the outer edge of Chinatown, at Telok Ayer Street. Literally translated from Malay, this is 'water bay street'. Modern visitors might be quite puzzled by the name, as the seafront is nowhere in evidence. But in the earliest days of the colony, this was where ships disgorged their armies of migrants. When the newcomers landed, after being rowed to shore in frail *sampans*, they were understandably thankful for a safe conclusion to a long, uncomfortable and hazardous sea journey.

The Oldest Temple?
Exactly which temple is the oldest in Singapore is still a matter of dispute. Some scholars say Heng Shan Teng (Gathering at the Hillock of Heng)

Temple, southwest of Chinatown at the junction of Jalan Bukit Merah and Kampong Baru Road, is the oldest. The year 1828 is inscribed on a gilded wooden plaque, and a stone stele recording the building of the temple and the names of the donors was erected in the tenth year of Emperor Daoguang, or 1830. Unlike Thian Hock Keng, Heng Shan Teng is small and rather inconspicuous. Temple records say that the builders were from Zhangzhou and Quanzhou in southern Fujian province.

Others insist the recently defunct Soon Theng Keong Temple, well northeast of Chinatown in Malabar Street, was even older. Some years ago, a stone tablet found in the temple led a scholar to believe that there was a sizeable Chinese community of 500 souls in Singapore before Raffles' founding of Singapore in 1819. It fails, however, to answer an important question: Was the temple already in existence at that time? An answer is not likely to be forthcoming because the structure was demolished to make way for Bugis Station, one of the stops on the Mass Rapid Transit railway. Six hundred devotees said goodbye as the temple's deities rode a truck to a shophouse in nearby Albert Street.

Chinese pavilions are often decorated with scenes such as these

equivalent of All Souls' Day, when graves are swept and prayers offered to ancestors.

Nearby, at Block 4 in Sago Lane, check out Chun Chun, a Chinese medicine hall and tea shop. Patients are diagnosed and medicine is dispensed here as in any doctor's clinic, except that a patient can have his cure brewed for him, or if it is a common remedy he needs, down a ready-brewed draught from the rows of clay medicine teapots at the shop. Herbal tea stands, some dispensing goodness from large stainless steel urns, others from modest red enamel teapots, tend to be family-run businesses, and each proprietor has a stock of tales to tell. Interest in alternative medicine in the West has rebounded here, with a growing younger clientèle gravitating to the herbal habit.

Though there is no museum in Chinatown, an antique shop at 86 Neil Road comes close. Chan Pui Kee, run by the son of the founder, overflows with Chinese antiques, much of it there to be restored and repaired by Mr Chan Hong Cheong, whose reputation in antique restoration is such that people are prepared to wait years for him to carry out the work.

Club Street

The Club Street area on Chinatown's eastern fringe is quiet but certainly not godforsaken, for it is populated by more Taoist and Buddhist deities per square foot than possibly any temple. At Lim Aik Thuan Idol Maker, where Club Street turns east into Gemmill Lane, it is hard to tell which deities lurk in the logs being worked on by the sculptors. Half created on a shop floor littered with wood shavings may be a kitchen god or monkey god — or any other of the hundreds or perhaps thousands in the heavenly pantheon. Two other shops, the Say Tian Hng Buddha Shop at Gemmill Lane and Say Tan Kok in Club Street, also make carvings of deities.

Thong Chai Building

One of the few surviving examples of Chinese architecture in Singapore, apart from religious buildings, is a grand Chinatown structure, the Thong Chai Medical Institution building in Wayang Street. Built in the 1890s with the help of public donations, it was a centre of traditional medicine, where the poor could consult the *sinseh* (doctor) and get herbal medicines — all for free. The institution predates the building considerably, having been set up in 1867, and now carries on its good works in a modern, multi-storey building nearby. The original edifice is a minor palace of a building, its gabled roofs, high ceilings and sun-washed courtyard said to have been designed by an architect from Beijing. It has been preserved since 1972 as one of Singapore's national monuments and is the only building owned by the Preservation of Monuments Board.

Kampong Glam

'At the end of Kampong Gelam there stood two or three huts of the Sea
Gypsies, the Orang Laut of the Gelam tribe, who spent their time making
awnings and sails from the bark of the *gelam* tree. For this reason the place was
called Kampong Gelam,' wrote Abdullah bin Kadir, a language teacher and
scribe closely associated with Raffles.

If Colonel William Farquhar, who governed Singapore in its earliest days as
an English settlement, had had his way, Kampong Glam would have become a
business area and not the domain of royalty. This area, east of what was then
the European town, was instead allocated to Sultan Hussein Shah of Singapore
as Raffles wanted the business district to be south of the Singapore River.

The royal palace is not on any city tour itinerary, nor can visitors walk
through to admire its architecture. Now rather rundown, it does not have much
of a royal aura at all. But if you happen to be in the vicinity of Sultan Gate, it is
difficult to miss the Istana Kampong Glam, a large yellow mansion built in the
Palladian style. The existing building was constructed sometime between 1836
and 1843 to replace the original wood and *attap* (coconut thatch) structure.

Sultan Hussein was granted a large tract of Kampong Glam amounting to
nearly 23 hectares (57 acres) in 1823. By this time he had already begun to
build his istana to accommodate the family and entourage he had brought with
him from Riau (now part of Indonesia).

Other Malays from Malacca, Riau and Sumatra settled on the fringes, as did
Syed Mohammed bin Harun Al-Junied and his nephew Syed Omar bin Ali Al-
Junied, well-to-do Arab merchants from Palembang in south Sumatra who
came to Singapore in 1819. When Raffles revised his town plan, the Arabs
were given land east of the allotment for wealthy Europeans and Asians and
adjoining the part of Kampong Glam allotted to Sultan Hussein.

Mary Turnbull notes in *A History of Singapore 1819–1975* that the Malays
did not respect Hussein as their leader and that, debt-ridden, he moved to
Malacca where he died in 1835. Although his son Ali returned to Singapore in
1840 and took over his father's property in Kampong Glam, the English would
not recognize him as sultan.

By the mid-18th century, Kampong Glam and its environs were home to a
mixed community of Arabs, Bugis, Javanese, Malays and Chinese. By the turn
of the century there was also a sizeable community of Jawi-Peranakan,
descendants of Indian Muslims who, because of a dearth of Muslim womenfolk
from India, had married Malays. The Arab Street area, with its batik and textile
merchants, perfectly mirrors this mix of communities, as do the surviving
street names.

Kampong Glam acquired a Bugis flavour from very early on. Bugis traders
sailed to Singapore in September or October, where they would anchor their
craft just off the beach at Kampong Glam. While there, the boats functioned as
floating shops until the northeast monsoon took the Bugis home in November.
Many of these traders, who came from Dutch-controlled ports in Borneo, the
Celebes and Timor, were in fact smugglers, since the Dutch at that time were

trying to stop the ports in these areas from trading with Singapore.

While the royal fortunes declined in Kampong Glam, the temenggong's line prospered out in Telok Blangah under Daeng Ibrahim, the son of Temenggong Abdul Rahman, who along with Ali's father had signed the original treaty with Raffles. In 1855, Ibrahim made a treaty with Ali in which it was decided that Ali would become sultan, while Ibrahim would rule Johor. However Ali's son lost the title of sultan, and the Kampong Glam royalty declined further. Abu Bakar, Ibrahim's son, moved to Johor Baru and in 1885 was recognized as sultan of Johor.

Kampong Glam was very different in Singapore's early days. When Abdullah came to Singapore from Malacca about four months after Raffles first set foot on the island, he noted that there were no houses on the far side of the river, in the Kampong Glam area.'It was covered with jungle, mangrove and mud. People lived only on the near side. Sultan Hussein Shah was just starting to build his palace at Kampong Gelam but the area was covered with mangrove and there was no means of approach over the land. People going to Kampong Gelam used only the route along the shore. They feared the journey through the swamp though they had some fear also of the shore route. Every day without ceasing murders took place along the road to Kampong Gelam. There were policemen on duty here and there [but] they themselves were often murdered,' Abdullah reported.

Early Singapore was as lawless as you would expect a frontier town to be. The followers of the temenggong and sultan often fought with Malays from Malacca, and daylight robberies and stabbings were commonplace. This changed in the late 1820s. With the help of convict labour, mostly from India, the mangrove swamps at Kampong Glam were drained, roads were built and houses were constructed. Within a decade one fifth of the land was built up. Streets were laid out that still carry such names as Arab, Baghdad, Bussorah and Muscat.

Jalan Sultan, or Sultan's Road, was one of these streets. The best-known landmark here today is Sultan Mosque. Some people say there was already a mosque on the site before Raffles' arrival, but there seems to be no proof of this. What we do know is that the sultan asked Raffles for money to build a mosque and that in June 1823 Raffles promised him some. Kampong Glam's first mosque was built in 1824, but the oldest mosque in the area is the Masjid Hajjah Fatimah in Beach Road.

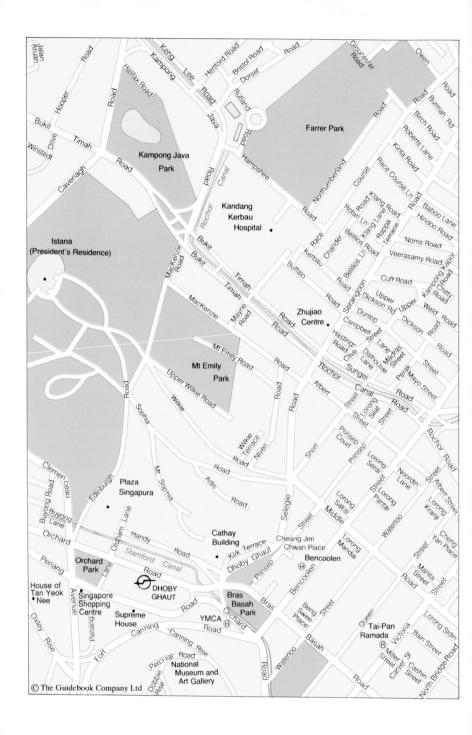

© The Guidebook Company Ltd

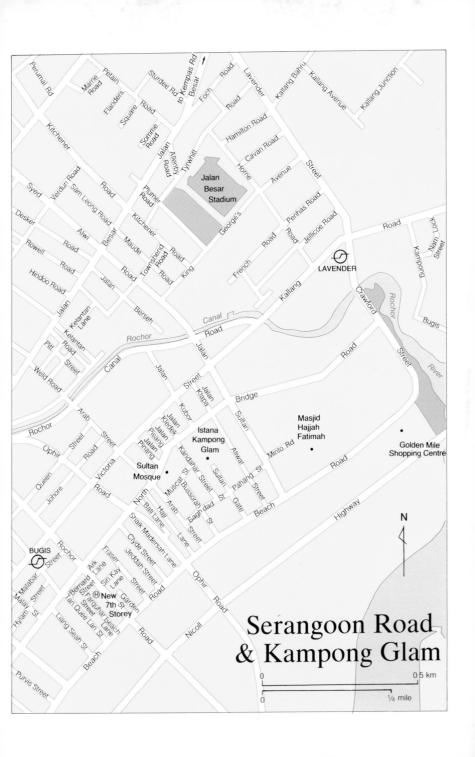

Serangoon Road
& Kampong Glam

It was at the Thong Chai building in 1983 that public interest in Chinatown's future was first sparked during a pioneering exhibition of historic photographs set up by the Archives and Oral History Department. The exhibition drew an audience of about 30,000 people, and the kindling of nostalgia caught fire later that year when Singapore turned out to say its goodbyes to Chinatown's street hawkers, who were being shooed off the streets and into the Chinatown Complex. For many people, the hawkers had been the essence of the place.

Little India

Serangoon Road, or Little India, is not so much a place as an experience, one that can be enjoyed even blindfolded. The air is perfumed by chains of roses, margosas, orchids and jasmine that hang from the ceiling of the garland makers, whose storefront may be the sidewalk, a narrow space under a stairway, or a counter in a 'deity department store' crammed with gods and goddesses rendered as plaster figurines or in framed portraits in bright blues, pinks and reds.

On feastdays, such as Deepavali, the Festival of Lights (see page 199), when garlands of fairy lights brighten the crowded streets, the deities keep the flower people extremely busy assembling innumerable orders of tinsel-bound garlands of heady jasmine. Though one can still see garland makers stringing together individual blossoms, plastic garlands seem to be gaining in popularity. 'If it gets dirty, can wash. Very practical,' says one entrepreneur, who adds that his paper garlands are also hot sellers. Real flowers are a bother, he continues, since the garland business has to rely in part on flowers brought in from Malaysia.

Just off the main road, Buffalo Road still snuggles up to Kerbau Road (which can be confusing since *kerbau* means buffalo). Here, a row of 28 pre-war shophouses and a bungalow are being refurbished to house traditional traders resettled from Serangoon Road. Their façades are to be kept, and the plan is to fill the row with shops selling Indian spices and cookware, flower garlands and Indian food. The public housing authority, the Housing and Development Board, expects to redevelop other buildings in the neighbourhood over the next few years.

While it enjoys the title of Little India, this part of Serangoon Road is not the only place in Singapore with an Indian flavour. There is High Street, in which Sindhi, Gujerati and Sikh merchants' saree shops and jewellery shops now sit side by side with an electronics emporium. South Indian dockworkers cluster near the port and railway station in Tanjong Pagar or at the opposite end of Singapore, around the naval base in the north. The very first settlers from the subcontinent headed for Chulia Street, an area in town where Indian moneylenders, shopkeepers, bankers and lawyers originally set up shop and where many still do business. But for Indians at large, including the thousands of visitors who flock to Serangoon Road from India and Malaysia, Little India is everything — the place to meet, eat, shop and live.

Over the years, Little India's residents have grown to expect the daily parade of outsiders through their lives, the shopkeepers here benefiting more from the open wallets of bargain-hunters from the subcontinent than from the busloads of tour groups. Lone visitors and smaller groups who walk in Little India's side streets are far more likely to receive friendly smiles of welcome. This has as much to do with the locals' feeling that they are being taken advantage of by tour companies as with the fact that individuals and smaller groups are much more likely to be paying customers in the shops and restaurants. On your own, you are also more likely to be able to enjoy the delights of poking your nose into the delightfully named Racing Parties Bar (a relic of the days when nearby Farrer Park was a race course) and the jewellery shops a-glitter with earrings, lockets and nose rings, all in distinctively Indian designs.

An old landmark, the wet market known to the Chinese as Teck Kah Pasat (*pasat* being a corruption of the Malay *pasar*, which means market) is long gone, supplanted by the Zhujiao Centre on the opposite side of the main thoroughfare from the old Teck Kah. It is still a wet market and still reeks of freshly slaughtered mutton, but the new market is part of a vast complex of apartments, shops and stalls. A major crowd-puller are the restaurants that serve generous portions of spicy food as delicious as it is cheap. As late as the mid-1970s, two could feast on *thosai* (thin, crisp pancakes made from a batter of lentils soaked and ground with rice and eaten with a relish of coconut and chillies) for less than $1 — less than you paid for your coffee, a brew thick with milk and sugar. Count on spending at least twice that much now. Masala thosai is the same pancake wrapped around a kind of vegetable stew not unlike *ratatouille*.

Several upmarket, air-conditioned eateries have sprung up in the area, but an old favourite remains Komala Vilas, at the first traffic light from the head of Serangoon Road, a great place to stop after an afternoon spent in the saree shops ordering *choli* (the snug-fitting blouse worn with a saree) and *shalwar kameez* (the blouse and baggy trousers worn by Punjabi women). You can also indulge in Indian sweets so sugary your teeth seem to curl around them on contact.

The best time to be in Little India is early in the morning, when the vendors, called *dudhwallas*, arrive to get fresh supply of milk from the dairymen. Pasteurization and refrigeration were unheard of in the days when they made house calls with cow or nanny-goat in tow and one could drink the creamy stuff straight from the pail, still warm and forthy (no skim milk then). Now the milk sloshes around in aluminium cans, is decanted into glass bottles that have been used and re-used a hundred times (no one has heard of no-deposit, no-return containers here) and then transported in bright green canvas saddlebags slung across bicycles, scooters and motorbikes. Most of the remaining vendors are old, and the increasing popularity of supermarket-fresh milk may soon drive the itinerant milk-sellers out of business altogether.

Like the milkmen, many of Little India's other institutions are found on the streets and by the roadside. One of the most popular is the yoghurt vendor who has been dishing out the *thairu* from her pails in Campbell Lane for the last 40 years. Thairu is made into a drink called *lassi*, either sweetened or salted, and is a staple on the Indian dinner table to exercise a counteracting 'cooling' effect on 'heaty' curries.

Once the inner man is satisfied, one can be more attentive to the rest of Little India's street culture. At almost any time of the day one can find the birdmen of Serangoon Road's sidewalks practising parrot astrology. They whisper the customer's name and birthdate to the bird, who then picks out a card with the 'right' fortune on it. Other fortune-tellers use trained parakeets to select numbered bamboo sticks, then look up the customer's fortune in well-thumbed tomes.

Little India's own fortunes are not doing at all badly. A recent influx of tourists from India has brought a new prosperity for many shopkeepers, especially those who sell the electrical and electronic goods avidly sought by their foreign clientèle. Colour television sets, video-cassette recorders and washing machines are as common a sight as spice shops. Yet, for all the sophisticated electronics in its shops, Little India is still fighting to keep things the way they were. Here, more than anywhere else in Singapore, it is most possible to leave the 20th century behind for a while.

No one quite knows how Serangoon Road came by its name. It might have been derived from the Malay word *ranggong,* a small marsh-dwelling bird. One charming (if doubtful) hypothesis presented in a book called *Singapore's Little India* has it that the name was derived from a Malay phrase *serang dengan gong*, which means 'to attack with gongs or drums' and recalls that the area was once the jungle sanctuary of snakes and other wild animals that had to be scared away.

If Serangoon Road once harboured wild animals, they were soon supplanted by cattle, who for years had free run of Serangoon Road, then a centre of Indian cattle-traders. This heritage survives in the name of the nearby maternity hospital (Singapore's largest) called Kandang Kerbau, which means water buffalo pen.

The cattle have been gone for more than half a century, banished from the municipality in 1936 by a polite if unequivocal notice in the government gazette. Cow pats have been replaced by more lethal pedestrian hazards measured in horsepower, but Little India lives on.

The Heathens
in their Midst

*T*he first St. Andrew's Church, which was completed in 1837 and
ceased to be used in 1852 as it was in a dangerous state, will be
remembered as the alleged cause of the first two "head scares"
among the Chinese, Malays and Indians. The first scare is recorded
by Abdullah in his Hikayat. He related how he himself made
inquiries into the rumour that the blood of thirty-six men was
required for the sanctification of the new church, and how he
argued with several persons who really believed the truth of the
rumour and how he failed to allay their fears. The matter became
worse after respectable and intelligent Chinese had made inquiries
and believed that nine heads had already been secured. What was
the origin of the rumour or who was responsible for it remains a
mystery.

In 1853, the Press reported a most extraordinary delusion
prevailing amongst the native population, and especially the
Chinese section. . . Placards in Chinese appeared all over the town
that the Governor and all the Europeans had left off worshipping
in St. Andrew's Church, owing to the number of evil spirits there,
and that in order to appease the spirits, the Governor required
thirty heads; and had ordered the convicts to waylay people at
night and kill them! The Governor, with a view to allaying the
panic, issued a notice declaring the reports to be false and offering
$500 reward for the discovery of any person propagating such
reports. As this notice only called forth other Chinese placards of a
very improper nature, some thirty of the leading Chinese
merchants, at the request of the Government, signed a long appeal
to their countrymen in which they pointed out the benevolence of
the English Government, and its anxiety to protect the lives of all
persons under its care, even to the extent of offering rewards for
the destruction of the tigers which killed people. This appeal was
lithographed and distributed, and in two days the fears of the
Chinese population were dispelled.

Son Ong Siang,
One Hundred Years' History of the Chinese in Singapore

North

Rural is a word that in Singapore applies only to the north, if at all — and then only in the most qualified way. Yes, there is farmland, and one can still see neat rows of vegetable gardens and compact orchards, especially from the air. One might wish to label this area the ricebowl, breadbasket or fruit bowl of the country, but the fact remains that the produce of Singapore's 40 square kilometres (10,000 acres) or less of farmland would leave its people quite hungry. Old-fashioned poultry farms (actually modernized beyond recognition into virtual factories) are now considered unsuited to a Singapore which has the world as its supermarket. Could this be the same country where tigers roamed only 50 years ago?

The tiger menace was first reported in the 1830s, and by the 1850s the man-eaters were said to be claiming a victim a day at least. The situation grew even more dire in the 1860s. The naturalist Alfred Wallace, who visited Singapore some 120 years ago in search of specimens, wrote thus of his explorations on Bukit Timah, 'We heard a tiger roar once or twice in the evening, and it was rather nervous work hunting for insects among the fallen trunks and old sawpits when one of these savage animals might be lurking close by, waiting an opportunity to spring upon us.' Towards the end of the 1800s, the terror had turned into target practice for local huntsmen, and by the 1940s there were no more tigers, only trophies. According to legend, the last tiger in Singapore was shot under the billiard table of the famed Raffles Hotel. And who are we to spoil a good story?

North of the city the predominant colour is green — for a reason. Reservoirs and greenery dominate the landscape because this is the country's prime water catchment area. The north has the lion's share of the 320 square kilometres (80,000 acres) of Singapore not claimed by buildings. The green is forest, marshland, fish pond, plantation, farm holding and military firing range. Greenest of all are the country club golf courses sculpted out of land fringing the inland waters of Seletar, MacRitchie and Peirce reservoirs. Parts of the reservoirs' foreshores are public parks, a verdant escape from city concrete.

MacRitchie Reservoir is the closest to the city of the three and can be entered by Lornie Road near Thomson Road. It has a jogging track frequently used for cross-country competitions. Runners start within the reservoir and jungle reserve, emerge near a golf course of Singapore Island Country Club and then run the long stretch of Lornie Road back to the reservoir. Band performances are a weekend tradition at MacRitchie. At night the scenery changes, for MacRitchie becomes Singapore's best known lovers' lane.

Woodlands

This is the gateway to Malaysia, specifically to Johor Baru, the capital of Malaysia's southernmost state. For Singaporeans, even those who do not live in Woodlands, Johor is a friendly nearby suburb — except that you need your passport to get in. There are checkpoints on both sides of the Causeway (the territorial boundary being on the bridge itself). The Causeway is just over a kilometre (0.6 miles) in length. It links the countries by road, rail and water pipe (Singapore drawing much of its drinking water from Johor, and returning some to the state purified). Three-day weekends mean a bumper-to-bumper crawl on the Causeway. It is a little better on non-holiday weekends, but the crush has become so heavy that the authorities on both sides are considering building a second link, probably at some other point.

Johor Baru can be reached by bus service 170 from Queen Street or Bukit Timah Road. The fare is 80 cents. An express bus leaves Bansan Street Terminus every 10 minutes (fare $1.50). You can also take a taxi, but Singapore taxis cannot ply in Johor. A railbus (actually a stripped-down train) service from the railway station at Tanjong Pagar is planned.

Barely 50 metres (yards) from the Woodlands checkpoint is Kampong Fatimah (*kampong* meaning village in Malay). This village was formed in the early 1930s and is still something of an idyll. Many of the houses are built on stilts over the water, and villagers say that when the tide is exceptionally high their homes get flooded. This is not what makes the community unique, though it is among the last of the 'floating villages' in Singapore. What distinguishes this village from other kampongs is that it has one foot in Malaysia and the other in Singapore. It is the only kampong that has on duty an immigration officer, who checks the IDs of Singaporeans and the passports of Malaysians entering the village. Trains rumble past the village regularly. The village stands partly on land belonging to the Malayan Railway Administration (MRA), which runs the railway network whose southernmost terminus is Singapore. Since the MRA is a state body, the land it owns here belongs to the Malaysian government. Yet, more than half of the village homes stand on Singapore land, which is an advantage of sorts, since the rent is a fraction of what neighbouring householders pay for the privilege of living on 'high rent' (about $10 a month) railway property.

Kranji War Memorial

A peaceful memorial park dedicated to the Allied troops who died defending Singapore in World War II, Kranji is to Singapore what Arlington National Cemetery near Washington, DC is to the United States. The broad expanse of white grave stones tells of the tremendous toll of the war in this tiny state alone. Reading the memorial tablets, one realizes how young many of the dead were. A dwindling group of war veterans and representatives of foreign

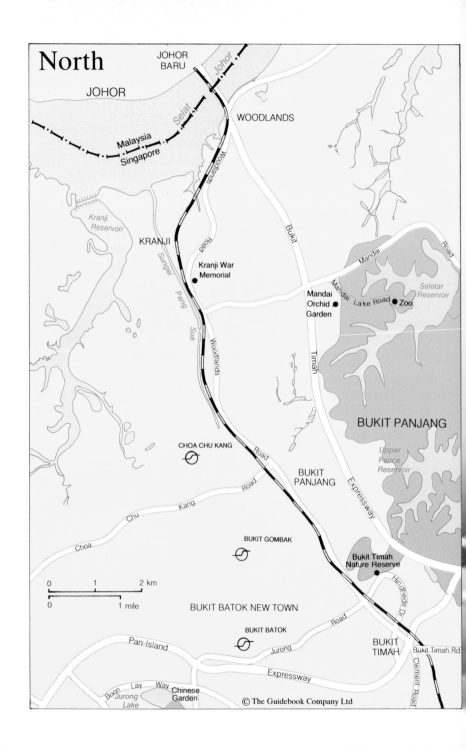

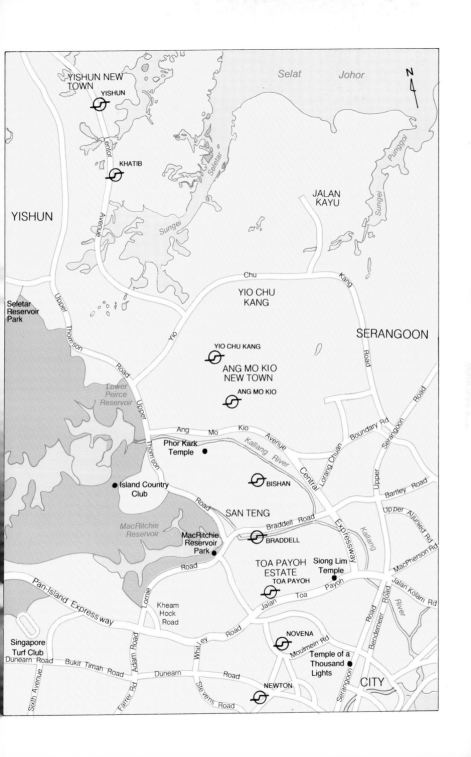

military forces here attend annual services here. Additional services and ceremonies are often held for visiting VIPs laying wreaths at Kranji.

Bukit Timah

It could only be in Singapore that one finds a nature reserve within easy walking distance of three shopping malls. This is Bukit Timah, or Tin Hill. This forest-covered granite outcrop, which stands more than 160 metres (525 feet) high, is the country's tallest hill and has been a nature reserve since 1951. The reserve is only a half-hour car ride from the city centre and can be reached by bus. Once in the reserve, forget about driving or cycling. At any rate, the road to the top could be conquered only by a four-wheel-drive vehicle.

Easy access makes this last true refuge of the rainforest a favourite weekend spot for nature lovers, walkers and the merely energetic. Armed more often than not with Walkmans or portable radio/cassette players, more than 60,000 people tramp through the reserve each year.

Some Sundays the place is so busy that its more popular paths feel rather like busy platforms at a railway station, and at least twice a day explosions from a nearby quarry shatter the calm of Bukit Timah. A favourite route to the summit lies through Jungle Fall Path and up Rock Path. At the top, the *kraa kraa* call of long-tailed macaque monkeys sound above any tape player. Weekdays are quieter, and if one keeps off the asphalted road there is tranquillity enough in the reserve's 75 hectares (185 acres). Here you can almost believe you are not in Singapore; at the same time, the reserve is small enough that it would be quite hard to get lost.

Though it is a protected reserve, Bukit Timah's survival is threatened because some of its characteristic giant trees, which are to the tropical rainforest what the redwoods are to California, are not regenerating. The giants form a protective canopy keeping the forest cool, shady and humid, but the canopy here has been broken by tree falls. On its fringes, sunlight stimulates secondary growth, known locally as *belukar*, which grows more aggressively than primary forest and thus crowds it out.

The most impressive of the forest giants are *Dipterocarp* trees. Among these are the *Seraya* or *Shorea curtisii*, which are often home to the lanky giant forest ant, or *semut temenggong*. Though they may look fearsome, these ants are far less interested in nipping unwary visitors than in zipping in and out of the tree trunk. Watch out for the *kerengga*, the red weaving ant. These ants nest in leaves that they weave together with silk from their own larva. They are very aggressive and bite if disturbed, so be careful what you brush against as you walk along. The kerengga are known as the dairy farmers of the forest because they milk the mealy bugs that live off plants. The *Crematogaster borneensis*, which 'milks' excretions from scale insects, is another insectivorous 'dairy farmer'. It makes its home inside the hollow stems of the *Macaranga triloba* tree.

If it has rained recently, mushrooms and other fungi will be in full 'bloom', sprouting pink, beige and grey from old tree stumps and rotting branches. The bird's nest and elk's horn ferns, which look down on you from tree perches, are among the 100 species that have survived out of some 170 recorded here since the early 19th century. About 80 varieties can be found only here in the reserve. The best place to see these shade-loving plants is in Fern Valley. Large fronds weigh down the tree ferns, which can grow to a height of three metres (ten feet). At the other end of the spectrum are the 16 species of filmy ferns that are just one cell thick and found only in this valley.

The animals in the reserve are rather shy, except for the macaques. Some of these monkeys will eat from your hand, but resist the urge to feed them. They are curious beings and would happily make off with your whole picnic basket or anything else you are carrying. Forest birds are heard but not seen because the most successful birds are those that best manage to disguise themselves. Instead, listen for calls or songs that stand out from the insects' droning sound. Among the birds you might see is the greater racket-tailed drongo (*Dicrurus paradiseus*), which lives high in the trees and is sometimes mistaken for a crow. The drongo has distinctive tail-feathers drawn out into a long spike ending in a tuft of feathers called a racket. If you hear a *chonk-chonk-chonk-chonk* sound, that would be the stripe-throated tit babbler. Close to the ground, one may hear the preep of the tailor bird, so called because it sews up the edges of a leaf to make a nest. The chatterbox of the forest-floor is the short-tailed babbler, whose constant calls keep one company.

Small mammals such as rat-like tree shrews, scaly ant-eaters (or pangolins), civet cats and squirrels, including red giant flying squirrels, still live here, and with a torch at night, you might be able to spot a flying lemur or a common flying fox, which is the largest bat in the world, with a wingspan as wide as one and a half metres (five feet). Early morning, twilight or after dark are the best times to observe wildlife, as some species, such as the reticulated python, one of Singapore's most common snakes, are nocturnal as well as shy.

The hill lies at the end of Hindhede Drive, which begins at the 12-kilometre (7.5-mile) mark on Upper Bukit Timah Road.

Zoological Gardens

British military families here helped to found the Singapore Zoological Gardens on Mandai Lake Road, though not intentionally. It all started with a military menagerie at an air base, formerly the Royal Air Force base at Tengah. When the British pulled their forces out of Singapore, families returning to Britain left their pets in the mini-zoo at Tengah. At one time it

held some 30 animals; including ducks, monkeys, tortoises, rabbits, sun-bears, a mousedeer and a civet cat. When the Tengah airmen finally went home themselves, the animals were moved to Mandai and became part of the new zoo, which opened in 1973.

The first residents of the zoo included zebras, Malaysian tapirs, Sikar deer from Hong Kong and Sambar deer from Malaysia, a pair of young tigers from the Rangoon Zoo, pelanduk or mousedeer, giraffes, leopards, jaguars, panthers, rhinos, cheetahs, lions, kangaroos and wallabies. Also among the earliest to call the zoo home were an assortment of orang-utans, more than a dozen of whom were adopted in 1971 when it became illegal in Singapore to keep them as pets. The zoo now has the world's largest social colony of orang-utans. It also has the only Bawean hog deer outside Indonesia, the only polar bears in the region and the only bearded pigs in captivity. It used to be easy to see every animal here in the course of a morning stroll, but there are now more than 170 species housed in 60 landscaped exhibits, so that morning stroll now takes the better part of a day.

The zoo's most famous animal is undoubtedly Ah Meng, the orang-utan. Since 1982, Ah Meng, a mother of three, has been taking turns with other orang-utans having breakfast with visitors. Some of her breakfast companions hardly notice the food, seeming content to sit back and gape until it is their turn to spend a few minutes being photographed with her. Breakfast (American-style or vegetarian) with an orang-utan costs $14. A local dish served in the breakfast buffet is fish with rice porridge. If you are there at tea time, you can have high tea with primate babies and get a picture of yourself cradling one in your arms. Elephant and pony rides are also available.

There is no need to book a tour. Take the Zoo Express, an air-conditioned coach with 11 pick-up points in the city. Call 235–3111 (during office hours) or 777–3897 (after office hours) to arrange to be picked up. The Zoo Express costs $18.00 for adults ($11.50 for children), which includes admission. The tram ride in the zoo grounds costs $1.50 ($1 for children under 16). Children under three years old do not need a ticket to enter or ride the tram.

The zoo is open every day from 8.30 am to 6.30 pm. Admission is $5 ($2.50 for children), but the animal shows are free. Orang-utan and snake shows are at 10.30 am and 2.30 pm, and elephant and sea lion shows at 11.30 am and 3.30 pm. For more information, call the zoo on 269–3411.

Mandai

The **Mandai Orchid Garden** was set up on Mandai Lake Road much earlier than the zoo; it was started by John Laycock and Lee Kim Hong when the land was leased from government by Singapore Orchids in December 1950.

The acreage was expanded to four hectares (ten acres) more than 20 years ago. After the founders died (Laycock in 1960 and Lee in 1969), the gardens

On the Outside Looking In

*B*eing American was part of my uniqueness. There were few
Americans in Singapore, and though the last thing I wanted to be—
after all, I had left the place for a good reason—was the glad-hander,
the ham with the loud jokes and big feet and flashy shirts saying, 'It
figures' and 'Come off it' and 'Who's your friend?', and 'This I gotta
see', it was the only role open to me because it was the only one the
people I dealt with accepted. It alerted them when I behaved
untypically; it looked as though I was concealing something and
intended to defraud them by playing down the Yankee. In such a
small place, an island with no natives, everyone a visitor, the
foreigner made himself a resident by emphasizing his foreignness.
Yardley, who was from Leeds, but had been in Singapore since the
war—he married one of these sleek Chinese girls who turned into a
suburban dragon named Mildred—had softened his accent by
listening to the BBC Overseas Service. He put burnt matches back
into the box (muttering, 'These are threepence in U.K.'), cigarette ash
in his trouser-cuffs and poured milk in his cup before the tea. The one
time I made a reference to the photograph in the Bandung of the
Queen and Duke ('Liz and Phil, I know them well—nice to see them
around, broo-reh-ah!'), Yardley called Eisenhower—President at the
time—'a bald fucker, a stupid general who half the time doesn't know
whether he wants a shit or a haircut'. Consequently, but against my
will, I was made an American, or rather 'the Yank'. When America
was mentioned, fellers said, 'Ask Jack'. I exaggerated my accent and
dropped my Allegro pretence of being Italian. I tried to give the
impression of a cheerful rascal, someone gently ignorant; I claimed I
had no education and said, 'If you say so' or 'That's really
interesting' to anything remotely intelligent.

It was awfully hard for me to be an American, but the hardest part was playing the dumb-cluck for a feller whose intelligence was inferior to mine. The fellers at the Bandung reckoned they had great natural gifts; Yates, in his own phrase 'an avaricious reader', would say, 'I'm reading Conrad' when he was stuck in the first chapter of a book he'd never finish; Yardley pointed to me one night and said, 'I wouldn't touch an American book with a barge-pole', and Smale ended every argument with 'It all comes down to the same thing, then, don't it?' to which someone would add, 'Right. Six of one and half a dozen of the other'. They were always arguing, each argument illustrated by anecdotes from personal experience. That was the problem: they saved up stories to tell people back home; then, realizing with alarm that they probably weren't going home, wondered who to tell. They told each other. Stories were endlessly repeated, and the emphasis and phrasing never varied. The silent fellers in the Bandung were not listening; they were waiting for a chance to talk.

I was the only genuine listener—the inexperienced American, there to be instructed. But the funny thing was, I had a college education and almost a degree. It was no help in the Bandung to say a bright truth, for even if someone heard it he was incapable of verifying it; and on the job it created misunderstandings. I recall meeting an Irish seaman on one of my 'meat runs', as my ferrying of girls into the harbour was called. Hearing his brogue, I said, 'I'm crazy about Joyce' and he replied, 'That the skinny one in the yellow dress?'

I said, 'You guessed it!' and he went over and pinched her sorry bottom through a fold in her frock. Later he thanked me for the tip-off. He was right and I was wrong: education is inappropriate to most jobs.

Paul Theroux, Saint Jack

were run by Amy and John Ede, who have been associated with the company since 1953. The first orchid sales started at the gardens in 1956, and soon after that orchids began to be marketed overseas, first in London, and now in more than 30 countries. Many visitors come to see the orchid display and enjoy the Water Garden, which is landscaped with tropical plants. Mandai Orchid Garden is open seven days a week from 9 am until 5.30 pm. Admission is $1 (50 cents for children). Tel. 269–1036.

If orchids leave you cold, how about lunch at a fish pond? The name of the restaurant is itself rather a mouthful — **Ng Tiong Choon Sembawang Fishing Pond Seafood Restaurant**, but it began as a small operation catering to the sport anglers who needed to be fed while waiting for the fish to bite. The anglers were hooked, and the small kitchen that served them became a restaurant in 1986, according to Khng Eu Meng (a food writer with *The Straits Times* who, incidentally, recommends the baked crab, banana and scallop fritters). Bump along to 59 Lorong Chuntun, off Mandai Road, to check it out. On weekdays, lunch is served between 11 am and 2 pm, and dinner from 6 pm to 11 pm (to midnight on Sundays). Expect to spend at least $20 per person.

If you would rather fish, the restaurant will rent you a proper rod and reel for $20 or a bamboo job for $8. The price difference not only separates the men from the boys, but sets out which of the two ponds you can fish at. Both are stocked with several varieties of carp. Fishing hours are 8 am to 10 pm Sunday to Friday, and on Saturday the place stays open overnight through Sunday morning for diehards who would rather fish than sleep. The redoubtable Mr Ng Kee Soon, who owns the place, will also cater for anglers who would like to picnic ($15 to $25 per person) or hold a barbecue here. For information and reservations, call 754–1991 or 257–7939.

Siong Lim Temple

Chinese agriculturists were already settled in the interior before Raffles arrived to set up his trading station in 1819, and they founded many temples that are now 100 years old or more. Most of the largest and most popular, however, are 20th-century creations.

Siong Lim Temple in Toa Payoh is one of the best-known temples outside the city area. Its address is 184-E Jalan Toa Payoh, but directions are almost superfluous once you are on the road because the temple is so large that it is impossible to miss.

The full name of the temple is Lin Shan Shiong Lim Shan Si, which translates to the Twin Groves of the Lotus Mountain Buddhist Temple, commemorating the birth of Buddha in a grove of trees and his death under a Bodhi tree, the same kind of tree under which he achieved enlightenment. Siong Lim Temple was founded around the turn of the century, its benefactor a Buddhist philanthropist Low Kim Pong, who donated four hectares (ten acres) of land on Balestier Plain and asked a visiting abbot to build a temple there with the $500,000 he helped raise. The central building, containing the main altar, was finished in 1904, and a hall of the Four Heavenly Kings was finished the following year. Officially, the temple was completed in 1908, but building never seems to stop.

Different manifestations of the Lord Buddha (Amitabha, Sakyamuni and Maitreya), the Goddess of Mercy, Kuan Yin, Si Da Tian Wang (or Four Heavenly Kings) and the 18 lohans preside over smaller shrines in the temple dedicated to ancestral figures, including the founder, Low Kim Pong. The temple has had facelifts in 1919, 1935 and 1950, but neither these, nor large-scale repairs and the addition of new buildings, have diminished its appeal. The arrival of the Pan-Island Expressway cut through woodland that used to screen Siong Lim Temple, and the road now puts the temple on permanent show to anyone driving through. The grounds were halved in the 1950s when the land was acquired for public housing. Despite that, Siong Lim Temple remains one of the largest in Singapore and its carved panels, worked ceilings and statues are among its most photographed objects.

Phor Kark See

From relatively modest beginnings, Kong Meng San Phor Kark See has grown into a multimillion dollar city whose golden roofs spread over seven and a half hectares (19 acres) of land on Bright Hill Drive, which is opposite Ang Mo Kio on the south side of Ang Mo Kio Avenue and the Kallang River. The temple complex has been the backdrop for many scenes in locally made *gongfu* films. One wonders how they can shoot anything but close ups now, with the towering blocks of public housing drawing ever closer. Already among the largest temple complexes in Southeast Asia, Phor Kark See is itself still growing, and building is as much an activity as prayer.

There are halls for prayer and meditation, a two-storey Buddhist library and a senior citizens' home set among the many temple buildings. Inside a temple dedicated to the Goddess of Mercy, Kuan Yin, is a nine-metre (30-foot) tall statue of this incarnation of Buddha. The statue was carved out of a single block of marble by two Italian sculptors working from sketches. On feast days, volunteers dish up free vegetarian food in one-metre (three-foot) wide woks permanently set into huge kitchen ranges.

Cremation is now the norm for all but Muslims in Singapore, and the columbaria — or urn vaults — at Phor Kark See are the final resting place for many Singaporeans. Their ashes repose in funeral urns stacked to the ceiling. On virtually any day there will be several funerals going on in a large, almost hangar-like, crematorium.

Among the most interesting occasions on which to visit the temple is Qing Ming, a kind of All Souls' Day that falls in March or April. This is when Chinese visit and clean family graves, and make offerings. A particularly good time to visit is Vesak Day (in May), the most important festival for Buddhists because it marks the birth, enlightenment and death of Buddha. Devout Buddhists circle the complex, prostrating themselves every few steps and ending in front of the main temple, where a priest uses a bunch of chrysanthemums to sprinkle the moving ranks of the faithful with water.

Bukit Turf Club

Established in 1842 as the Singapore Sporting Club, the Bukit Turf Club is among the oldest of the country's clubs. The club moved in 1933 to its present verdant setting in Bukit Timah, in the middle of some of the country's choicest residential areas. In 1988, it became the Bukit Turf Club.

Regular admission to the stands is just $5. The first race of the weekend starts at 2.15 pm on Saturdays. A club tour designed with visitors to Singapore costs $48 on any weekend. Your ticket price includes a free copy of *Racing Guide*, covering the day's races, as well as transfers by air-conditioned coach between the club and the Orchard, Dynasty, Crown Prince, Westin Plaza and Pan Pacific hotels. Pick-up time is between 11 and 11.45 am (depending on the hotel), and the coach returns at 5 pm. After lunch in the Members' Restaurant, you can view the races from the Members' Section on the fifth floor. Between races, there is a guided tour of the paddock.

Passports are required on this tour. The dress code for men is a shirt with a collar, tie, slacks and closed shoes. Women are expected to wear a blouse and slacks or a dress. No jeans, shorts or slippers are permitted. Reservations can be arranged through RMG Tours (298–3944), Siakson Coach Tours (336–0288) or Singapore Sightseeing (737–8778).

Singapore has 32 weekend race days a year. On the other weekends, off-course race meetings at the Malaysian capital of Kuala Lumpur, Ipoh or Penang are televised live at the club on a 6 by 18-metre (20 by 60-foot) Diamond Vision TV screen. You should check ahead (tel. 469–3611) to see if racing is on or off course. Events to watch for are the Singapore Derby (March), Singapore Gold Cup (June and July), Pesta Sukan Cup (July), Lion City Cup (October) and Queen Elizabeth II Cup (October and November).

Riding

If you would rather ride than watch, the Singapore Polo Club at Thomson Road charges $30 per 45-minute period. (Tel. 256–4530.) Or you can call the Saddle Club at 466–2782 for more information from Tuesday to Friday (8 am – 5 pm) and Saturday (8 am – 12 noon).

East

In the old days, the East Coast was the traditional weekend refuge of the moneyed classes, civil servants, Europeans and Straits Chinese. The wealthy built seaside bungalows, some with their own beaches and jetties. These private enclaves have now been left high and dry by massive reclamation, which has pushed the seafront southwards, and leisure for the masses has found a new home in East Coast Park, a long and narrow stretch of parkland and beaches. The park extends all the way from the western end of Benjamin Sheares Bridge, which spans the Kallang Basin, to the airport at Changi on the eastern tip of the island, though one long stretch of it, greened and manicured at considerable cost, is the grounds and golf course of the Tanah Merah Country Club, one of the country's newer enclaves for the well-heeled.

When one mentions the words 'East Coast' to a Singaporean, they evoke thoughts of seafood restaurants and sea sports, camping and condoland. A drive along East Coast Road, Upper East Coast Road and the East Coast Parkway readily confirms these impressions. There seem to be more restaurants here than there are traffic lights — and goodness knows there are enough of those! Bedok, once a place where seafood enthusiasts opened and ate steamed cockles and crabs on rickety wooden tables, with the waves virtually lapping at their feet, has lost its seafront. But it has kept and even added to its collection of seafood restaurants, which are packed every weekend. A newer seafood haunt close to·the waves is the UDMC Seafood Centre on East Coast Parkway. The park's seaward expanse was designed with watersports in mind, and any weekend, especially when the wind is blowing, will find bronzed windsurfers and colourful catamarans riding the waves. Condomania also rules the East Coast. Towering glass-sheathed apartment blocks have sprung up anywhere developers have been given half a chance. If, for one reason or another, you cannot live here, you can still camp at the People's Association's campsite at the far end of East Coast Park.

Kallang

Kallang was once synonymous with airplanes, for this land surrounding the Kallang Basin was the civil airport for Singapore. Seaplanes were a common sight in the early days. But the airport moved to Paya Lebar and, in 1981, moved again to its present location at Changi, on the eastern tip of Singapore. What was once the airport building is now part of the People's Association from which the country's network of community centres are directed.

The beaches on the banks of the Kallang River are not natural but the result of a decade-long clean-up conducted by the government. The clean-up ended with a massive landscaping and tree-planting effort, which saw tons of

clean sand poured on to create a sandy, palm-shaded beach where none had existed. The area is also used for waterskiing tournaments.

It is hard to believe that Kallang was once an industrial area and the river, well known for its shipyards, was also a conduit for waste and pollutants. Close by, the profile of the Kallang Gasworks (one of the oldest surviving industrial plants in Singapore and still the only source of city gas) is a prominent reminder of that past.

During the soccer (football) season, lights towering over the **National Stadium** blaze like gargantuan candles on an octogenarian's birthday cake. Soccer, while not the consuming passion it is in Latin America, is undoubtedly the national sport. The Malaysia Cup, the series of soccer league games most closely followed here, pits Singaporean and Malaysian teams against each other. To find out when matches are scheduled, call the Singapore Sports Council on 345-7111. Local newspapers also carry details of these and other sporting events.

The Sports Museum opened at the stadium in 1983, but, because of its peculiar and somewhat out-of-the-way location, it sees few visitors other than those who happen to be visiting the Singapore Sports Council, which set it up.

Because there are relatively few Singaporean athletes who have won medals in the Olympics and other international meets of note, the museum's Hall of Fame is somewhat modest. Singapore's Olympic medallists can be counted on the fingers of one hand—well, actually, just one finger! Tan Howe Liang won a silver medal in weightlifting in the Rome Olympics in 1960. The medal, along with the leotard and belt he wore are exhibited here. Another prominent Olympic exhibit is a case of porcelain spoons commemorating the 24th Olympiad in Seoul in 1988. These were originally presented to the Prime Minister, Mr Lee Kuan Yew.

The 1,200-seat **Kallang Theatre** sits rather strangely next to the National Stadium—and nowhere near any other theatre. It used to be a cinema, and is now used for everything from ballet performances and Bible rallies to Chinese opera and acrobatic displays.

Nearby the Singapore Indoor Stadium, a mammoth arena which can seat some 10,000, has already played host to operatic tenor Placido Domingo, the Moscow State Circus and exhibition tennis matches among other shows.

Not far off is the **Gay World,** a name that never fails to amuse. Stranger still is that the name was actually changed to Gay World from New World. The stadium has an association with basketball and recently with martial-arts displays. The Geylang area in which it stands has a somewhat sleazy air, aided by a proliferation of bars and, so it is said, houses of ill repute. Secret societies once ruled the *lorongs*, or lanes, in the Geylang area, making the area as well known for its vice as for its excellent food. Far better to eschew the bars and brothels for the certain pleasures of the rather rough-and-ready establishments that call themselves restaurants. One can soak up the atmosphere and a backstreet supper under the stars at Fatty Restaurant in Lorong 1, Geylang, immediately opposite a major bus terminus. The restaurant stays open into the wee hours, primarily for patrons who tank up in the bars before heading here for a good meal.

Geylang Serai

Among the more interesting areas in the eastern part of the island is Geylang Serai. This is an irregularly shaped zone bounded by several major roads: Aljunied Road, Guillemard Road, Dunman Road, Joo Chiat Road, Jalan Alsagoff and Paya Lebar Way. Historically and culturally fascinating, the area began to be settled in the early 1840s when the *Orang Laut* were moved out of their floating village at the mouth of the Singapore River. They moved eastwards and inland to this area, which for a time was known as Geylang Kelapa, a name borrowed from a copra factory set amidst coconut plantations. (The word *geylang* itself is believed to be a corruption of the Malay word for factory, *kilang*.)

Javanese and Boyanese (from Bawean, an island between Java and Sumatra) migrants came to Singapore, and by 1860 there were about 3,000 of them living in Geylang Kelapa, which had become a working-class neighbourhood. It was then that wealthy Arab families bought large tracts of property in the area. The Alkaff, Aljunied and Alsagoff families, who made fortunes in the spice trade and from the land they owned, lent their names to roads in this and other areas of Singapore. They also made a name for themselves in civic leadership.

The Alsagoffs were among those who developed the cultivation of lemon grass or *serai*. This was pressed into citronella oil, which was also used as an antiseptic and in treating rheumatism. In the West, the oil was then in great demand for use in perfumes and soaps. Thus did Geylang Kelapa give way to Geylang Serai. Before the end of the century, though, the demand for citronella oil had fallen and the cultivators returned to coconut cultivation, worked on rubber plantations or turned to vegetable and poultry farming. During World War II , tapioca replaced coconut and rubber, and part of the area is still known as Kampong Ubi, or Tapioca Village. But the name Geylang Serai stuck, and the area as a whole is still known by that name today.

In all of Singapore, this is the one place that most strongly retains a Malay

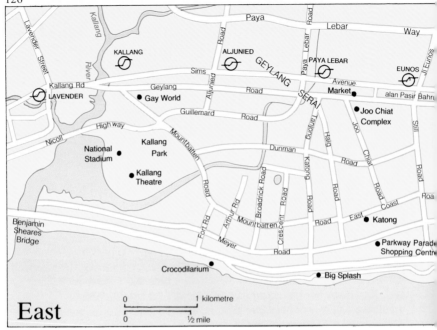

East

0   1 kilometre

0   ½ mile

flavour. Though its residents are no longer overwhelmingly ethnic Malay, Geylang Serai remains a magnet for Malay Singaporeans. To Malay visitors from Malaysia, Indonesia and Brunei, this is a shopping, meeting and eating place in which they feel quite at home.

Hari Raya Puasa, which marks the end of the Ramadan fast, is one of the best times to visit Geylang Serai. Weeks before the holiday, fairy lights are strung across streets and buildings, and they are lit every night until shortly after the holiday. Busloads of visitors — many of them from Malaysia — descend on the area nightly to enjoy its bazaars, food stalls and cultural performances.

The area looks set for an even livelier scene now, with a new Malay cultural village, or *kampong*, soon to open on a 1.8-hectare (4.5-acre) site in the heart of Geylang Serai. Its shops and kiosks will sell traditional crafts, and there will be at least one restaurant, as well as outdoor and indoor areas for cultural performances and demonstrations by kite makers, batik printers and *gasing* (top) carvers.

Geylang Serai's heart is its market, a hub for Singapore's Malay families, even those who live miles away. As a place to have breakfast or lunch, or just a snack of favourite traditional foods, the market is unbeatable. It offers fast-food, Singapore-style: Javanese *gandos* (savoury semi-circles of rice flour and shredded coconut baked over charcoal), *pisang goreng* (deep-fried

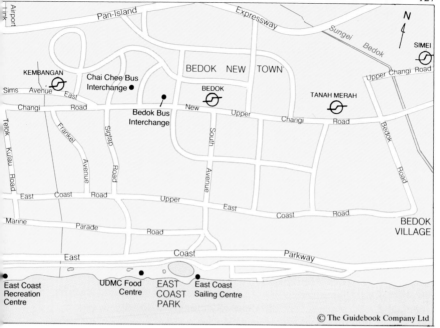

bananas) and an endless array of sweets and savouries.

People come from all over to shop for meat and produce, as well as for sundries seldom found in such quantity or variety anywhere else on the island. This applies especially to fruit and other fresh produce. One example is *jering*, a flattened nut-like fruit. The older fruit, eaten raw or boiled, is said to be a cure for diabetes. Another local oddity is the *petai*, a smooth-skinned, light-green bean from a long, fibrous pod. As with the jering, a taste for petai is acquired — but easily. Cooked or eaten raw, it is good for the kidneys, or so a vendor maintains. Then there is home-made *belacan*, cakes of fermented shrimp used extensively in cooking local dishes, and *cincalok*, a sauce of fermented fried shrimp. Usually these are imported from regional manufacturers.

Among the market's sweetest-smelling pleasures is the *bunga rampai* stall, where housewives stop to buy an aromatic salad of petals, blossoms and finely shredded *pandan* leaves (a variety of the pandanus, or screwpine plant). Dressed with jasmine oil, this gives a wonderfully fresh scent. Gilt wedding ornaments and fancy hairpins essential to the bridal coiffure are among the characteristically Malay products sold in the shops fringing the market. One of the shops, Mini Arloji, displays diamante and gilt tiaras, gilt veils and shiny bracelets and belts, most imported from Indonesia. Another offers prayer mats, shawls and *songkok*, the rimless velvet caps often worn by

Malay men on festive occasions or at prayers. Occasionally one may still spot women streaked white with *bedak sejuk*, rice powder pellets ground into a paste said to refine the complexion. Geylang Serai is also the place to look for *ubat periok* (dried flowers, herbs and roots used in traditional preparations for women after childbirth), and *jamu*, herbal teas and medicinal draughts from Indonesia.

Joo Chiat

Cross Changi Road to the Joo Chiat Complex, where Feroz Khan carries on the traditional medicine business started by his father more than 40 years ago. Under a modern plastic signboard advertising 'Perubatan Tradisional', the shop also carries beauty care potions that owe nothing to Estée Lauder. Inside, a wall of shelves carries cures for anything that ails you. If you see a long turnip-like root hanging from the shelves, it is probably *pasak bumi*, a root used in many medicines.

At 116 Joo Chiat Road is one of the few remaining tinsmiths in Singapore, a family business well known for made-to-order, hand-crafted pans. This is the place for nostalgia buffs hankering for a traditional zinc-lined watering can, non-plastic buckets, cake tins and jelly moulds in novelty shapes, including Christmas trees and Mickey Mouse.

Some of the finest examples of local architecture are in the Joo Chiat area, which is home to many Straits Chinese. The area was named after a local landowner, Chew Joo Chiat. Chew bought the land from the Alsagoffs, wealthy Arabs who settled in Singapore in the 19th century. He had the lots subdivided and sold for building. Since the area lacked roads, he constructed those, too. The row houses on Joo Chiat Road, as well as those on adjoining Koon Seng Road, were built in the 1920s and 1930s. From the turn of the century until just after World War I, it was fashionable to ornament the façades liberally. On adjoining Koon Seng Road, two colourful rows of terrace houses, elaborately gingerbreaded and with exquisite exterior mouldings, face each other across walled courtyards. They are among Singapore's most frequently photographed buildings.

Katong

Antiquarian Peter Wee is an expert on Straits Chinese or *Nonya* culture and customs, as well as an oft-consulted authority on its distinctive porcelain, silver, beadwork and other antiques. One has to call for an appointment as he is not always at the Katong Antique House at 208 East Coast Road. One cannot really call the place a shop, though its front room displays porcelain, beaded slippers, basketry and furniture for sale. It is more like a museum that happens to put some of its collection on sale. The back room is a convivial area that may be chock-a-block with boxes of traditional sweetmeats in the weeks just before the Chinese New Year.

East Coast

If the weather is fine, you might want to try the outdoor sun and fun spots at East Coast Park. Get your sea legs at the **East Coast Sailing Centre**. Six hours of windsurfing lessons spread over two days ($80) will usually give you enough courage to stand up on (and fall off) your own board. There is a special four-hour crash course ($50) tailored for tourists who do not have six hours to spare. This is offered only on weekday afternoons.

You must first be able to swim 50 metres (yards), albeit with a lifejacket on. The instructors start you on a board almost straightaway, but this one will take some wind to tip over, since it is anchored firmly in the sand. When you get more proficient, you are allowed on the water in the safety of the lagoon. Its calm (if often mucky) waters make you believe every manoeuvre is a cinch — then you graduate to a humiliating dunking in the sea, in full view of arrogantly proficient windsurfers and a tanned assortment of beach boys who may be kind enough not to laugh out loud.

The centre is open every day from 9.30 am to 6.30 pm. If you are already a proficient windsurfer, you can rent a sailboard for $20 for the first two hours and $10 for each additional hour. Call the centre at 449–5118.

Yes, there are crocodiles here. No, they are not in the water, but in the **Singapore Crocodilarium** at 730 East Coast Parkway. The crocodilarium is said to have more than a thousand crocs bred here — or enough of the real thing to turn any Lacoste shirt green. Feeding time is at 11 am every Tuesday, Thursday and Saturday. If man-to-man wrestling is too tame for you, have a look at crocodile wrestling, which is on at 11.45 am and 4.15 pm every day, except when it rains. Then shed crocodile tears when browsing through the reptile-skin goods on sale here. Open daily from 9 am to 5.30 pm. Admission is $2 ($1 for children). Show times and feeding times have sometimes been erratic, so call ahead at 447–3722 to confirm.

The East Coast Recreation Centre on East Coast Parkway (tel. 449–0541) has Singapore's only public courts for racquetball. The centre is open between 7.30 am and 11.30 pm every day. There are three courts that cost $5 an hour before 4.30 pm and $7 an hour after 4.30 pm. The centre also has squash courts. The glass courts rent for $12 an hour, while the others rent for $4 (before 4.30 pm on weekdays and before 1.30 pm on Saturdays) and $6 at other times.

Big Splash, nearby on East Coast Parkway, has water slides in graduated heights, a children's pool (deep enough to splash about in), a flow pool and a wave pool. It is open from noon to 6 pm on weekdays (except Wednesday) and from 9 am to 6 pm on weekends and public holidays. Admission is $3 ($2 for children). Call 345–1211.

West

The West is for work and play. The main port of Singapore and the Jurong Industrial Estate are here, but so too are parks and gardens. Major attractions include Tiger Balm Gardens, Jurong Bird Park, the Chinese and Japanese gardens and the Singapore Science Centre and Omni-Theatre, a planetarium and cinema for Omnimax movies designed to be shown on hemispheric screens.

Less well known are the West's historical links, especially its royal connections, some traces of which remain in this part of the country largely unvisited. The West is a quickly developing area, and as we go to press some attractions are being redeveloped and improved and new ones created.

Telok Blangah

Royalty once lived here. Temenggong Abdul Rahman's house and village at the foot of Mt Faber are documented in a well-known period print. The Temenggong and Sultan Hussein Shah were the ones who signed a treaty with Stamford Raffles authorizing the East India Company to set up a trading post on the island. The Temenggong and his entourage of about 600 people were moved west to Telok Blangah from Singapore Town in 1821, and this area subsequently became a hub for immigrants of Arab, Indonesian and Malay stock.

The royal graveyard, or Tanah Kubor Temenggong, on Telok Blangah Road near Kampong Baru Road, holds Temenggong Abdul Rahman's remains. His nephew Ibrahim and other close relatives are also buried here in the graveyard in the grounds of the State of Johor Mosque, or Masjid Jamek Jerahaan Johor, on Telok Blangah Road. According to Norman Edwards and Peter Keys, the authors of *Singapore: a Guide to Buildings, Streets, Places,* the mosque was originally a pavilion of the old *istana* (palace) and there are still traces of old baths.

Abdul Rahman died in 1825. His younger son, Daeng Ibrahim, who was only eight years old in 1819 when he was brought to Singapore, was installed as temenggong only in 1841. Daeng Ibrahim established a monopoly over the *gutta percha* (a kind of gum) trade in east Sumatra and south Malaya, and as the harbour developed his land appreciated in value.

But Telok Blangah lost its royal connection when Ibrahim's son, Abu Bakar, who became temenggong in 1862, moved to Johor and was later acknowledged as sultan.

A Cultural Chasm

arricades had gone up all over Singapore, at which all were searched before they were allowed to proceed, or were refused passage, as the whims of the sentry dictated. At one barricade a Chinese pedalling a loaded tricycle was told to stop. He did so, but the moment the sentry turned away to deal with someone else, he made off as fast as he could. He was overtaken and manhandled, made to kneel down and was clouted on the head until he fainted. When he came to, he was thrashed until he fainted again. All this was done in the sight of hundreds of pedestrians who passed that way, and had a salutary effect on them. Thenceforward the sentry did not find his duties too onerous. Every order was instantly obeyed, and if he playfully dropped his rifle on a foot, the victim smiled appreciation for the signal favour.

That sentry was neither more zealous nor more brutal than his fellows. He was, as would seem, of a more kindly disposition than most, for when someone presented a slip of paper bearing the inscription in Japanese— "Please let me pass; I'm looking for my family,"—he let the man pass at once. But he could ill-treat the tricyclist, and many others, whom after manhandling, he made to kneel by the roadside for hours, giving them his wrathful attention whenever he felt inclined! One must conclude that it was an instance of imperfect sympathy, neither understanding the other's point of view. How could the Japanese soldier, accustomed to giving instant and unquestioning obedience to orders, how could he understand the slovenly Chinese who seemed so inclined to greet an order with airy badinage and to brush it aside with a wave of the hand? How could he, to whom chastisement was a matter of routine, which he received from a superior and administered to a subordinate, how could he understand the resentment that smouldered in the eyes of the Chinese whom he had so justly punished? No wonder he was exasperated, and dealt all the more savagely with the offenders.

The Chinaman, on his side, with his inherited and ingrained misprizing of all that appertained to war, was incapable of understanding the Japanese sentry. How could he know that the Japanese was such a fanatic for discipline, loving it for its own sake, as the only key to the enigma of life, that to him a command was sacrosanct, tardy compliance with which was not a mere peccadillo, as the Chinese fondly imagined, but an affront to the Emperor himself? As for failure to bow to him, the sentry, it was sacrilege, for he, the sentry, was the viceregent for the nonce of **Tenno Heika**—that very god of very god, child of the Moon Goddess, holding sway over gods and men.

N I Low, **When Singapore was Syonan-to**

Mt Faber

A blind man started the first rush to Mt Faber, which bore the name of Telok Blangah Hill until 1845. According to the story, the man fell asleep between two trees on the hill. In the course of his afternoon nap, he dreamt of being told to go to a nearby spring to wash his eyes. Upon waking, he went to the spring, where he bathed his eyes and recovered enough of his sight to find his way home unaided.

Word spread and many people visited the spot to get the water. It was a windfall for canny locals who charged visitors a dollar a bottle in the days when one cent was real money. Day and night, there would be people letting off firecrackers and generally making a nuisance of themselves, until the authorities finally put a stop to it by pouring concrete over the 'magic' spring and chanelling its waters underground.

There is no magic to Mt Faber any more, but this 116-metre (380-foot) high hill off Kampong Baru Road offers a panoramic view of the port and is a common stop on city tours. It is a good place to get your bearings on the city and a great place to be on New Year's Eve, when the ships in the harbour sound off in a cacophony of horns, bells and sirens on the stroke of midnight.

The hill is the start of the cable car ride across the harbour to the resort island of Sentosa. Unless you are driving or being picked up, it is better to take the cable car from here to Sentosa and return by ferry to the World Trade Centre. If you ride the cable car the other way, you may not find a taxi at the Mt Faber end.

Labrador Park

At first sight, Labrador's beach seems to have little to commend it — still less at low tide, when the rocky shore looks even more desolate and even farther from most people's notion of a great beach. However, a closer look at this half-kilometre (0.3-mile) slip of beach near the British Petroleum jetty at Tanjong Berlayar can be quite rewarding.

This is one of the few stretches of Singapore seashore untouched by reclamation or other development and relatively undisturbed by the usual seaside crowd. It is still home to a rich variety of marine flora and fauna, including coral, crabs and different types of seaweed. The area between high and low water — the intertidal zone — can be comfortably explored at low tide, which occurs twice a day. (Tide times can be checked with the Tide Tables issued by the Port of Singapore Authority and swimming times published in the daily newspapers.)

Canvas shoes, a hat and a willingness to get your feet wet are all you need. If you want help in identifying your finds, take along a copy of *A Guide to Seashore Life*. This inexpensive ($5) handy-sized book is available in most bookshops as well as at the Singapore Science Centre.

Some of the creatures you can expect to see in the intertidal zone are the hermit crab, bottle-brush tube worm, sea cucumber and many types of coral. Tiny gobies or anemones stranded by the ebb tide can often be found in rock pools and even in shallow niches in exposed rocks. An easy way to sightsee is to lift up a rock — but carefully and with gloves on. That spot might be home to a stone fish (venomous) or glass worm (non-venomous but able to leave painful 'glass' bristles in your flesh). Rocks are often covered with barnacles. Remember also to replace rocks and stones as you found them.

Haw Par Villa

The second incarnation of Haw Par Villa, often referred to as Tiger Balm Gardens, was created by the Aw family.

The exciting Wrath of the Water Gods Flume ride takes only eight minutes and part of the ride plunges you headlong into the drink. Live shows and robot shows make up the rest of the entertainment.

At Spirits of the Orient Theatre, a multi-screen slide show with special effects gives you an insight into Chinese culture. Hoy Hay, a robotic old codger, tells tales from Chinese mythology at the Legends and Heroes Theatre.

Take the SBS 10, 30, 51 or 143 buses or the west bound MRT to Buona Vista and then the SBS 200 from there. Parking is available at a restaurant car park opposite the theme park. Haw Par Villa is at the 10 km (six mile) or Pasir Panjang Road. Admission covers all rides and shows and is $16 for adults and $10 for children under 12. Children under three go free.

Singapore Science Centre

Opened in 1977, the centre's chief mission is education, but its five galleries, in which the emphasis is on participatory exhibits, graphics, live specimens, huge models and multi-media presentations, are entertaining. It is well worth a visit.

The main galleries are devoted to the physical sciences, life sciences (the genetics exhibits being among the most interesting) and aviation, but exhibits are also found in the atrium (a favourite shows how mice can live underwater) and in a gallery specially designed for young people.

The Discovery Centre, funded by Esso, exhibits interesting if well-worn exhibits, which are repaired every week in the wake of hordes of enthusiastic young visitors. Light, sound and mechanical gadgets make the place feel like a playroom designed and built by eccentrics (in this case, chiefly the imaginative staff of the centre).

Simple interactive computer games that teach colours and numbers can keep younger kids occupied for the better part of an hour. Older children will appreciate the postage-stamp-sized Walk-in Forest, a 'landscaped' patch of

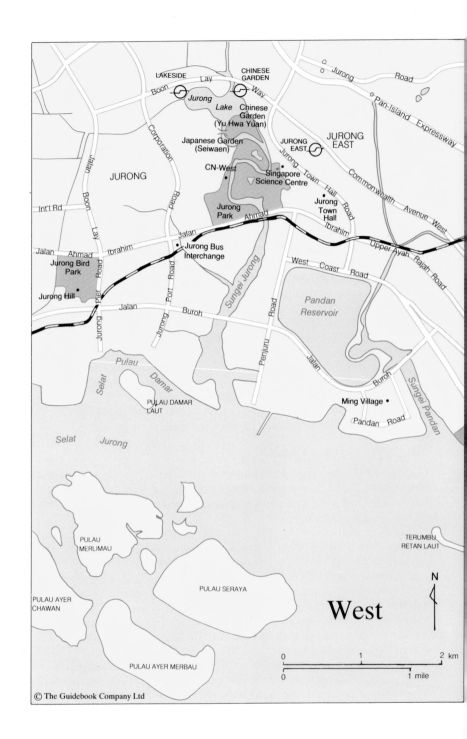

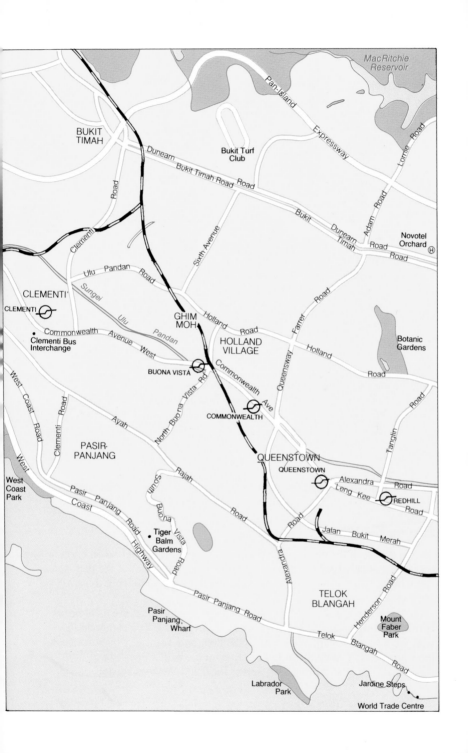

green carpeting with lifesize local fauna, either the real thing stuffed or models. Life in the Sea, a crawl-through aquarium designed for children, is a winner with all ages, including grown-ups. The fish are contained in small aquaria set into lighted windows in the cavern.

The Aviation Gallery, sponsored by Singapore Airlines, is one of the newest additions. A favourite with schoolboys is the simulator that lets them make believe they are pilots. The gallery's six areas show flight through the ages, principles of flight, and the development of engines, airframes and aircraft systems. The Aviation Theatre's multi-media show uses 15 projectors to trace the history of aviation from man's first attempt to fly. The Physical and Life Sciences galleries also screen multi-media, video and slide shows.

Admission is $2 (50 cents for children under 16), with concessional rates for groups of 30 or more. Opening hours are 10 am to 6 pm Tuesday to Sunday, including public holidays. Closed Monday except public holidays.

Omni-Theatre

Lean back and enjoy the experience in the Omniplanetarium, whose massive hemispheric screen draws you right into the picture. Omnimax films are double features and the main movie changes about every six months. '

The 284-seat theatre has space for ten wheelchairs and a special entrance near the top of the theatre through which the chairs can be wheeled. Admission is $6 ($4 for children between four and 12 years). Children below four are not admitted. Discounts are available for groups of 30 or more. Hours are 3 pm–8 pm Tuesday to Friday, 12 pm–8 pm Saturday, Sunday and public holidays. Call 560-3316 for show schedules. All shows begin on the hour, and the last show is at 8 pm. Closed on Monday except when Monday is a public holiday.

The Omni-Theatre and Singapore Science Centre are served by SBS services 79, 97, 157, 335 and TIBS services 178 and 852.

Jurong Bird Park

As you approach the park on Jurong Hill, it is not unusual to find an egret or two sitting nonchalantly by the roadside. They could be part of the park's 3,800 birds, many of whom are uncaged and unfettered and wont to go a-visiting.

A cuckoo clock welcomes you at the entrance, which leads to a colourful corridor of bright-hued macaws in the new entry plaza. You can breakfast with the birds (the feathered kind) on the Songbird Terrace, which overlooks the whimsically named Swan Lake, a hub for the park's free-flying waterfowl. The Water Front Cafe serves local and Western cuisine.

Also new is the Fuji Hawk Walk, where you can see the white-bellied sea eagle, golden eagle, Harris's hawk, lugger falcon, wedge-tailed eagle, bald eagle, king vulture and prairie falcon.

Should these birds of prey go AWOL, they can be tracked electronically. When the keeper gets close enough, he calls the birds, who are trained to repond to a whistle.

Many of the park's residents are rare birds. The park's flamingo pool and a large exhibit of scarlet ibises are among its most photogenic attractions.

Shows include the Hornbill Chitchat: 11 am and 3 pm, Fuji World of Hawks: 10 am and 10.45 am, King of the Skies: 3 and 4 pm, Wonderful World of Birds: Noon, 1 pm and 2 pm, and Getting to Know Us, 11.30 am, 12.30 pm and 1 pm. Pelican feeding at the Swan Lake 9.30 am to 2.30 pm. $5 for adults ($2.50 for children) and $10 for the family package (two adults and three children). For more information, call 265-0022.

There is a tram ride with recorded commentary, but it does not allow you more than a glimpse of many of the smaller birds and caged exhibits. A principal stop on the tram route is the walk-in aviary. It encloses a tropical forest complete with man-made waterfall, which splashes 30 metres (100 feet) down into a valley spanned by a suspension bridge.

Opened in 1971, the park is now in the middle of a five-year re-development plan. A children's farmyard and an icy enclosure for penguins and puffins are planned. Admission is $5 ($2.50 for children). Family package (two adults and three children) costs $10 and the hours are 9 am–6 pm daily, including public holidays.

Jurong Hill and the bird park are on Jalan Ahmad Ibrahim. To get there, take SBS service 10 and 30 (from Clifford Pier) or 198 (from Supreme House) to Jurong Interchange, then services 250, 251, and 253 to the bird park.

The Jurong Bird Park Roadrunner, an air-conditioned express coach, runs twice daily from Orchard and Havelock roads to the park ($10 return, $6.50 one way). Call Journey Express at 339-7738 details and to book a seat. Daily conducted tours can be arranged at most hotel tour desks for about $24, including transfers and admission. By taxi, it costs about $12 from Orchard Road. For more information, call 265-0022.

Next to the Bird Park is the Jurong Crocodile Paradise where you can see more than 2,500 crocodiles. Crocodile-wrestling displays at 11.30 am and 3 pm daily. Admission is $4.50 for adults and $2.50 for children.

Garden of Fame

At last count, there were 30 trees planted by royalty and other heads of state
and government in this 0.9-hectare (2.2-acre) garden. The first was planted in
1969 by Britain's Princess Alexandra before the gardens opened, the last in
1984 by Dr Albert Winsemius, economic adviser to the Singapore
government. The tree he planted occupies a unique status in this garden of
VIPs, as Dr Winsemius was neither royalty nor head of state or government.

The lookout tower in the garden on Jurong Hill, near the bird park, offers a
good view of the industrial area and the southern islands. Coming down to
earth, you find names like Britain's Queen Elizabeth II and Prince Philip, the
Chinese leader Deng Xiaoping, and the late Shah of Iran. A new garden of
fame outside the Jurong Town Hall continues the tradition.

Chinese Garden

On Sundays, public holidays and all through the eighth lunar month, this
garden turns into an outdoor wedding-photo studio. The Chinese Garden, Yu
Hwa Yuan, figures in more wedding albums than almost any other place in
Singapore, apart from the Registry of Marriages. It is not unusual to find
bridal couples posing for a souvenir picture with other visitors to the garden,
usually Japanese tourists. On especially auspicious days for weddings, you
might find couples queuing up to be photographed at the three-metre (ten-
foot) tall bronze statue of Confucius, and the Garden of Fragrance.

Yu Hwa Yuan is also a popular spot during Chinese festivals, especially
the Mid-Autumn Festival (also called the Lantern Festival) and Chinese New
Year. The 13.5-hectare (33-acre) garden on an island in Jurong Lake was
designed along Song Dynasty lines. A refreshment stand and shelter from the
rain are provided on Moon Inviting Board, a stone boat styled after the one in
Beijing's Summer Palace.

The garden is full of poetically named sights. Ascend the Cloud-Piercing
Pagoda (the tallest of three in the garden) for a view of both the Chinese and
Japanese gardens and environs. Then there is the Tiger Roar Fall, Cloud-
Wrapped Pavilion, Moon-Receiving Tower, Jade Splashing Bridge and the
romantic Place to Convey Lovers' Wishes. The Herb Garden is landscaped
with plants long used as homeopathic cures. Miniature plants from China,
Malaysia and Thailand join locally cultivated specimens in the Bonsai
Garden.

Admission is $2.50 (50 cents for children), and there is a 50-cent camera
charge. Entry hours are 9 am – 7 pm Monday to Saturday and 8.30 am–7 pm
Sunday and on public holidays. The garden is cleared at 7 pm.

To get there take SBS bus service 10 and 30 (from Clifford Pier) to Jurong
Interchange and change to service 240, 242 or 406. From Orchard Boulevard,
take service 7 to Jurong East Interchange and change to service 98. The taxi

fare from Orchard Road is about $12. (For return by taxi, call the Jurong Taxi Stand at 265–4553 and 268–4233). There is also the Jurong Bird Park Roadrunner (see page 136).

Japanese Garden

Slightly smaller than the adjacent Chinese Garden, the 13-hectare (32-acre) Japanese Garden, or Seiwaen, is still one of the largest Japanese gardens outside Japan and in many ways is more interesting than its neighbour. Cobbled pathways, steeply arched wooden bridges, pools of carp and stone lanterns create a tranquil atmosphere. Some 500 tons of Japanese stones and 1,800 tons of local stones were used to landscape the garden.

Professor Kinsaku Nakane of Kyoto designed the garden in the style of the Muromachi period (1392–1568) and the Momoyama period (1568–1615), when the art of gardening is thought to have achieved its peak in Japan. The dry garden, or Keiseien, is of a style developed along Zen lines in the Muromachi period. The arrangement of stones gives the impression of mountains and valleys, with white pebbles representing streams.

Admission is $1 (50 cents for children), with a 50-cent camera charge, (a combined admission to both gardens cost $2.50, or $1.20 for children). Hours are 9 am–7 pm Monday to Saturday and 8.30 am–7 pm Sundays and public holidays.

CN-West Leisure Park

Water slides, bumper boats, a wave pool, a wading pool and a motorized boat ride through a circular flow pool are some of the features of this water playground. It has a restaurant, and catering for groups can be arranged.

The address of the leisure park is 9 Japanese Garden Road, Singapore 2261; tel. 261–7374. Admission is $2 ($1 for children under 12, and infants under one year old free). Hours are noon – 6 pm daily (closed Monday) and 9.30 am – 6 pm on weekends and public holidays.

Ming Village

Reproductions of antique Chinese porcelains are made here at 32 Pandan Road. Apart from visiting the showroom, which contains thousands of pieces of Ming, Yuan, Song and Qing porcelains, you can see the reproductions being made. The village will handle shipping of purchases. Call 265-7711 for more information.

Islands

In 1969, Singapore had 62 offshore islets — give or take a few reefs. Now it has about a half dozen fewer. Islands have been merged, their identities submerged, and reefs have been elevated, literally, to the status of islands. Take Terumbu Retan Laut, which was once a reef exposed only at low tide. Reclamation added 15 hectares (37 acres) because this spot, only one kilometre (half a mile) off the west coast of Singapore, seemed ideal for boating and sailing. So one year it was a reef, the next 15.8 hectares (39 acres), and now 24.6 hectares (61 acres). Terumbu Pesek began as an underwater reef and has now attained island status as Pulau Pesek, with a completely respectable acreage of 67.1 hectares (166 acres), though at a cost of some $12 million.

A handful of Singapore's islets can be visited fairly easily. Pulau Kusu, St John's Island and Sentosa are on scheduled ferry routes. The most visited is Sentosa, a resort island just a five-minute boat or cable-car ride away. It is a picnic spot, a place for revisiting Singapore's history and observing its natural history, a weekend disco and, only lately, a place where one can enjoy the arts.

The situation is now a far cry from that in the early 1800s, when J Johnson, a surgeon in the Royal Navy, described Singapore's islands thus, 'They are covered with woods, have a great variety in their shapes, and are indented on all sides with pleasant little bays and sandy coves where the finest turtle is found in great plenty. The passage between these islands is in some places so narrow that we might have almost thrown a biscuit on shore; yet the water was deep, clear and smooth as glass.' The water is no longer clear or smooth as glass, but then it would be unrealistic to expect that in one of the world's largest and busiest ports.

There are no scheduled ferries to **Pulau Hantu** or the **Sisters Islands**, which are south of Singapore and good for swimming, snorkelling or just getting a tan. Pulau Hantu does not look half as sinister as its name, which in Malay means 'ghost island'. Some say it got its name because it was the place where the ancient warriors duelled to the death. On weekends it is often visited by anglers and picnickers. The Sisters Islands, so named because the pair of islands face each other across a narrow channel, are just as good for a suntan, swim or snorkel. Do not attempt to swim from island to island, however, as there is a strong undertow here, which can be lethal especially at the turn of the tide.

Few of the islands are now permanently settled, and the villagers on **Pulau Seking** (see page 150) are about the last who can really be called a community, though they, too, lack a regular ferry service. These people, who are almost all Muslims, know it is only a matter of time before their island

idyll ends. They cannot bury their dead on Seking but must lay them to rest on the main island of Singapore.

Boats to Pulau Seking, Pulau Hantu and the Sisters Islands can be chartered from Clifford Pier or Jardine Steps. If you are leaving from Jardine Steps, you can fill up a picnic cooler at the Cold Storage mini-supermarket on the ground floor of the nearby World Trade Centre.

Several of the southern islands are used by the military for training and live-ammunition firing exercises. These, of course, are no-go areas, as is **Pulau Brani**, near Sentosa, which is a naval station. Other islands are industrial workplaces in the petroleum and petrochemical industries and are generally off limits to visitors. These include Shell's Pulau Bukom, which has been a workplace since 1892, Pulau Ayer Chawan, or PAC, which flies the Esso flag, and Pulau Ayer Merbau, which is the site of a $2 billion petrochemical plant.

Also off limits are the lighthouse islands, which are the property of the Port of Singapore Authority. The three best known are **Sultan Shoal Lighthouse**, **Raffles Lighthouse**, which watches over the southern waters, and **Horsburgh Lighthouse** at the eastern entrance to Singaporean waters. Sited on Pedra Branca (White Rock), Horsburgh was Singapore's first lighthouse and the first in the region to be built of granite.

Sentosa

Sentosa, the Isle of Tranquillity, was once a military base. Until its transformation into a pleasure island early in the 1970s, it was called Pulau Blakang Mati, (Malay for Island Where Death Lurks Behind). Its 375.5 hectares (928 acres) lie just half a kilometre (a quarter of a mile) away from the main island. In its present sunnier incarnation as Singapore's only resort island, visited by some two million people a year, Sentosa offers half a dozen museums.

Perhaps Sentosa's most unusual 'museum' is the **Butterfly Park**, where one can walk through a landscaped garden fluttering with thousands of live butterflies representing more than 50 species ranging from the 25-millimetre (one-inch) *Eurema sari* to the 15-centimetre (six-inch) *Papilio iswara*. Visitors can also inspect some 4,000 mounted specimens in the insectarium.

Another living museum is **Underwater World**—Asia's biggest Oceanarium—which replaces the old Coralarium. It contains over 2,000 species of fish and other marine life indigenous to Singaporean waters such as soldier fish, cardinal fish, yellow sea horses, mandarin fish and fluorescent corals. Younger visitors can handle sponges, crabs, coral and starfish in the Touch Pool and watch sea anemones opening and closing in the Tidal Pool.

A 100-metre (91-yard) moving walkway through a Perspex tunnel brings sharks and stingrays within touching distance and poisonous puffer fish and ferocious moray eel can be viewed in safety. The 25,000-square-metre (six-acre) site close to Fort Siloso and within walking distance of the New Ferry Pier also has a 100-seat audiovisual theatre running 6-minute shows on the underwater world.

The **Rare Stone Museum**, which claims to be the only one of its kind in the world, houses what may be the world's largest collection of rocks, with 4,000 specimens, including a 600,000-year-old stalagmite, gold nuggets and fossils. Natural colouring and flaws in the stones recall images of Chinese deities and historical figures or suggest unusual scenes or objects.

Choreographed by computer, the dancing jets of water at the **musical fountain** pirouette and polka to music. Built on reclaimed land at Imbiah Bay, a ten-minute walk from the ferry terminal, the fountain is a collection of pools and a rock-wall waterfall. One watches the show from the viewing gallery, which can hold 1,500 people. Showtimes are 7.30 pm, 8 pm, 8.30 pm and 9 pm daily, with disco fever seizing the scene Saturday and Sunday evenings from 9 to 10.30. There is an extra show at 9.30 pm on public holidays.

A weekend favourite with the locals are the island's two food centres, **Rasa Sentosa** and the **New Food Centre**, where one can dine al fresco on local hawker fare, the kind that used to be sold on the streets from pushcarts. The three-storey **Ferry Terminal Building** has a restaurant, coffee lounge, viewing gallery, souvenir kiosk, fast-food restaurant and information counter.

The island offers visitors who have a little more time to spare an evocative look into Singapore's history. The waxworks of the **Surrender Chamber** show the British surrender to the Japanese during World War II and the Japanese surrender to the Allied forces at the end of the war. Previously in City Hall, which also housed the Foreign Ministry and the prime minister's office, these historic tableaux were moved out to Sentosa, and the **Pioneers of Singapore** tableaux was added to complete the story. In all, there are 109 life-sized figures in the display, which is enhanced by audio-visual material including actual combat footage, archival films and special sound effects.

One can still see the guns of **Fort Siloso**, which guarded the western approaches to Singapore in the 1880s. A complex of ammunition bunkers, tunnels, gun emplacements and cannon covering four hectares (ten acres), Fort Siloso was used by the Coastal Artillery until 1956, when it was disbanded. The fort was occupied by the Gurkhas until 1967, then by the Singapore Combat Engineers until 1972, when the island was developed as a resort. An audio show, 'The Sounds of Siloso', recreates the tense days before the fall of Singapore to the Japanese in World War II, and there is a permanent exhibition on the fort's history.

At the **Maritime Museum**, take a walk through the history of the world's

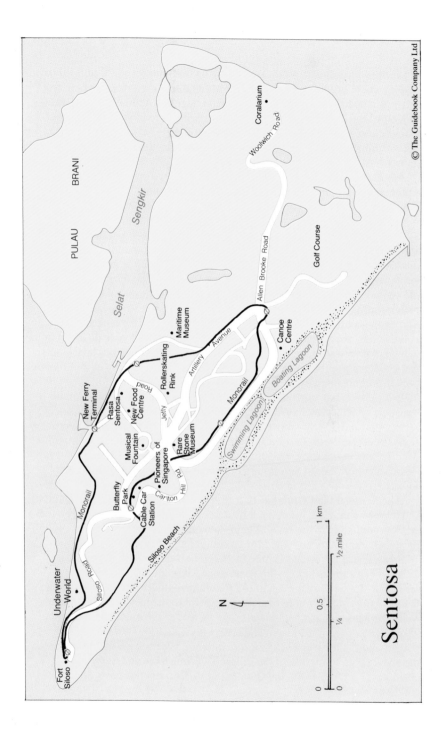

© The Guidebook Company Ltd

BRANI

PULAU

Sengkir

Selat

Coralarium

Woolwich Road

Allen Brooke Road

Golf Course

Maritime
Museum

New Ferry
Terminal

Rollerskating
Rink

Artillery   Avenue

Canoe
Centre

Rasa
Sentosa

New Food
Centre

Road

Jetty

Boating Lagoon

Monorail

Monorail

Musical
Fountain

Pioneers of
Singapore

Rare
Stone
Museum

Swimming Lagoon

Butterfly
Park

Carlton Hill Rd

Cable Car
Station

Siloso Beach

Monorail

Siloso Road

Underwater
World

Fort
Siloso

N

Sentosa

0   0.5   1 km

0   ¼   ½ mile

busiest port. Local watercraft, some only museum pieces now, are also on display in the Primitive Craft Gallery, which traces their development from rafts, skin boats, bark canoes, coracles and dugouts. Another section shows models of the trading vessels that called at Singapore in the 19th century — Chinese junks from Fujian and Hainan, East Indiamen, tea clippers and opium clippers. Special exhibits are held from time to time, and there are daily films shown at the theatrette.

For those wanting to stay overnight, there are two campsites with running water and bathroom facilities at the **swimming lagoon**. Tents, barbecue pits, skewers and campbeds can be rented on the island. There is a youth hostel with 130 beds that can be rented by groups of ten or more.

Energetic visitors may opt to take the 1.3-kilometre (0.8-mile) **nature walk**, which shows bits of virgin tropical forest, including the carnivorous pitcher plant, on the way up Mt Imbiah. They can also ride along a 4.7-kilometre (2.9-mile) **bike track** (bikes are for rent at the ferry terminal and the swimming pool), take a few turns at the 12,000-square-metre (three-acre) **rollerskating rink,** or head for the swimming lagoon to canoe or boardsail. The **canoe centre** has single- and double-seater canoes for rent. Canoeing, boardsailing and scuba-diving classes can be arranged. People do swim in the lagoon, but its waters are not inviting. **Siloso Beach**, which has beach huts and changing rooms, is often a better bet. Pedal boats, aquabikes and funbugs (which are propelled by underwater fins) can be rented here.

If it gets too hot, hop on the Swiss-built **monorail**. The island's main transport system, which opened early in 1982, travels between three and six metres (ten and 20 feet) above ground level at a speed of about 14 kilometres (nine miles) per hour. Its 13 trains chug one way around the six-kilometre (four-mile) loop of track, stopping at five stations: Ferry Terminal, Singapore Tennis Centre Chalets, Swimming Lagoon, Cable Car Station and Fort Siloso.

The **Sentosa Golf Club** has two 18-hole, par-71 golf courses. Though it is a membership club, limited public access is allowed. Weekday green fees are $50 per player ($100 on weekends and public holidays) plus $20 caddy fees. Golf clubs may be rented for an additional $15. (Tel. 472–2722.)

Sentosa also has an **art centre** showing the works of 40 Singaporean artists. The centre is next to the Rare Stone Museum.

Tickets for Sentosa are $3.50 ($2 for children under 12), which includes the ferry ride, admission to the island, musical fountain, swimming lagoon, Maritime Museum and nature walk, and the use of the monorail and buses. The ticket is good until 11 pm and costs only $3 (still $2 for children) if bought after 5 pm. The $7 ($3.50 for children) day-package includes all of the above, plus admission to the Pioneers of Singapore and Surrender chambers, Fort Siloso and the Coralarium. After 5 pm this costs $5 ($3 for children).

The Sentosa Discovery package costs $19 ($14 for children) and includes admission to all attractions except the Rare Stone Museum and Butterfly Park, access to all rides, and transfers by air-conditioned coach from the Sheraton Towers, Hyatt Regency, Mandarin, Boulevard, Shangri-La, Orchard, Hilton International and Glass hotels. Reservations can be made at the front desk.

Admission prices and opening times for individual attractions are: Rare Stone Museum ($2, or $1 for children; 9 am – 9 pm daily); Fort Siloso (same); Coralarium ($1, or 50 cents for children; 9 am – 7 pm daily); and Butterfly Park ($2.50, or $1.50 for children; 9.30 am – 5.30 pm Monday – Friday, 9.30 am – 7 pm weekends and public holidays).

To get to the World Trade Centre (WTC)/Jardine Steps Cable Car Station, take bus service 143 from Orchard Road, service 10, 20, 30, 97, 125 or 146 from Collyer Quay, or service 61, 143, 145 or 166 from Chinatown. Get off at the WTC stop.

The Port of Singapore Authority operates ferries between WTC and Sentosa at 15-minute intervals starting at 7.30 am every day. The last ferry leaves Sentosa at 11 pm Monday – Thursday and at midnight Friday – Sunday and on public holidays.

Cable cars run 10 am – 7 pm Monday – Saturday and 9 am – 7 pm on Sunday and public holidays. The 1.8-kilometre (1.1-mile) return trip between Mt Faber and Sentosa costs $6 ($3 for children). The service is apt to be crowded on weekends, particularly later in the evening.

Call 473–4388 or 270–7888 for more information.

Pulau Kusu

Legend has it that a Malay and a Chinese caught in a storm at sea were rescued by a giant turtle that turned itself into an island. This is why Kusu is also known as Pulau Tembakul, or Turtle Island. According to another story, Kusu's religious pull derives from an Arab and a Chinese, both holy men. They fasted and meditated on the island and became sworn brothers.

The island's main attractions are its modest Malay *keramat*, or hermit's shrine, on a hillock and an unassuming Chinese temple on the beach. Between them they notch up tens of thousands of visitors each year. Some come from Malaysia or even Indonesia and Hong Kong to visit the shrines. The season lasts for the whole of the ninth month of the lunar calendar, though the shrines are visited year round by worshippers as well as by day-trippers.

There are few documented clues to Kusu's origins. Malay and Chinese elements are intermarried in the religious ritual peculiar to this island. Red banners with Chinese characters in gold hang at the Malay shrine on the peak. The shrine is believed to be inhabited by spirits called *datok-datok*.

Depending upon the lunar calendar, the Kusu festival comes in October or November.

The Chinese temple dedicated to Tua Pek Kong is more crowded and very much the centre of the ninth-month festivities. The Chinese temple got its start in the 1920s from a donation by a wealthy businessman, Chia Cheng Ho. Some worshippers come to pray for good husbands (or for radical improvements to an existing model). Many ask in their prayers for children, or more usually, sons. Here, too, you will find the unavoidable throng of 'fortune hunters' who believe the deities can provide winning numbers for the illegal four-digit lottery or help them strike it rich in the monthly Singapore Sweep.

Off-season, Kusu is just another picnickers' haven. The island now measures 7.8 hectares (19 acres), but it started as two outcrops on a one-hectare (2.5-acre) reef. Kusu grew in the mid-1970s along with a few other offshore islands that were part of a $50 million scheme to create new beaches for swimmers and picnickers. Man-made swimming beaches stretch from either side of the Chinese shrine and there are picnic benches and shelters, toilets and changing rooms. There are even public telephones for those who must stay in touch.

Kusu is about 20 or 30 minutes away from the main island by ferry. On weekends 9 am – 5 pm, there are eight scheduled departures to Kusu from World Trade Centre. The last boat leaves Kusu at 6 pm. The same ferry also visits St John's Island. On weekdays, there is just one ferry in the morning and one in the afternoon, which also takes the last load of day-trippers back to the ferry terminal. During the pilgrimage season, there are more frequent departures, and if you want an authentic pilgrimage experience, take a bumboat there at the crack of dawn.

Pulau Ubin

More than three times the size of Sentosa, Pulau Ubin is spread out over 1,019 hectares (2,518 acres) in the Straits of Johor, off the eastern corner of the main island. You can hoof it from the jetty, but the way to get around the island is by taxi. These are actually beat-up vehicles retired from the fleet on the main island and driven by local residents who also double as guides.

The island has never been a resort, though students do come out here on holiday outings. Ubin has long been an industrious island, and its granite quarries have been worked for more than 140 years; today the granite is cut way below sea level. Granite slabs taken and shaped on this island were carried nearly 60 kilometres (40 miles) to the rocky outcrop of Pedra Branca when the Horsburgh Lighthouse was being constructed there. Today, Pulau Ubin continues to feed the building industry on the main island. The extent of land used for rubber plantations, once a good living for the islanders, has shrunk to almost nothing as it has been cleared for other uses.

Man-made embankments delineate modern prawn farms on Ubin, and, just offshore, floating fish farms perched on plastic pontoons supply the so-called 'live' seafood restaurants. On this island, however, the restaurants used to have no names, no tablecloths and no pretensions. It might have been the sea air, the long wait for the food or the cook's expertise that made for such a good meal, but the combination seldom failed. However, civilization has caught up with Pulau Ubin.

If you fancy roughing it in Singapore, Pulau Ubin could be about as rough as it gets. That is probably why the Outward Bound School (run by the military) and the National Police Cadet Corps use Ubin as a training ground. You can pitch your tent almost anywhere on the island or stay at the seafood restaurant's rather basic resthouse (no lights, no air-conditioning, no ceiling fan — and bring your own mosquito repellent) or at the Longhouse, which can take up to 40 people in dormitory-style accommodation and has canoes, sailboards and other sports equipment for rent. Canned drinks, sweets, sundries and some fresh produce are available from the town area near the jetty.

The ferry costs 80 cents and leaves from Changi Point on the hour between 6 am and 11 pm.

Pulau Seking

Seking, or Sakeng, as it is sometimes spelt, is the only offshore islet with an authentic community of islanders. Its plank houses are built on stilts over the water, and there are no homes inland because it would be too laborious to transport fresh water here. At high tide, the villagers bring in jerry cans of water from nearby Pulau Bukom, where the Shell refinery maintains a water pipe from the main island. Also lacking are electrical mains. The government resists putting in more facilities on Seking because it expects that all the islanders will soon go ashore for good.

The village homes on stilts are quaint, but visitors should not expect spectacular scenery. Goats, chickens and cats roam at will. Here, instead of fencing up the animals, they fence up the few vegetable patches and trees — with chicken wire and corrugated steel sheets — to protect them from the animals. Even the thorny bougainvillea has to be shielded from the goats. So Seking's neat little gardens are creations of cactus, coral and seashells.

The island's only school closed in the mid-1980s, and its teachers' quarters had been empty and boarded up for about ten years before that. To get to school, the island children take a ten-minute boat ride to Pulau Bukom and ride the Shell company's hovercraft to the jetty at Pasir Panjang and then complete the rest of the journey by bus.

The community centre, housed in a large, airy, yellow and blue building, organizes activities like *sepak takraw* —a kind of volleyball in which a rattan ball is butted about with the head, feet and just about any part of the body except the hands. An annual highlight is the sea sports held during the National Day festivities in August. The most eagerly awaited events are the *jong* races. This is a macho sport, a man's game, though one might be tempted to compare it with playing with boats in a bathtub. The unmanned, scaled-down sailboats are in three sizes, with two-, three- and four-foot hulls, which determine racing class. They can fairly rip along with a good wind, and handlers can get injured trying to catch one when the wind fills its sails.

Though the tiny slipper-shaped island of Seking is less than an hour away from the main island of Singapore, it seems like a foreign country light years removed from Orchard Road's traffic lights, cash registers, department stores and attractive shop windows. There is no need even for a bicycle here since one can walk around the island in minutes. But there are shops — four at last count — where the shopkeepers stuff their takings into drawers and tins. The shelves are stocked with basics like onions, garlic, salt fish, tinned milk and mosquito coils. In the largest shop there are also kerosene lamps, aluminium kettles, cooking pots, inexpensive cosmetics and perfumes in aerosol dispensers, which seem like luxury items on the plain wooden shelves. This shop is run by three brothers, the only Chinese on this island, and it functions as the island's pharmacy with its assortment of Western patent medicines and Chinese curatives.

One of Seking's two public telephones can be found in the home of the *penghulu*, or village head, Mohamed Yatim bin Akib, who also happens to run a grocery shop from home. His clientèle is dwindling. The 1980 census counted some 300 people, and many of the 79 homes on the island are now empty. Most people of working age have moved to the main island and visit only on weekends. Sometimes there are more visitors than residents on the island.

Kelongs

A *kelong* is not strictly an island but a man-made fish trap on stilts made of nipah palms driven 1.5 metres (five feet) or more into the seabed. This device was introduced to Singapore by Malaccan fishermen, according to Abdullah bin Kadir, a Malay scribe in whose autobiography much of the colour of Singapore's history can be found. According to him, a Malaccan named Haji Mata-mata built large fish traps with rows of stakes. The tide would carry the fish into the trap along lines of converging stakes planted in the water. 'In the first kelong which was put up off Teluk Ayer, they caught no small number of tenggiri fish; in such vast surfeit that the fish could not be eaten and had to be thrown away. Their roes were taken out, put into barrels containing salt,

and sold as a regular commodity to ships. The people of Singapore were
surprised to see the number of fish caught in this way.'

The traditional keeper's day began at about 3 am with a quick breakfast of
fish and squid — fresh from the net traps below. Then it would be time to
haul up last night's catch and ferry it to the fish market. Five or six times a
day, the nets would again be lowered for a few hours and winched up by
hand to check the catch, which was brought up with a long-handled scoop
net. The catch could be anything from silvery scraps of *ikan bilis* to a baby
shark.

In the old days, owners and their families lived on their kelong, but now
many of them commute to work every night from their apartments on the
main island or from Pulau Ubin. By 9 am they are on their way to the fresh
fish market at Punggol, northeast of Singapore Island, and by evening, much
of the catch is dinner for the fastidious gourmets who patronize Singapore's
many seafood restaurants. Rainy weather means a poor catch, and in any case
today's catch is no longer as bountiful as it was.

The workforce on a kelong was once exclusively male. Traditional
fisherfolk staunchly believed that women brought bad luck to the kelong, but
this superstition rarely poses a problem now.

Once commonplace, the fish traps used to mark a trail of neat chevrons in the seas off Singapore, and anglers could always buy fish at one if they had not managed to catch any themselves. When the catch dwindled in the mid-1970s, some owners started renting their kelongs out for parties and, in recent years, have converted them into fish farms. Building contractors, traders, accountants and others have sunk up to half a million dollars into sea-farms, which produce about a quarter of the fish that Singapore consumes, the rest being imported mainly from Indonesia and Malaysia. When the price is right, the rewards can be rich. The spotted grouper at one time commanded up to $120 per kilogram, a price guaranteed to choke anyone other than the most exacting of seafood connoisseurs.

Fish farms are not built to accommodate visitors, but if you rent a boat and arrive at the right time, you may find the fish being fed in their nylon cage nets. Feeding time is fighting time. When the meal of chopped up 'rubbish' fish is dumped in, the waters churn as the seabass and grouper fight for their share. This is a good place to buy one's dinner. Though prices are no cheaper here than ashore, one is assured of freshness.

Singlish as She is Spoke

Singapore is a reassuring Asian destination for a visitor. Particularly if he speaks English. Particularly if his notions of the exotic East have been culled from old Hollywood movies. Particularly if all he knows about Singapore is that it is the place where a drink called the Singapore Sling was first concocted.

The first reassuring surprise is that all the signs in the airport terminal are in English (when they are not international pictograms, that is). On stepping out of his hotel (its name writ large in English), the visitor discovers that street names are also in English and that almost everyone he meets seems able to understand at least some of the visitor's own English. Indeed, for the most part, Singapore functions in English, though it is only lately that English has become the main teaching medium in schools.

But what English? The first linguistic hurdle for a stranger is to understand . the rapid-fire pace of much of Singaporean speech. Pace is complicated by the second, perhaps larger, hurdle of Singlish, a distinctive variant (some would say perversion) of colonial English. In essence it is an English whose syntax and vocabulary have not only been invaded, but in some cases subjugated, by Hokkien (a dialect from the southern Chinese province of Fujian) and Malay. It is not simply a difference in accent, pronunciation or vocabulary. Nor is it just poor, contracted or contorted English. It is all of these in different measures, spoken differently by different people in different contexts and, in many cases, quite unintelligible to a non-Singlish-speaking person.

Among Singlish's most useful phrases are all-purpose gems like 'Is it?' (usually pronounced eezeet), which can stand alone or be used as a postscript to a sentence. Depending on the tone of voice in which it is said, it can be an expression of sarcasm, horror, wonderment, uncertainty or polite disbelief. It can also be a request for confirmation, a bridge over an awkward conversation gap, a substitute for 'Really?' or an acknowledgement that you are listening. Of course, it can also be a simple question.

'Where got?' may sound like a question, but more usually it is an expression of utter disbelief or denial. As a one-word comment, 'Wow!' comes close to 'Shiok!' (pronounced as spelt but sometimes extended for emphasis until it is almost two syllables). 'Can die one!' may sometimes suggest 'shiok', depending on its context, but it can also mean the speaker is dead tired or plain fed up. Commonly uttered is the suffix 'la', which punctuates many Singlish sentences and softens their brusqueness.

'Can' means possible, but when said with some finality it means 'yes'. 'Can, can' means a definite yes, but this may be only tactical agreement. On the other hand, 'Can do, la' is a standard shopkeeper's answer to the question of how his business is doing. To say that one's business is doing well is to invite trouble, the Chinese believe. So if you do ask, you will most likely be told 'Can do, la' or 'Can survive, la' — the latter immortalized as the title of a book by Margaret Sullivan about Singapore's craftspeople.

Forget about subjects and predicates and the appositeness of anything. Forget in fact about articulating consonants clearly, as the Singlish attitude to this Anglo-Saxon requirement is rather laid-back to say the least. All you need do is walk into a shop and look interested in the merchandise and you will likely be greeted by a salesgirl thus, 'Kairh ai hep choo?' (Can I help you?)

If, after monopolizing her attention for an hour, and then confessing that you were only window shopping (or as the locals might say, 'look-see, look-see ohnee'), you might be told, 'Now then you say!' or 'Early-early don't say!' Translated straight from Chinese, they mean exactly the same thing, 'Why didn't you say so earlier?'

Creeping into Singlish are Cantonese expressions like 'one-leg kick', a literal translation of an idiom that means doing a task (particularly drudge work) or doing business on one's own. Simple Anglo-Saxon words like 'dirty' may not always mean what you think. If a certain house, place or stretch of road is said to be 'dirty', it is haunted. 'Ai kee Madonna mai?' has nothing to do with the pop star. It means 'Do you want to go to McDonald's?'

A Chinese Singaporean who speaks with an American or English accent (or a Chinese American or British national of Chinese descent) is likely to be labelled in the most contemptuous tone, 'Real banana!' (that is, yellow on the outside, white on the inside): But that is, as some might say, 'not your pasal, don't champoh!' which means, more or less, that you should mind your own business.

Downers include Singlisms like 'No mood la' or 'Moody da!' The first is shorthand for 'I'm not in the mood' and often implies 'Go away' as well. The second implies anger, frustration, or boredom. If the situation is really dire, it is 'habis for you!' (*habis* being Malay for 'finish'), but it could be 'lagi worse' (literally 'even worse').

The best Singlisms are those that blend Hokkien, Malay and English, like 'Ee baru ki offit', which virtually any Singaporean will understand to mean 'He just left for the office'. The Hokkien-Malay-Hokkien-English sentence is one of many supplied by local Singlish pundit Paik Choo. She has compiled two books on the subject — *Eh Goondu* and *Lagi Goondu*. *Goondu* is something akin to 'village idiot' — which is what you may feel like till you get clued in.

Shopping

Singapore is a shopper's city mainly because of the tremendous variety of goods it offers, the ease of moving between shops, the pleasant (and safe!) shopping atmosphere, the long shopping hours and the lack — so far — of a sales tax. The country is an international emporium, stocking its shelves from what the rest of the world produces. Almost all imports enter the country duty free.

There are still bargains to be had, but the savings are not what they used to be when the country first earned a reputation as a shopper's haven. Cameras, musical equipment and other electric and electronic goods, especially if they are well-known Japanese makes, may be only a little cheaper here than back home. What remains unbeatable, however, is the range of goods, particularly of new products. Everything seems to be available virtually everywhere in Singapore and not only in the large stores. Even small shops carry an impossibly wide range of makes and models, and if you ask for something they do not happen to have on their shelves, they will usually offer to secure it for you from a nearby stockroom, branch store or friendly neighbour.

The Ropes

It is impossible to avoid Orchard Road if one is a shopper. This is the main shopping strip, and while it is a delight to explore the other areas, you can be quite contented if you never get beyond it. Shopkeepers in other areas may tell you that their price is 'cheaper than the Orchard Road price', and it is true that some things may be cheaper off this main shopping strip. But it is not only in a high-rent area that one can get clipped. Comparison shopping is your best insurance against being overcharged anywhere. If you can, check prices with a department store and two other stores. Also, if you are buying a camera or a piece of electronic equipment, find out which accessories are included in the price.

One may still bargain in Singapore, but as a rule not in the major department stores where prices are fixed. Curiously enough, you may find that some shops displaying 'fixed price' signs rather prominently may offer a discount 'special for you' just as you start out the door. You are in fact expected to bargain in shops that sell cameras, VCRs and any electronic equipment. Always haggle in shops that deal in watches, jewellery, curios, antiques and oriental carpets. If you enjoy the fun of bargaining, you can haggle your way through most of the shop units in the multi-storey centres. But if you lack the appetite for it, just ask for a discount. Discounts are a way of shopping life in Singapore. Some stores issue their own discount cards to regulars.

Frequent and free-spending patrons are not the only ones who benefit; members of unions affiliated with the National Trades Union Congress get discounts at the Metro stores, for instance. A number of enterprising operations sell membership cards to 'subscribers' who can use them to obtain discounts at certain shops and food outlets. Tourists are better off sitting out this game.

Most stores, even fairly small establishments, accept credit cards, with Visa and MasterCard preferred over Diners Club and American Express. A few also accept Carte Blanche and an increasing number take JCB. However, discounts — if given at all — are generally only for cash purchases. If you intend to use your credit card, it is better to say so up front to avoid a misunderstanding later on. Many shops in the Orchard Road area will accept US dollars, sterling and Malaysian ringgit (and occasionally other currencies as well) in payment. However, you would most likely be better off making a detour to the money changer (most shopping centres have several and they generally offer a better rate than banks) as store rates are seldom as favourable. Travellers cheques are also widely accepted.

Cash register receipts are usually given as a matter of course, and some stores will also provide a written receipt. Others will give an itemized receipt upon request. It is good practice to ask for one for insurance purposes, if yours is a costly purchase. Even if it is not, you should ask for one as proof of purchase (cash register slips are often unreadable) should you want to return it. Be warned, though, that most stores do not accept returns. If they do, there is a time limit and a restriction on what it can be exchanged for. There are no cash refunds. You should inspect what you buy before you pay and insist on trying out any electrical/electronic equipment in the store to see if it works. You may also need a written receipt for customs inspection in your home country.

If you are buying something on which there is a warranty, be sure to ask for and inspect the warranty card (conditions of guarantee and serial number among other details) before paying for your purchase. Some electrical and electronics goods are brought into Singapore as parallel imports, that is, not through an authorized distributor. While this practice is not against the law, it may mean that your purchase has only a restricted warranty, perhaps requiring you to send it for servicing to — say — Paraguay. Or worse, there may be no guarantee at all. Even if you are prepared to live with that, it would be as well to check out if you need to. Complaints should be directed to the Singapore Tourist Promotion Board at Raffles City Tower 36–04, 250 North Bridge Road, Singapore 0617. Or telephone 339–6622.

While Singapore has been described as the safest shopping city in Asia, there are a couple of important caveats: Beware of pickpockets and beware of touts. Crowded stores — especially on Saturday afternoon, which is when all Singapore seems to descend on the shops — provide prime pickings for gangs of petty thieves. Where a department store has a courtesy counter, it may be prudent to check shopping bags so you have less to keep your eye on. Tangs Department Store offers a convenient service if you're planning to do a lot of shopping in the store. Take a shopping number (a plastic tag) at the information counter and show it to the salesperson when making a purchase. When you're through, you pick up your purchases and pay for everything in one shot, a boon especially when using a credit card. They will also deliver, free of charge, purchases above $200 to your hotel or local address.

The second caveat: beware of touts. These generally button hole would-be customers on the sidewalk or in shopping centre corridors. They do their best to hustle you into the tourist traps from which they can earn a commission. A taxi driver or tour guide who leads you to a particular store may also be cut in on this deal. Respond to unsolicited store recommendations with extreme caution or, preferably, not at all. Although touting or soliciting for business on the street is not allowed, it goes on nevertheless and often fairly openly at popular shopping places such as Lucky Plaza, Orchard Towers and Far East Shopping Centre.

Service ranges from pleasant to indifferent, but most people would agree that the annual courtesy campaign promoted by the government has reaped dividends. Most sales staff in the larger stores can speak English, but here as elsewhere do not expect a high level of product knowledge, as training tends to be rudimentary. The tremendous growth in the retail industry between the 1970s and the 1980s has resulted in many young people hopping from store to store.

Most of the larger stores that carry bulky or breakable goods can often have your purchases delivered to where you are staying. There may be a delivery charge. Many stores will ship out purchases for you. Ask at the information counter. Tangs and Centrepoint also maintain counters where one can purchase tickets for major theatrical and musical performances.

Opening times vary considerably from centre to centre and from store to store, but most are open between 10 am and 6 pm. Department stores stay open until at least 9 pm every day, and some close even later. The only department store that closes on Sunday is Tangs. Many shops stay open even on public holidays, though the first day of the Chinese (Lunar) New Year is a holiday for an increasing number of stores.

Fashion goods give about the best value for money in Singapore. If you are thinking of arriving with an empty suitcase or no suitcase at all (since luggage is fairly inexpensive here), it will not be the first time a visitor has done so. Because the stores cater equally to Asian and larger Western sizes, it is easy for all visitors to find clothes that fit. Custom-tailoring can be completed quickly, and many tailors and dressmakers offer 24-hour service, though at a premium and sometimes at the risk of a less-than-perfect fit. The best buys are in summer clothing, since Singapore's daytime temperature is never far from

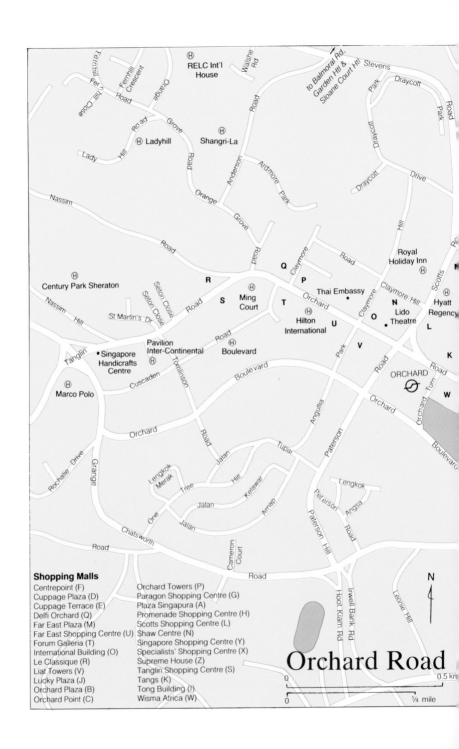

Orchard Road

Shopping Malls

Centrepoint (F)
Cuppage Plaza (D)
Cuppage Terrace (E)
Delfi Orchard (Q)
Far East Plaza (M)
Far East Shopping Centre (U)
Forum Galleria (T)
International Building (O)
Le Classique (R)
Liat Towers (V)
Lucky Plaza (J)
Orchard Plaza (B)
Orchard Point (C)

Orchard Towers (P)
Paragon Shopping Centre (G)
Plaza Singapura (A)
Promenade Shopping Centre (H)
Scotts Shopping Centre (L)
Shaw Centre (N)
Singapore Shopping Centre (Y)
Specialists' Shopping Centre (X)
Supreme House (Z)
Tanglin Shopping Centre (S)
Tangs (K)
Tong Building (I)
Wisma Atrica (W)

0   0.5 km

0   ¼ mile

N

30°C (85°F). But if you are interested in purchasing heavier clothing, a number of speciality stores, notably Fook On (its main store at 83/85 South Bridge Road, and a branch at 03–82/83 Lucky Plaza) and Windy Bay Apparel (02–69 Far East Plaza) cater for travellers. They carry woollies, gloves and winter coats year round. Some upscale boutiques in Orchard Road (mainly in the Promenade and Paragon shopping centres) regularly carry the fall/winter collections of European and other designers. In between the highly functional and the highly fashionable are the increasing number of factory outlets that carry not only sweaters but also anoraks (parkas) and winter coats. International chains such as Benetton (Centrepoint, Forum Galleria, Scotts and other centres in the Orchard Road area) and Esprit (270 Orchard Road) also carry a surprisingly large selection of sweaters and unsummery clothing, a testament to the powerful and pervasive air-conditioning as much as to the Singaporean yen to travel. There are also a number of leather boutiques and even fur salons.

A minor irritant is the lack or inadequacy of labelling, especially in some of the smaller shops. Ask the origin of a shirt or pair of shoes and the answer will often be just one word: 'Imported.' That usually means it is from Hong Kong or Taiwan, or occasionally from Malaysia, Thailand or Indonesia. In many shops one may search high and low for a 'Made in Singapore' label and never find it because of long-standing prejudice in favour of imports. This is changing now, especially in the department stores, many of which have developed their own house names. The expanding influence of Singaporean designers, whose ready-to-wear clothes are carried in some stores as well as their own boutiques, has also helped. Among the more wearable mid-range designers are Esta for women and Bobby Chng for men.

In Singapore, shops tend to move with the shoppers. The newest shopping centre to offer a packed programme of promotions, fashion shows and other entertainment tends to be the flavour of the month, for which the crowds will readily abandon last month's favourite — to be followed by the shop-owners. Possibly no other city has seen so many malls and shopping complexes spring up in so short a time, nor so many foreign department stores which have jumped in to carve out a share of the market.

Orchard Road

For visitor and resident alike, Orchard Road is synonymous with shopping. In the last 15 – 20 years, this street (actually an area that includes Scotts Road and perhaps Tanglin Road) has become the easiest place to shop and, for most people, the only place. Whether it is haute couture or inexpensive souvenirs you are interested in, Orchard Road has it all.

One way to do the area systematically is to run a loop starting at Plaza Singapura near the head of Orchard Road, then thread your way through the aesthetically forgettable though quite friendly complexes of Orchard Plaza, Orchard Point and Cuppage Plaza, then to Centrepoint.

Between Cuppage Plaza and Centrepoint is **Cuppage Terrace**, a row of refurbished shophouses, whose rewards are to be found on its upper floor. First, there is **Babazar Design Market**, where antiques and almost-antiques sit cheek by jowl with modern stoneware table settings from Bali, primitive art from Southeast Asia, carved furniture from India, rattan settees from the Philippines, ethnic hand-woven fabrics made into modern garments, painted wood table-pieces, and unusual postcards of Singapore. A few paces away is the **Della Butcher Gallery**, a good place to view and purchase original paintings, prints and ceramics done by artists working in Singapore. There are frequent exhibitions of local art. Many Singapore artists found their first gallery space with Ms Butcher, who was one of the earliest to promote their work. Down the corridor from her gallery is **Petnic's Enterprise**, a small antique shop that specializes in the treasures and bric-a-brac of the Straits Chinese. Its silver ornaments, porcelain and beadwork are much prized by collectors in Singapore and Malaysia but are still largely unknown outside this region.

Some of the best shopping on Orchard Road is at **Centrepoint**. This complex offers seven levels of shopping anchored by **Robinson's**, the country's oldest and once most venerated department store, and **Cold Storage**, the main store of the dominant supermarket chain. The original Robinson's in Raffles Place was devastated by a fire in the 1970s. While it was finding its feet again in the 1970s and 1980s, competitors fought over its previously unchallenged title as the country's premier store. Robinson's may never regain that title, but the store is once again a pleasure to visit and a good place to shop for mid-priced-to-expensive clothes and accessories. The second level has a Louis Feraud corner and a newly opened Fratelli Rosetti shoe boutique. Centrepoint also has the best selection of local boutique names — **Trend**, **Mims**, **Blum** and **China Silk House**. **Chomel**, a fast-growing chain selling inexpensive women's clothing and accessories, has a new flagship store here. Two discount clothing stores — **Factory Outlet** and **Stockmart** — are tucked away in the aisles off the main concourse but are not difficult to find. Stockmart carries some well-known American names including Banana Republic, The Gap, and Calvin Klein (labels are usually ripped or cut off). Browsers head for **Times the Bookshop** or its rival, **MPH Bookstore**, which face each other across an atrium. Apart from the usual array of bestsellers and respectable magazines, both have a fair collection of local fiction and non-fiction. A must-see is the new **Cora Jacobs** boutique that features this Filipina designer's imaginative handbags using shell, lace and dyed basketweave.

Father Knows Best

And what about life here? I received from my father advice which he received from his, the accumulated wisdom of Singapore ancients, as it were; and I am only too glad to pass it on.

'If you want to be healthy, never take an entirely cold bath, never sleep at night with your stomach uncovered, put disinfectant immediately on any kind of a cut or a skin abrasion, and use alcohol just as a sane-living person would in Europe.

'If you want to be happy, remember that the country is just round the corner waiting to black-jack you. Don't admit that you are living in an Oriental country; live as neatly as possible as you would in Europe. Read plenty, the mind needs more exercise than the body; keep yourself up to date; have your own things round you, and as much beauty as you can in your home. Above all, never wear a sarong and baju; that's the beginning of the end!'

The fact is, that every white man who goes to the Orient has a mental and spiritual fight before him; he must always keep up his guard or the country will down him. It has been said that Singapore is a paradise for second-class people, and so it is in one way; but, however second-class their talents may be, only first-class people can remain captains of their souls, and that goes double for the Orient.

So far as creature comforts are concerned, Singapore will do you proud—all kinds of sport all the year round, a good table, owing to cold storage, and a magnificent fish supply, comfortable houses, lovely green gardens, superb roads on which to motor, and plenty of places to go by road, rail, or sea. Perhaps the best thing about our life is that we are forced to take longish periods of leave, so that we get better chances of seeing the world than our opposite numbers at home, most of whom take a fortnight or a month each year for their annual holiday and go nowhere much when they take it.

Roland Braddell, The Lights of Singapore

OG, an inexpensive local chain popular with office workers and young people, has its own store just up the road. From there it is a short walk up Orchard Road (against the traffic flow) to the beautifully designed **Esprit** store and the **Paragon**, which has a collection of designer boutiques and generally upscale shops, including **Gucci** and a new **Emporio Giorgio Armani**.

Bylos, Issey Miyake, Matsuda, Ralph Lauren, and **Louis Feraud** are some of the names at Promenade. Others to note are **Man and His Woman, Tyan, Le Bijou and Glamourette. Art Forum** carries the work of foreign and local artists. **Unlimited** is a slick showcase of fashion and decor items, and **Abraxas**, an amusing emporium of high-priced, high-tech high jinks in home decor.

If you are really in the mood to indulge — or dream — look in at the **Rolex Centre**, which occupies the lofty ground floor of the adjacent **Tong Building**. Next door is **Lucky Plaza** with several hundred shops, many of them catering chiefly to the tourist trade to judge from the plethora of luggage shops and money changers there. Anchor tenant **Metro Grand** occupies the entire fifth floor. Do drop into **Good Old Days** on the fourth floor, which carries antique and vintage watches.

Tangs, arguably the best department store in Singapore, is situated strategically at the Orchard/Scotts crossroads. Despite having five large floors for its merchandise, the store has decided to depart from the tradition of having only a flagship store and has opened **Tangs Studio** next door at **Scotts**. This is very much a 'lifestyle' (read yuppie) store, with prices to match. Scotts began life as an upmarket collection of shops, moved down-market somewhat and is now settling into a liveable mix spanning the spectrum from inexpensive sportswear (**Heshe**) and affordable chic (**Bylines**) to expensive elegance (**Casa Luisa, Mondi, Diane Fries**).

The **Lanvin Shop** is about all that is left of the **Hyatt Regency's Serendipity Row** of upmarket boutiques.

One of the largest shopping centres in the country is **Far East Plaza**, which boasts 800 shops. The main action, though, is at the large **Metro** store, the centre's anchor tenant, just below street level.

A pedestrian walkway across Scotts Road leads to another Metro store and a **Bally** shoe boutique. Move on to **Shaw Centre**, whose shopping floors are starting to come alive again. Two shops here that are fun are **Fay-Fay**, a tiny boutique that deals in naughty (but nice) lingerie, and **Knick Knacks**, which sells bric-a-brac, old brass and ceramics, handprinted stationery, locally made soft toys and costume jewellery. Knick-Knacks also has a small rack of casual clothes, many of them hand-printed or hand-painted.

Next stop is the **International Building**, beside the Lido Cinema. This is chiefly an office building, but the **Chinese Emporium** is worth the climb up the stairs for its imports from China, including silks, crafts, curios and soapstone chops, or 'signature' seals. (There is a fee for carving your name on the seal, but non-Chinese can have their names 'translated' for free.)

Past the Royal Thai Embassy are the two linked blocks of **Orchard Towers**, which once called itself Shoppers' City but is better known now for its nightlife than its shopping. Fashion, jewellery, factory outlet shoes and sporting goods are found in the front block (**Handloom House** for Indian silk and **Miss Ming** for Thai silk); a gift shop, drugstore and supermarket are at the rear.

Delfi's Orchard's main redeeming feature is **Hemispheres**, a showcase for young and often zany local design, whose trendy clothes and accessories often seem made not so much to be worn as exhibited. Escada, Etienne Aigner and other designer names may be found at Delfi Orchad, a generally upmarket and rather quiet centre which seems tailored to Japanese tastes. **Le Classique**, where Orchard Road turns into Tanglin Road, caters unabashedly to Japanese shoppers. Most, if not all its salespeople speak Japanese and are courteous and pleasant.

Cross the road to **Tanglin Shopping Centre**, which is a haven for art, curio and antique hunters. (If you're fatigued by now, step into **Steeple's Deli** on the second floor for a blueberry milkshake or something more substantial like a hot pastrami on rye.) **Tatiana** and **Antiques of the Orient** are not to be missed. Tatiana has an interesting collection of primitive Southeast Asian art, while Antiques of the Orient has just about cornered the market on antique maps and prints of Southeast and East Asia. The shop is almost a museum. There is also a section of old books and first editions of regional interest. **Ju-I Antiques** specializes in antique Chinese furniture, Buddhist figures and ancient ceramics.

The **Singapore Handicraft Centre** further up on Tanglin Road could be an alternative starting point for a shopping tour. The centre has about 30 shops that deal in the arts and crafts of Afghanistan, Bangladesh, India, Indonesia, Iran, Japan, Malaysia, the Philippines, Singapore, Sri Lanka, Thailand and other countries. There are *wayang kulit* (shadow play puppets) from Indonesia, Bornean tribal crafts and pottery from East Malaysia, opera masks from China, prayer mats from Pakistan and hand-screened modern batik made in Singapore. It may be more fun, however, to go there for the so-called Pasar Malam (night market) on Wednesday, Saturday and Sunday nights, when sidewalk traders set up stalls in its corridors. Some of the arts-and-crafts shops keep longer hours on these nights.

Moving back down Orchard Road, there is **Forum Galleria**, a new shopping complex dominated by **Toys R Us**, which takes up a whole floor.

The rest is a mix of fashion, sportswear, dancewear, jewellery, optical and other shops, including **Benetton** and **Bruno Magli** boutiques.

The **Singapore Hilton** is one hotel that takes its shopping seriously and luxuriously. Its shopping floors, including much of the ground level, are crammed with names like **Louis Vuitton, Loewe, Valentino, Missoni** and the jewellers **Bulgari**.

Far East Shopping Centre next door is distinguished (if one can call it that) by a jewellery shop that appears to have a sale on all year round. Next to it, **Liat Towers** is better known as the home of the first McDonald's restaurant in Singapore than for its two newer tenants, the French department store **Galeries Lafayette** and the **Hermés Boutique**. **Galeries Lafayette** has an in-house **Sonia Rykiel** boutique and some of the nicest casual wear for men under its Galfa house label.

Across the road is **Wisma Atria**, home to the Japanese retailer **Isetan** and a mix of couture names like **Chanel** and **Versace** and chain shops like **Trend**. The shopping floors of the **Mandarin Singapore** include boutiques like **Link** and **Bern Conrad**. **Specialists' Shopping Centre**, which housed Robinson's for many years, now has Robinson's sister company **JL** (previously known as John Little's) as anchor tenant. JL's main draw is inexpensive fashion for a younger and trendier crowd. In the basement is another large branch of **Times the Bookshop**.

If you cannot face a hot and humid walk down to the head of Orchard Road, hop into the subway and get off at the next stop, Dhoby Ghaut. From this station it is a short walk to **Supreme House** (which has a **Metro** store) and **Singapore Shopping Centre** (which has some interior decor shops but no other shopping to recommend it). The MRT station's underground tunnel links it with **Plaza Singapura**, the last shopping stop on Orchard Road. This was the hottest shopping spot in town once, and it was the place for young people to hang out even before McDonald's arrived. Though the shine has worn off somewhat, it has a well-established home decor floor with a good range of shops selling building materials, lighting, fittings and furniture. **Yaohan**, the Japanese department store chain, set up its first store here. The store sells everything from groceries and consumer durables to fashion and sports. **OG** has a large store on the ground floor with racks of inexpensive fashion and footwear.

Off Orchard Road

Shopping off Orchard Road requires a little more planning. Though it is usually not difficult to catch a taxi from other shopping centres, it is best to join the taxi queue well before closing time or plan on taking the bus or train back to your hotel.

Liang Court on River Valley Road is unmistakable because of its bright orange-tiled façade. Even if you did not know that it was part of the same complex as the Hotel New Otani, the presence of the **Daimaru** department store and the multitude of Japanese eateries and shops in the building would soon force you to acknowledge its distinctly Japanese flavour. Daimaru was not the first to place cafes and restaurants side by side with its selling area, but nowhere else in Singapore have the national passions of eating and buying been so closely and cleverly integrated as in the basement of Daimaru and the rest of Liang Court. Upstairs is its wide range of fashion, from ultra-chic couture to ultra-reasonable fashion under the house labels and cheap chic for young people. These and an in-between range of moderately priced imports are worth browsing through. Also in Liang Court, **Marusho** carries trendy Japanese clothes and bric-a-brac, and **Taisei** deals in coins and stamps. Credit cards are accepted.

People's Park really comes to life at night, though many of its shops are open in the daytime. The area has several large shopping centres, the best known being the **People's Park Complex**. Others in the area are **Pearl's Centre**, **People's Park Centre** and the flagship store of **OG**. People's Park Complex is crammed to the gills with electronics, electrical goods, cosmetics and cheap chic. **Tashing Emporium** sells mainly made-in-Taiwan goods, while the **Overseas Emporium** upstairs is a year-round made-in-China showcase. Both are worth a visit. One of the most established factory outlets is **Bond**, a good place for export men's shirts, which are longer in the sleeve than shirts made for locals. Credit cards are accepted in many shops.

Raffles City, the same complex that houses the two Westin hotels, is bright, brassy and rarely quiet. A high-decibel campaign heralded the arrival of the Japanese retail giant, **Sogo**, which promptly ran out of space and spawned several extensions in unexpected shop lots not directly connected to the main store. **St Michael's** (local scion of Britain's Marks and Spencer), **Mico Boutique** and a number of handicraft and gift shops add interest to a busy, buyable shopping scene. Credit cards are accepted.

Marina Square has overtaken all others as the largest shopping centre in Singapore. It has a multitude of anchor tenants including a large **Metro** store, a branch of **Habitat** (a local offshoot of Sir Terence Conran's brainwave store), the Japanese retailer **Tokyu** and **Kid's World**. **Athlete's Foot** is here, too, and an interesting corner for vanishing crafts. The half of Singapore not on Orchard Road at the weekend is undoubtedly at Marina Square — at least for now. Credit cards are accepted.

Parkway Parade is the largest suburban shopping centre, with **Isetan** and **Yaohan** taking up the lion's share of space. Inexpensive fashion shops, some with more than one branch within the same complex, are a big draw here. The biggest draw, though, may be its plethora of restaurants, fast-food outlets and basement food stalls. Credit cards are accepted at most non-food shops.

Flavours

A first-time visitor who cites food as his most compelling reason for visiting Singapore may be a somewhat unusual creature, but he is not unheard of. Once entrapped by that first perfect meal, however, a visitor may find the myriad flavours of Singapore ample reason for staying on and a compelling excuse for making a return visit.

Singapore's culinary charms stem not from a single cuisine elevated to the realm of high art but from the immense variety of food, which makes eating out a consuming adventure. One may breakfast on thick buttered toast and kaya (coconut jam) at a local coffee shop with the morning traffic as background music, stoke the coals at lunchtime with a fiery south Indian 'banana leaf' curry, seek refuge in high tea at 4 pm with a nibble at watercress sandwiches and scones served on fine China, indulge in a ten-course Chinese banquet at dinner-time and, at midnight or after, stuff any inner space still vacant with cubes of French loaf dipped in *soup kambing*, a spicy mutton soup — then start over again with a fresh menu of gastronomic challenges the next morning.

Singapore is a nation that eats out — and eats well. Visitors may be surprised at the number of restaurants and other food outlets in the hotels, but, unlike those in many countries, hotels here depend considerably on regular local walk-in custom. Therefore, any hotel worth its salt has at least one decent Chinese restaurant (and sometimes two) as well as a coffee shop whose patrons are largely local. As an institution, the 24-hour coffee shop is more than 20 years old and still thriving, thanks mainly to local patronage.

As new eateries open (and some close) each week, it is quite possible to spend a lifetime here without once being compelled to eat twice at the same food stall, lunch counter, coffee shop or restaurant. There is no record of anyone succeeding in the attempt, but a growing colony of food writers and journals (compared with none in print a scant 20 years ago) does its best to keep up with new establishments and track down old favourites that have relocated. The most handy references are *The Food Paper*, a monthly newspaper published and largely written by the country's best-known food writer, Violet Oon, and a compact guide published by Guides and Annuals Publishers entitled *Where to Eat and Drink in Singapore*. Food news and reviews also appear in *The Straits Times* and its sister papers *The Sunday Times* and *The New Paper*.

Eating out is generally inexpensive, by big-city standards, and the notion of a brown-bagged sandwich for a desk-top lunch is still anathema to many who grew up expecting a hot lunch and a complete meal (which to many means a meal with rice). Food is an important social event here. It is common for colleagues to lunch together and occasionally have dinner out together, too — more usual, in fact, than going out together for an after-work drink. Many restaurants are packed on weekends, especially for Sunday lunch, when it is customary for people to dine out *en famille*.

Peranakan (Nonya) Food

The food of the Straits Chinese community, which evolved through the intermarriage of Chinese and Malay elements, is unique to this area. Coconut, candlenut, turmeric and fragrant lemon grass are essential to this cuisine, though none are used in Chinese cooking. Pork is also one of the most common ingredients, making it different from Malay food which, as Malays are traditionally Muslim, never contains pork.

Peranakan food (or Nonya, as locals call it) migrated south with the early settlers who came in droves from the older settlements of Malacca and Penang on hearing news of Stamford Raffles' new trading post. Purists still debate whether a certain dish has more of a Malacca or Penang Nonya flavour, though for the uninitiated it may be difficult to detect any difference. Ironically perhaps, it was in Singapore that Peranakan (pronounced *pranakahn*) food was reported to be a dying cuisine not so long ago, and it is here that it has now spawned so many new restaurants.

Nonya desserts and snacks, many of them based on rice and coconut, are if anything more popular than the rest of the cuisine, and one does not have to go to a restaurant for these. Breakfast is a good bet at **Sin Tiong Wah Coffee Shop** (47 East Coast Road), where one can feast on *Nonya kueh*. There is *dodol*, a glutinous rice and brown-sugar cake; the multi-coloured, many-layered *kueh lapis*; *onde onde*, or coconut-covered balls with a liquid centre of brown palm sugar; and *agar-agar santan*, a jelly of agar and coconut milk. Much of this is supplied by housewives who live in the area. A meal in themselves, Nonya rice dumplings stuffed with sweetened minced pork can be bought at **Sin Wah Coffee Shop** (62 Joo Chiat Place).

There are now at least half a dozen establishments that serve fairly decent Nonya food, apart from hotel coffee shops that have some dishes on the permanent menu and occasionally lay on a Peranakan buffet. Try the **Baba Cafe** (25B Lorong Liput in Holland Village), **Nonya and Baba Restaurant** (262 River Valley Road), **Peranakan Inn** (210 East Coast Road) and **Guan Hoe Soon Restaurant** (214 Joo Chiat Road). Ask for *ayam buah keluak* (tamarind-flavoured chicken stew with *buah keluak*, a kind of nut), *babi pong tay* (beef and bamboo shoot stew), *pong tauhu* (pork, crabmeat and beancurd meatballs in a clear soup with bamboo shoots), *chap chye* (a stew of mixed vegetables) and *otak otak* (a kind of fish pâté wrapped and cooked in banana leaf).

As good as it can be, restaurant Nonya food remains essentially fine domestic cooking translated into commercial cuisine. This explains why

An Innocent Abroad

Consider the case of a certain gawky young Wandervögel who stayed at Raffles in 1911. Though Herman Hesse is now considered the peer of Thomas Mann and Stefan Zweig, and has achieved something of a cult status in the West, he was still unknown outside Germany when he joined the Swiss painter Hans Sturzenegger for a trip out East. On the last leg of their journey they spent ten days in Singapore, where Sturzenegger's brother had a business; and from Hesse's diary, which has only recently been published, we get his views of the place, warts and all:

Wednesday 25 October: Tired arrival. Mail at last. At dusk walked along the magnificent avenue of the esplanade and through High Street, where we visited Chinese, Japanese and Indian shops. I like Singapore better this time, we are staying expensively but well in Raffles Hotel. The food is bad here too. In the shops, treasures of all kinds, a delight for the eyes. I bought toys and photographs. In the evening unpacking and writing, the gigantic hotel is horrible acoustically and echoes like a drum in its vast corridors and staircases.

Thursday 26 October: Sociable lunch. In the evening, trip to the Botanical Garden. Dinner in the hotel, as always with music, the boys are dressed all in white, the supervising waiters all in black. At the next table a jolly drunk amuses us and everybody else, he loses his patent leather shoe and retrieves it with his foot etc. He is an English administrative officer, who has been here for years and sits at his hotel table almost every evening as drunk as this. Trip to the German Teutonia Club, where we joined in an English bowling game until after 11 o'clock, with ten pins and absurdly large and heavy balls, we sweated awfully and became dead tired.

Friday 27 October: Excursion by tram and riksha unending coconut groves with kampongs and European houses, beautiful beach. The Chinese coolies mostly wear blue linen trousers, one leg rolled down, the other rolled up to the knee. Pretty young female Chinese in a riksha. Lunch in the Singapore Club, refined with Hock punch, afterwards buying photographs, all terribly expensive. Rain. In the evening very hot in dinner jacket, because we visited a Chinese acrobatic performance in the Town Hall.

Sunday 29 October: Last night in the large stone paved game hall of our hotel there was roller skating until midnight, of which, however, we saw nothing. . . Afterwards, when we returned at one o'clock, a few tipsy young Englishmen played around in the hall with the brutality of football players, shattering the shop window of the poor postcard dealer to smithereens and shouted, fooled wildly around and fought with each other half the night like pigs. In the morning we went to Johore by train. English Sunday: no music during meals, miserable food.

Tuesday 31 October: Sunny, piercingly hot. Morning stroll through the nearby Chinese quarter, extremely busy but at the same time almost quiet, often reminding me of Italy, but more active and without the childish shouting, with which in Italy every matchstick boy calls out his bagatelle wares. In the evening I wanted to go to the Star Opera with the Sturzenegger brothers, but there was nothing new on, we turned back. . . when Hasenfratz turned up. As it was the last evening with him we took a whisky together and the three of us returned to Chinatown. These night rides or walks in the Chinese streets are always magnificent. The Chinese brothels, that look very pretty, seem to be only for the yellow people. We were only accosted and invited by the Chinese women; for the white people there are brothels in other streets with Japanese females. Incidentally, the majority of the brothels, which run at a high profit, are supposed to be owned by (Portuguese or French) mission fathers. . .

Friday 3 November: In the evening there was Sturzenegger's big reception in the hotel, elegant dinner with about 20 guests, drinking and unrestrained merriment, afterwards three of us roamed around the brothel streets till three o'clock at night, a fight involving a raving Englishman, many Russian whores.

And there we will leave him, a slightly bemused figure frowning through his pince-nez not quite at home in his surroundings, wondering perhaps what the price will be, and whether it might not be best, after all, to go back to his hotel.

From Raffles: The Story of Singapore *by Raymond Flower*

virtually every Nonya restaurant emphasizes the 'home-cooked' flavour of its food. Few dispute the assertion that to taste the best Peranakan food, one must still hold out for an invitation to someone's home.

Hawker Food

While some regard Peranakan food as the closest thing to a national cuisine, it is more true to say that a truly Singaporean cuisine is still in the making. Paradoxically, 'local food' has most definitely arrived. The food once served from a street hawker's cart (usually unlicensed) and often eaten on the run (with a watchful eye out for the arrival of the hawker inspector) is now served in restaurants — in and out of hotels. It is also served nowadays at the ubiquitous food centres that dot the island, but locals still call it 'hawker food'. They are generally one-dish meals, but friends and family may often order a selection and share.

Some dishes to try are *char kway teow* (broad, flat rice noodles fried with shelled cockles, slices of Chinese pork sausage, shrimp and beansprouts in thick soy sauce), *laksa* (coarse rice vermicelli, shrimp, fishcake and occasionally shredded chicken in a chilli-spiced soupy gravy made with coconut-milk), *meesiam* (fine vermicelli with shrimp, chives and slices of hard-boiled egg in a sourish-sweet shrimp-based gravy) and *murtabak* (a south Indian fried bread enclosing minced mutton and onions — like a calzone). Wash it down with soya bean milk, sugar-cane juice, barley water, mixed fruit juice, *bandung* (a rose syrup and milk drink) or *sarabat* (a steaming ginger brew usually served with milk). While one may insist on scouring the island for authentic hawkers' carts — few and far between and probably unlicensed — it is far easier to head for the nearest food centre or a hotel.

Food Centres

Food centres were started to get the hawkers off the streets and into more hygienic surroundings with running water and proper washing facilities. Most were built by the government but have proved so popular that the private sector has followed suit. The hawker centre, as locals call it, is not only a place to have a relatively inexpensive meal but also a place for visitors to absorb the Singaporean way of life, a major part of which is spent eating. Locals like to eat at **Cuppage Centre**, a food centre above what is called a "wet market". The building is connected to Centrepoint shopping centre via a staircase at the rear. The biggest disadvantage is that it is ill-ventilated. Another popular food centre is at **Newton Circus**, which is within walking distance of Orchard Road. Despite being rather touristy (and consequently more pricey than other centres), they remain popular haunts for locals, as the food is still very good. While Rasa Singapura's stalls are busier in the daytime and close fairly early in the evening, Newton is the place to enjoy a late dinner or midnight supper of grilled seafood, barbecued chicken wings or noodles.

Most stall-holders can take orders in English, and where verbal communication breaks down, sign language never fails. At food centres the Chinese stalls and Muslim stalls are generally kept apart. One may sit at any table, but at some places Muslim stall owners may decline to serve you in areas where pork is served. So take care where you sit when ordering Malay food, like *mee rebus* (boiled yellow wheat noodles in thick shrimp gravy), *soto ayam* (spicy chicken soup) and *satay*, or Indian Muslim dishes, like *biryani* (rice pilaf with curried mutton or chicken). If one orders both Muslim and Chinese food, the cutlery and crockery they come with should be used separately. Recently, this problem has been circumvented at some centres by the use of disposable plastic ware. This innovation, detested by some, is apparently gaining acceptance among most patrons.

Food Courts

Disposables were first introduced in what has become known as 'food courts' — the upmarket, air-conditioned version of the food centre. The first and still the most popular is **Picnic Food Court** at Scotts Shopping Centre, in Scotts Road. Probably the most popular counter here is the one that dishes out beef noodles in a thick dark gravy that tastes better than it looks. There is a story behind this concoction. It was cooked up in a local coffee shop, made headlines some years ago when it won its originators the Hawker-of-the-Year Award given by a local newspaper, found itself over-run by a whole new clientèle, changed tack and moved upmarket. It has adapted well to assembly-line cooking and still draws crowds, though some old customers moan that things ain't wot they used to be.

Picnic's counters offer, among other foods, Japanese *tempura* and *sushi*, Chinese vegetarian vermicelli with mock meats, *nasi padang* (Indonesian curries) and Peranakan food, but they also dish out *satay meesiam* and frozen yoghurt. A new generation of fast-foodies, already well trained in self-service by McDonald's, made Picnic a roaring success from the start. Inevitably, it has spawned a new breed of like-minded gentrified hawker-style enterprises, including **Rasa Marina** (Marina Square), **Lucky Plaza** (6th floor) and **Wisma Atria** (basement). What has also happened is that these new places have transformed simple questions—like choosing a place to have lunch—into a mind-boggling exercise.

A National Dish?

The real pioneer in the gentrification of hawker food was the Mandarin Singapore. It all started in the 1970s when this hotel put Hainanese chicken rice on the menu in its 24-hour coffee shop, **Chatterbox**. That inspiration undoubtedly came from a resident genius who reasoned that customers who grew up enjoying hawker food would like it even more in air-conditioned comfort. The hotel's innovation was to serve up the poached chicken deboned in a boat-shaped dish. Soup and savoury chicken-flavoured rice came in separate bowls, and the three condiments — ground chilli, ginger and thick, dark soy — came in individual sauce dishes. The complete meal was presented on a round wooden tray, a formula since aped and adapted by most restaurants. Other local dishes have since found their way into all hotel coffee shop menus, but none appears as popular as chicken rice. Some think it ought to be declared the national dish because it can be enjoyed by all except vegetarians. Muslims prepare it with *halal* chicken, which has been slaughtered according to Islamic dietary law.

Until the Mandarin Singapore transformed chicken rice, the best-known version was almost regarded as the trade-marked property of **Swee Kee**, at 51/53 Middle Road. This rather more downmarket eatery still serves chicken rice at its original premises, which are in an area settled by many Hainanese from south China.

Chinatown, My Chinatown

Though extensive urban renewal has greatly changed the ethnic character of the older parts of Singapore, some of their traditional flavour persists. The riverside area around Ellenborough Market, where the Teochew community dominated the wholesale fish and vegetable trade, still offers some great Teochew food. The wholesale business was generally concluded in the coolest time of day, in the early morning hours. Around sunrise, when most people were starting their day, the traders would have their dinner. Because of this, the stalls at Ellenborough Market see nothing odd in serving up ten full courses at breakfast time. Your meal might include braised goose, crayfish fried with black beans, deep-fried liver rolls called *ngoh hiang* (a kind of pâté wrapped in soy skin), steamed pomfret (pompano), fried crabmeat dumplings and braised belly pork with preserved vegetables.

Ban Seng (79 New Bridge Road) and **Hung Kang** (38 North Canal Road) are some old favourites. More plebeian surroundings with prices to match can be found at **Liang Kee** (Tew Chew Street, 02–406 Block 1) in a high-rise apartment block overlooking the Singapore River. Whichever one chooses, this area is seafood heaven, as the Teochews are extremely fastidious about the freshness of the catch.

Some of the best-known Cantonese restaurants of old still survive at the southern end of Chinatown. This is an area as well known for its food as for its ladies of the night. **Majestic Restaurant** (31–37 Bukit Pasoh Road) and **Spring Court** (291–A New Bridge Road) are two of the old-style restaurants here.

A determined attack by Hong Kong-style nouvelle Chinoise cuisine has been spearheaded by new chic restaurants outside Chinatown. A never-fail favourite is the **Garden Seafood Restaurant** (Goodwood Park Hotel, Scotts Road), where the dim sum (or *dian xin*, as it is rendered in Mandarin) is consistently good. At last tasting, the best of the new wave also included **Tsui Hang Village** (Hotel Asia, Scotts Road), **Fook Yuen Seafood Restaurant** (South Bridge Centre, South Bridge Road, and Paragon, Orchard Road) and **Tung Lok Shark's Fin Restaurant** (Liang Court, River Valley Road).

Hokkiens are the country's largest Chinese dialect group, but their hearty, stick-to-the-ribs, southern Chinese food has tended to be overshadowed by Cantonese, Sichuan (Szechuan), Beijing and even Teochew cuisine. Much of Singapore's Chinese hawker food, though, has Hokkien roots. *Popiah* (soft-skinned spring rolls), *oh chien* (oyster omelette), *hae mee* (yellow wheat noodles with shrimp and slices of boiled pork in a rich shrimp stock) and fried Hokkien *mee* (yellow wheat noodles stir-fried with seafood and pork) are some favourite dishes. Restaurants to try are **Beng Thin Hoon Kee** (05–02 OCBC Centre, 65 Chulia Street), **Teck Lim Restaurant** (01–169 Blk 91 Zion Road) and **Beng Hiang Restaurant** (20 Murray Street), all on the fringes of Chinatown.

In or out of Chinatown, Singapore is definitely the place to sample the spicy cuisine of Sichuan: the **Cherry Garden** (Oriental Singapore, Marina Square), **Golden Phoenix** (Hotel Equatorial, 429 Bukit Timah Road) and **Min Jiang Sichuan Restaurant** (Goodwood Park Hotel, Scotts Road) are recommended, as are **Moi Kong Restaurant** (22 Murray Street) for Hakka food (chicken in rice wine, Hakka *yong tow foo*) and **Lee Do Restaurant** (Kempas Road Block 11, 01–79) for Hokchiu specialities like chicken in red wine mash. The latter two are hearty rather than elegant.

Be warned though that in many Chinese restaurants, the departure of a chef can mean the difference between a divine meal and disaster.

A Passage to India

One cannot get more ethnic than in Serangoon Road, the heart of an area known as Little India. The reason for the name is clear even before one crosses an invisible boundary at the crossroads. Women in sarees, men in dhotis, and the covered sidewalks — or five-foot ways as they are called here — are redolent of tumeric and chilli. Breakfast at a coffee shop here is not to be missed. *Roti prata*, not unlike a pizza in preparation, is performance art you can eat. Starting with a ball of dough well greased with *ghee* (clarified butter), the *prata* man flattens and spreads it on a counter-top, then with fingertip control, whizzes it around in the air until it is tissue-thin and translucent. He folds it back on itself on a wide cast-iron griddle to make a many-layered savoury pancake. You eat it with a generous sprinkle of sugar or with a thick lentil curry. *Thosai* (pronounced *toe-say*) is an enormous, crisp pancake served rolled up with coconut and chilli relish on the side.

Banana leaf curry is another southern-Indian delight not to be missed. This is not, as one might think, a curry made from banana leaves, but an assortment of south Indian curries served on a banana leaf. Some restaurants, like **Komala Vilas** (76/78 Serangoon Road) and **Madras New Woodlands** (14 Upper Dickson Road, just off Serangoon Road) serve only vegetarian curries with rice or a choice of breads. A good, filling meal can cost less than $3 each. Others, like **Banana Leaf Apolo** (56 Race Course Road, parallel to Serangoon Road) and **Muthu's Curry Restaurant** (76/78 Race Course Road) serve meat, seafood and vegetable curries. The restaurants will supply forks and spoons, but the proper way to eat is with your finger, and purists swear it tastes better this way. A unique local variant here that one will not find in India is fish-head curry, featuring a large meaty fish head (eyes intact) in spicy-hot, tamarind-soured gravy. It tastes far better than it sounds.

Northern Indian cuisine tends to be more up market than its southern cousin and has acquired more fans in recent years. Tandoori chicken and prawns (marinated in spices then roasted in a clay oven), lamb in spinach sauce, and virtually any vegetable dish are easy fail-safe choices for first-timers. Be sure to order *naan*, a flat bread that comes plain, with garlic, mutton or even raisins. Rice-lovers should also experiment with the different *pilaus*. If one is prepared to queue, the food at **Naan n' Curry** (Funan Centre 07–31), is inexpensive and well worth the wait. Good food matched by moderate (not really cheap) prices can be found at **Moti Mahal** (18 Murray Street). The **Tandoor** (Holiday Inn Parkview) and **Omar Khayyam** (55 Hill Street) serve some of the best Indian food, but prices are steep.

A felicitous blend of north and south is found in the classy Indian vegetarian restaurant **Annalakshmi** (Excelsior Hotel and Shopping Centre, 5 Coleman Street, 02–10) where the food — prepared and served by volunteers —and the atmosphere are worth four stars. It used to be the best value-for-money vegetarian restaurant but has since gone dramatically upmarket with prices to match. But the lunch buffet is still worth the experience. You'll never see the same spread twice and everything tastes divine.

Malay and Indonesian Food

Much of the tastiest Malay food is served in food centres or along the east coast of the island in coffee shop-style restaurants. A local innovation not unlike a submarine sandwich, *roti john,* is a popular breakfast or lunch item at **Taman Serasi Food Centre** (Shukor Stall number 9) near the Botanic Gardens. It is essentially a French loaf dipped into a minced mutton, onion and egg mixture and fried till crisp, then eaten with cucumber slices and chilli sauce.

If you are more adventurous, and especially if you have a sweet tooth and hollow legs, try snacking your way through the market at Geylang Serai, which carries many food items, especially certain edible seeds, fruits, vegetables and convenience foods not found in other markets.

Singapore's cosmopolitan outlook is so pronounced that one should not be surprised to find one of its most popular Indonesian restaurants owned and mostly staffed by Chinese but bearing a name with a French flavour. **Rendezvous Nasi-Padang** (02–19 Raffles City Shopping Centre, North Bridge Road, and lunch only at 4/5 Bras Basah Road) is arguably the best known establishment for *nasi Padang*, curries that originated in Padang, a town in West Sumatra. One of Rendezvous' hallmark dishes is *beef rendang*, a dry curried beef that loyal offshore customers sometimes have flown out to them. Try the chicken curry, *egg sambal* (hard-boiled, then deep-fried and doused with chilli-hot sauce) and *sayor lodeh* (a mild, soupy vegetable curry). For many older Chinese Singaporeans, a meal at Rendezvous was their first experience of a cuisine other than their own.

Since then, many other Indonesian restaurants have come along serving food from other regions of Indonesia, like *opor ayam* (a relatively mild chicken curry), *tauhu telor* (beancurd omelette), *kicap tauhu* (deep-fried triangles of bean curd in sweet sauce) and *ayam panggang* (roast chicken). **Tambuah Mas Cafe Restaurant** (Level 4, Tanglin Shopping Centre, Tanglin Road) and **Sanur Indonesian Restaurant** (04–17/18 Centrepoint, Orchard Road) are consistently good and service is prompt. For Malay food, try the **Bintang Timur Restaurant** (02–08/13 Far East Plaza, Scotts Road).

The Rest of the World

One still hears the occasional Western chef complaining about how parochial Singaporeans are when it comes to food. One innovative young French chef left in disgust some years ago because beef steak seemed to define the outer limits of his clientèle's culinary desires. That may still be true in some cases, but there are enough adventurous souls to support several fine Italian restaurants (apart from the standard batch of pizza parlours), a few good

French restaurants and even a couple of establishments serving Mexican food (**El Felipe's Cantina** at Lorong Mambong, Holland Village, and **Chico's n' Charlie's** at Liat Towers, Orchard Road), complete with margueritas.

The **Brasserie** (Marco Polo Hotel, Tanglin Road) maintains a tradition of good food, but if you want to pull out all the stops, try **Le Restaurant de France** (Hotel Meridien, Orchard Road) or the **Harbour Grill** (Hilton Hotel, Orchard Road). **Restaurant Latour** (Shangri-La Hotel, Orange Grove Road), recently named Restaurant of the Year, is always booked out for its excellent lunch (starters and desserts come buffet-style, and you order your main course from a pretty wide selection). There is also **Maxim's**, a clone of the Parisian original, at the Regent Hotel (1 Cuscaden Road).

A restaurant called Gino's, now long gone, established a beachhead for Italian food in the 1960s, but it has taken these many years for high-quality Italian restaurants to become a viable proposition here. Great pasta, freshly made on the premises, distinguishes **Prego** (Westin Hotel, Raffles City) from the rest. Stalking **Pizza Hut** is a homegrown pizza chain called Milano Pizza, which had more than half a dozen branches. A relative newcomer, **Rocky's**, is making inroads into the market, not least because it delivers anywhere in Singapore. The clue is to order well in advance and have something to munch on in the meantime. Rocky's, especially its white pizza (three cheeses, no tomato sauce), is well worth the wait.

Asian cuisines including Indonesian, Korean, Thai and Vietnamese food are so well established with locals that they hardly count as imports. Thai food has really taken off in Singapore. In the Orchard Road area, **Parkway Thai Restaurant** (Parkway Parade, 80 Marine Parade Road) has a busy branch at Centrepoint (no reservations), plus another establishment at Cairnhill Place (Bideford Road just off Orchard Road), while up the road there is **Bangkok Garden,** across the road from the terribly popular **Her Sea Palace** (Forum Galleria, Orchard Road).

Japanese restaurants are so numerous that they are almost part of the furniture. One directory lists nearly 50, a good number of which are located in the Hotel New Otani/Liang Court complex. It is not only the food that is imported. **Sushi Kaiseki Nogawa** (Crown Prince Hotel) and Keyaki (Pan Pacific Hotel, Marina Square), with its beautifully landscaped surroundings. **Nanbantei Restaurant** (05-132 Far East Plaza), a branch of Yakitori Nanbantei in Tokyo's Roppongi district is where you eat everything in dainty morsels off skewers. **Nadaman** (Shangri-La Hotel) is also a branch of a Tokyo establishment of the same name.

The Swiss, English, Scottish, Polynesians and Scandinavians, among others, are also represented in food circles here, as are fast-food chains guaranteed to bring cheer to any homesick American — McDonald's, Burger King, Kentucky Fried Chicken, Church's Texas Fried Chicken, Denny's, Ponderosa—and sweet conclusions like Dunkin' Donuts, Famous Amos and Häagen-Dazs. Sadly, Wendy's closed shop, as did Mrs. Field's, who took her famous chocolate chip cookies home.

Americans — homesick or otherwise — are also to be found at **Steeple's Deli** (Level 2, Tanglin Shopping Centre), which has a growing yuppie and puppie (pubescent urban professional) following. Whether your hankering is for a tuna fish sandwich or hot corned beef on rye, you can satisfy the craving here and banish the blues with a fudge brownie or two.

Cultural Caveat

A word of warning is not amiss at this point. People here take their food seriously. They are quite capable of discussing food before, after and during meals. They are also apt, while devouring or digesting the meal at hand, to debate where the next one ought to be and to discuss the merits and demerits of the last. The discussion can easily be as spicy as the food, as dedicated foodies can be extremely vociferous when they disagree on matters of such importance. Interest in good food goes back at least a hundred years in Singapore, going by the experience of a visiting Chinese official in 1887 who wrote, 'Restaurants are not abundant in Singapore. There are only one or two Cantonese restaurants and European restaurants respectively. Most of the feasts are held in the gardens of private homes with both Chinese food and European food served.'

As Singapore's first recorded food critic, he probably had good reason for giving a review that, even a century later, sounds somewhat dyspeptic and far from generous. Undoubtedly, he would be amazed now if he were to return for seconds.

Festival City

Religion governs many of Singapore's traditional festivals, which are as varied as the multi-cultural origins of its people. Most festivals celebrated here also survive in the Asian countries where they originated, though not always in the same fashion. Thaipusam in Singapore and Malaysia is quite different from Thaipusam as celebrated in south India, to pick one example. Some festivals are unique to Singapore and Malaysia. Other celebrations have changed beyond recognition. Chingay, for instance, has shed its religious and Chinese clothes to become a thoroughly secular carnival-like parade involving other communities. One hardly thinks of religion when watching this annual parade down Orchard Road. Though it is unabashedly promoted as a tourist event, it is watched and enjoyed by thousands of native Singaporeans. Some festivals are imported, notably the Thai water festival called Songkran, and Christmas, which is celebrated here with gusto by Christians and non-Christians alike.

The disparate ways in which different communities in Singapore and Malaysia celebrate similar festivals makes for rich variety and uniqueness but can often be confusing. *The Illustrated Cycle of Chinese Festivals*, by C S Wong and Ronnie Pinsler, and *Chinese Temples and Deities*, by Evelyn Lip, contribute to untangling the complex relationships of Chinese festivals, while articles from the bilingual pages of the national daily, *The Straits Times*, help to explain the different facets of festivals celebrated by Indian Singaporeans. There are parallels between Indian and Chinese festivals, notably in the ninth lunar month of their respective calendars, which are very significant to both Hindus and Taoists/Buddhists. Both, for example, celebrate the first nine nights of the ninth moon.

Many festivals of Asian origin are based on lunar calendars, which vary significantly from the Western calendar and from each other. The Chinese, for example, follow a lunar calendar with a year regularly short of the 365-day solar year by seven or eight days. (They add an extra month to the lunar year every three years to keep in step.) Dates given here for such festivals are at best approximate. When in Singapore, pick up the Singapore Tourist Promotion Board's festival calendar from its Tourist Information Centre at Raffles City. This fold-out brochure gives the dates by the current calendar year and explanatory notes on each festival. Separate brochures on current major festivals are available at the centre. You can also check with any of the board's overseas offices, which are located in New York, Los Angeles, Auckland, Perth, Sydney, Tokyo, Hong Kong, Taipei, Frankfurt, Zurich, Paris and London. The festivals are listed here more or less in the order in which they come, depending on the year.

New Year's Day

The first of January is a public holiday in Singapore and a good time to sleep off the festivities of the night before. Most hotels and the larger restaurants (though usually not Chinese restaurants) hold dressy New Year's Eve dinners with live entertainment, champagne — the works. These, naturally, tend to be expensive. Nightclubs also get into the New Year's act, but an alternative that is lots of fun is the New Year's show produced by the local television station. Traditionally the show is on location, and this is a good, noisy place to be at midnight. Another prime spot to spend the dying moments of the old year is Mt Faber, where the harbour can be heard coming to life with a blast on the stroke of midnight, as ships blow their horns to welcome the new year.

Ponggal

There is no grain harvest in Singapore, but this has never stopped Tamils here from enjoying the winter harvest festival, which is celebrated as Ponggal in Tamil Nadu, the first day of the month of *Thai*. This festival, which usually falls in mid-January, marks the end of the rainy season and the onset of spring. Tradition requires that people get rid of their old clay cooking pots and old clothes by destroying them in a bonfire on Boghi, the day before Ponggal. The family must rise before dawn, bathe and put on new clothes, string up fresh mango leaves over the front door and draw decorative patterns, or *kolam*, on the floor and doorstep.

The festive dish, also called ponggal, of newly gathered rice cooked with cashew nuts, *ghee* (clarified butter), green peas, milk and raisins is cooked on a stove built over a kolam with a sun sign in the centre. The ponggal may also be cooked at the temple, although this festival is more a cultural than a religious event. The new pot has to have tumeric and ginger shoots tied around its neck before it is put on the fire. When it boils over, signifying plenty, the women and children shout, 'Ponggalo ponggal!' After the food is offered to the sun god, it is eaten by the family. The blessing of the food can usually be seen at the Perumal Temple in Serangoon Road. In Singapore there are also Ponggal soccer tournaments and variety and cultural shows, but these are not part of the traditional festivities.

Singapore Kite Festival

Local kite-fanciers use this opportunity to show off their creativity. It is organized by the Singapore Kite Association and has been held annually since 1982. There is no fixed location. The festival has been held in different years at East Coast Park, West Coast Park and Marina South — usually in January, which means a rain-out is not impossible.

Thaipusam

Chiefly celebrated by the Tamils from south India, who make up the largest group of Indians in Singapore, this Hindu feast honours Lord Subramanya. He is also known to the Tamils as Lord Murugan and by a host of other names, including Kumaran, Karthikeya and Shanmuga. Thaipusam as celebrated in Singapore appears to have been influenced by the Chinese, whose temple mediums go into trances and give flamboyant displays while in this state. The men who take part in the Thaipusam procession generally wear huge steel arches, or *kavadi*, adorned with peacock feathers and flowers and have their bodies pierced with spikes or hooks. Most are Indians, but it is not unusual to find Chinese men taking part in the procession. All have sworn a solemn vow to carry kavadi as part of a request made to the deities.

Devotees generally walk barefoot, but some wear spiked sandals. Spikes represent the *vel*, or javelin, which symbolizes the triumph of good over evil. The deity Murugan, who is associated with the vel, slew an evil chieftain named Taraka who could not be defeated by other gods. The big procession is in the daytime from the Sri Srinivasa Perumal Temple in Serangoon Road to the Sri Thandayuthapani Temple in Tank Road.

The morning before Thaipusam, there is another procession in which the Silver Chariot is taken from the Tank Road temple to Chinatown, specifically to the Vinayagar temple dedicated to Ganesa, the Elephant God. Ganesa is Murugan's elder brother and a popular deity. He is known and loved as the god who removes obstacles. You are quite free to take photographs inside or outside the temples — some of the penitents carrying kavadi will even pose for you — but remember to take off your shoes before going into a temple. Because of the huge crowds (and consequently the enormous number of shoes) you may be better off carrying your shoes with you.

Chinese New Year

The Lunar New Year is the most important time in the entire Chinese calendar and the only two-day public holiday. There is not a lot of street activity during these two days, as the new year is mainly a family occasion and a time to visit relatives and close friends. It is the custom for married people to give money to the unmarried in *hong bao* (red packets). The celebrations actually stretch over 15 days, though it is usual to do most of one's visiting in the first two days. Be warned that it is almost impossible to get a taxi when you want it at this time, as many Chinese taxi drivers are busy ferrying their own families around. The third day is a regular working one and it is customary not to go visiting on this day because it is believed that one will fall out with those who are visited. If you are invited to a Chinese home for the New Year, take two mandarin oranges (or any even number) and present them to your host. The reunion dinner on the eve of the

New Year is almost more important than the first day, for this is the one time that the extended family (all unmarried children, married sons and their wives and children) are expected to sit down to a meal together. It is the only holiday all year for some shops and, apart from Boxing Day (the first weekday after Christmas), the only time that the local newspapers do not go to press.

For about a month before the day itself, Chinatown is the focus of an extended orgy of shopping and eating. Waxed duck (ducklings preserved in oil), sausages and other seasonal delicacies from China, mandarin oranges, potted chrysanthemums and kumquats, melon seeds and sweets are some of the traditional purchases. For the last few years Chinatown's streets have been lit up at night and carnival stalls set up on vacant lots. Cultural performances including lion and dragon dances, acrobatic displays, and Chinese opera or *wayang* are also held at this time. There are also shows, pop and trad, at and on the Singapore River. This is also the time to settle debts and do spring cleaning. Many people have their homes renovated or redecorated in time for the new year, and the months before new year will see a large amount of old furniture and furnishings being abandoned on the rubbish heap.

Chingay

This parade, now an annual event on Orchard Road, has outgrown its religious origins. Though still basically Chinese in flavour, it has included a vintage car procession, Malay and Indian dances, nursery rhyme and cartoon characters in choreographed movements, Filipino dances, Morris dances and even demonstrations by German shepherd dogs. Stilt walkers, lion and dragon dancers, flag dancers, acrobats and a flotilla of decorated floats that change each year are among the staples of Chingay. In 1988, parade organizers initiated 'warm-up' acts along the parade route to keep the crowds entertained from about an hour before the start of the actual procession.

The parade begins at the junction of Orchard and Scotts roads and moves down Orchard to the junction just in front of the Istana, the official residence of the president of Singapore. It then turns off to the right to disperse on Clemenceau Avenue. The parade is held on the first Sunday after Chinese New Year's Day, though the date may change if the first Sunday is the second or third day of the year. The parade starts at 9 am and takes about an hour. Shutter-bugs will probably get the best photographs starting from about 7.30 am on Orchard Boulevard (parallel to Orchard Road) where the parade assembles. One of the best spots from which to watch the show is the second-floor balcony of the Lucky Plaza shopping centre.

Monkey God's Feast

Once upon a time, there was a huge rock atop a mountain called Hua Guo Shan. The rock gave birth to a stone and the wind fertilized the stone and transformed it into a stone monkey, which eventually came to life and became the King of the Monkeys. Popular in China, Singapore and Malaysia, the Monkey God is believed to be able to assume 72 different forms and to cure the sick and remove sins. No wonder his feast day is celebrated twice a year (spring and autumn) in Chinese temples. During the celebrations, the Monkey God's spirit enters into mediums, who skewer their cheeks and tongues with spikes and write charms in their own blood. This business is not for the squeamish, but all can enjoy the street opera and puppet theatre staged for the occasion.

Qing Ming

The Chinese equivalent of All Souls' Day is an annual occasion when the filial honour their ancestors. While it is not a mournful occasion, it is a serious family event, and some Chinese celebrants may dislike being photographed, though they would not object to strangers watching as they perform the rituals. The whole family visits the cemetery, cleans the ancestral graves, trims the grass around them and offers food and joss sticks at the graveside. The cemeteries along Kheam Hock and Lornie roads, Upper Thomson Road and Choa Chu Kang are some of the places where you can see Qing Ming observed. Since many people are cremated rather than buried and their funeral urns kept at temples, Qing Ming is also a big occasion at the columbaria (urn vaults) at the Mount Vernon Crematorium and the Buddhist temple complex, Kong Meng San Phor Kark See, which is on Bright Hill Drive.

Songkran

Thais living in Singapore have always celebrated Songkran within their community and had a good time throwing water over each other. Ritual bathing of religious icons is part of the festival. Lately, this Thai new year festival has been adopted by the appropriately named Big Splash aquatic sports complex at East Coast Park. In Thailand, Songkran is celebrated 13–15 April, but the highly commercial 'big splash' at the Big Splash is held for more than a week!

Birthday of the Third Prince, Ne Zha

Ne Zha's birthday is celebrated on the eighth and ninth days of the fourth moon. This child deity, depicted bearing a magic bracelet and sword with the wind and fire wheels at his feet, has a temple dedicated to him near the junction of Clarke Street and North Boat Quay. Here, temple mediums go into a trance and slash themselves with spears and swords, writing charms on yellow paper with their blood.

Legend says that, before he was born, Ne Zha's mother dreamed that a priest told her she would bear the son of a unicorn. When the child was seven years old he was already two metres (six feet) tall. The Third Prince accidentally killed a son of the Dragon King of the Eastern Seas, and to protect his parents from the king's anger, he gave himself up to him. In self-punishment he stripped his flesh to the bone. Ne Zha's master recreated him from the leaves of the lotus and the stalks of the waterlily, then taught him martial arts and equipped him with the wind and fire wheels so that he could travel at great speed.

Ramadan

The fasting month of Ramadan is also the feasting month. Muslims abstain from food and drink (and sex and cigarettes, too) between dawn and dusk throughout this holy month. Possibly at no other period on the Muslim calendar, however, is there so much good food available for the breaking of the fast.

Stalls are set up near mosques, most notably at Bussorah Street near the Sultan Mosque, which is regarded as the national mosque in Singapore, to sell cooked food for the breaking of the fast. These stalls provide non-Muslims with an excellent opportunity to try Malay delicacies. You might find *ayam percik lemper* (fingers of glutinous rice stuffed with shredded chicken — with dried prawns is another option), all manner of cakes and some non-traditional foods like doughnuts. Sweet dates from the Middle East are popular. Communal meals are not uncommon, and mosques provide free rice porridge known as *bubur lambuk* and other foods for ending the fast. At least one hotel, the Royal Holiday Inn, has initiated weekend 'breaking of fast' evening meals cooked by Muslim chefs and provides rooms for ablutions and prayers. At some workplaces with many Muslim employees, it is becoming customary to break the fast with colleagues.

Ramadan is also the time for Muslims to pay the *zakat* (religious tithe) to the *amil*, or tithe collectors, who are stationed at mosques. The money is intended for the welfare of the needy, and payment is compulsory for those who have the means. The Muslim Religious Council (MUIS) sets the rate of payment each year (the equivalent of 2.3 kilograms, or five pounds, of average-quality rice) and takes care of its collection and distribution. All Muslims who have reached puberty are bound to fast and to tithe. They are also encouraged to give alms to the poor during Ramadan. Paupers and destitutes are not the only ones who can benefit from this special fund. Those who are in debt for a good cause, people fighting for a religious cause, poor converts and travellers on long journeys are among those classified as 'needy'.

Hari Raya Puasa

The end of the month of fasting, Hari Raya Puasa, is a national public holiday. This is the community's biggest festival and an occasion for Muslim families dressed in new finery to offer prayers at mosques and to visit friends and relatives. For a few weeks before the big day and for several days after, Geylang Serai, the area most closely associated with the Malay community, is ablaze with fairy lights around its perimeter, another of the festive light-up programmes sponsored by the Singapore Tourist Promotion Board. Carnival stalls draw crowds from other parts of Singapore, and Malaysian tourists descend on Geylang Serai by the busload.

Community organizations keep up the celebrations for at least a fortnight with beauty contests, variety shows and *dondang sayang* evenings, which feature rhyming musical repartee.

Vesak Day

The most important date in the Buddhist calendar is Vesak Day, which marks the birth, enlightenment and death of Buddha. The celebrations begin the night before with candlelight processions in temple courtyards. There may also be processions on the night of Vesak itself. On Vesak Day, worshippers arrive at the temple before dawn to offer prayers and then to share a vegetarian meal at the temple. Anyone is welcome to eat. The food is usually donated by worshippers and cooked by volunteers.

On Vesak Day some temples hold special talks and exhibitions on Buddhist teachings. They may also conduct initiation and shaving ceremonies. One of the best places to see the Vesak celebrations is the Temple of a Thousand Lights in Race Course Road, where there is a 15-metre (50-foot) tall statue of Buddha. At Kong Meng San Phor Kark See, a temple complex in Bright Hill Drive, devotees circle the temple, prostrating themselves on the ground at every few steps. Though most Buddhist temples cater to the Chinese, there is a Thai Buddhist Temple at 50–B Jalan Bukit Merah and a Burmese temple at 17 Kinta Road. The Sri Lankaramaya Buddhist Temple, at 30–C St Michael's Road, and Mangala Vihara, a Buddhist temple at 30 Jalan Eunos, are visited by Sri Lankan and Indian Buddhists.

Singapore International Film Festival

A two-week bonanza of international films every April draws enthusiastic crowds and elicits visits from well-known actors and actresses. Festival organizers aim to programme a varied mix of social commentary, drama and comedy.

Dragon Boat Festival

Sport has superseded tradition in the Dragon Boat Races. A sizeable
international circuit has now been built up in Hong Kong and Australia,
Europe and the West Coast of the United States, so races cannot be held at
the same time in all countries. The old wooden boats have been replaced by
sleek fibreglass, but each boat still bears a dragons' head and tail, and
'dragon scales' along its length of nearly 12 metres (40 feet), and the guest of
honour at the races always dots the dragon's eyes (so they can see where they
they going) before the start of the races.

One wonders how many people remember the man whose death was the
original reason for the races. It all began with the ancient Chinese scholar and
poet Qu Yuan. Qu, a loyal state minister, was banished through court
intrigue. On the fifth day of the fifth moon, he drowned himself in protest
against the corruption of the state. To keep the fish from eating his body, the
people raced out to sea beating drums and thrashing the water. They also
threw rice into the water. Some say this was done to appease Qu Yuan's
spirit; others say it was done so the fish might eat the rice and leave his
corpse alone. Either way, this is why rice dumplings known as *bak chang* (or
zong zi in Mandarin) were traditionally eaten at this time. Now they are eaten
year round.

Hari Raya Haji

Also known as Hari Raya Korban (*korban* meaning 'sacrifice' in Malay), this
holiday is of special significance to Muslims who have completed the *haj*, or
pilgrimage, to Mecca. It falls on the tenth day of the month of *Zulhijah*, the
12th month, that of the haj. Unlike Hari Raya Puasa, the date of which is
determined in most Muslim countries by the actual sighting of the new moon,
Hari Raya Haji is the day following *wukuf*, or the day pilgrims stop at Mt
Arafat in the Holy Land.

Sacrifice is at the heart of this festival. Prayers are said and goats and
sheep sacrificed in remembrance of the willingness of the Prophet Ibrahim
(Abraham of the Old Testament) to sacrifice his son in obedience to Allah's
will. Because Ibrahim believed and trusted in him, Allah spared his son and
found a sacrificial animal, a sheep, to replace him. Muslims in Singapore
sacrifice some 3,000 lambs and a couple of hundred cattle.

Festival of the Hungry Ghosts

Small piles of burning paper, red candles, joss sticks and occasionally food
are placed by the Chinese in front of their homes to appease the spirits of the
dead. The offerings are made at the start of the seventh lunar month, when
the hungry ghosts are released from Purgatory, and at the end of the month.

In between, the spirits are at liberty to roam. In mid-month, on the 15th day of the seventh moon, paper clothes and 'Hell Bank Notes', or devils' money, are burnt.

Chinese opera or *wayang* troupes go on the road, and temporary stages are set up in open spaces and on city streets for performances. This is the best time to watch the *wayang*, and it is all free. Market stallholders, hotel employees and factory workers club together for elaborate celebrations at this time. These include the seventh-month auctions in which anything, from 'black gold' (dressed-up charcoal) and figurines of deities to bottles of cooking oil and sponge cakes, goes under the hammer. The sums they fetch bear absolutely no relation to their intrinsic worth — it is all in the value added. Sponge cake, or *huat kuay* in the Hokkien dialect, sounds like 'prosperity cake', and bids for a simple sponge can be in the hundreds of dollars. Most prized is the charcoal, for which bids have run as high as $20,000. Anything goes, it seems, to ensure a prosperous year ahead.

National Day

Singapore became an independent republic on 9 August 1965, and the anniversary is celebrated each year with an increasingly elaborate and sophisticated show, some years at the National Stadium and others on the Padang. In recent years, the show has commenced just before dark with a fly-past by the air force and ended with a laser light display and fireworks.

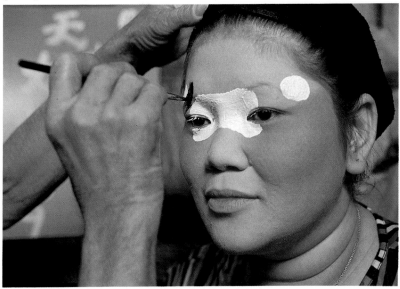

In the early days, the National Day Parade was more of a marchpast of military hardware. These days acrobatic riders from the police strut their stuff on motorbikes, the army's provost unit does a splendid precision drill, and brass bands galore march their music through the country's most important parade. You may also see a string of illuminated floats, generally unabashedly propagandistic, which are sponsored by large public and private organizations. Admission is free but by ticket only, most of which are distributed to civic groups, but there is sometimes a limited number of seats available for visitors. Ask at the Tourist Information Centre on the ground floor of Raffles City. The event is televised 'live' and, in recent years, shown on large TV screens in public areas.

Apart from the parade, there are other flag-waving events in celebration of 9 August. For some years there has been a National Day carnival with pop and cultural shows, food stalls and other entertainment, but there is no fixed location for this. A local hotel has launched a red-and-white soft-drink-and-disco night for young people, who have to come dressed in red and white, the national colours. One of the biggest non-parade events in 1987 was the Great Book. Thousands of Singaporeans congregated on Orchard Road to sign the huge sheets of paper as a kind of mass pledge of loyalty. The sheets were later bound into a book.

Mid-Autumn Festival

Westerners have their Man in the Moon, but the Chinese have a Lady in the Moon. A popular version of the legend tells us that Chang I was the wife of the archer Hou Yi, who shot down nine suns in the sky and so saved the earth from drought. Made ruler of the people he had saved, he became a tyrant and demanded the elixir of immortality. To save the people from his tyranny, Chang I swallowed the elixir herself and fled to the moon where she remains. Moon-viewing parties are quite the thing to hold at this time of year, when the moon is at its brightest.

Legend says the festival and the mooncakes figured in the strategy devised by the Chinese to overthrow the Mongols in the 14th century. The celebrations gave the people the perfect excuse to gather, while the necessity of cutting the mooncakes meant the people would be armed with knives. The call to rise against the Mongols was circulated in notes secreted in the mooncakes, and the resulting revolution gave birth to the Ming Dynasty. The 15th day of the eighth moon is the traditional day for a mooncake feast and for children to carry ornamental paper lanterns.

Mooncakes can be bought virtually anywhere in Singapore, but go to Chinatown for mooncakes with atmosphere. Good places are Tai Tong Hoi Kee, a teahouse in Chinatown's Mosque Street, and the New Nam Thong Teahouse in Smith Street. The Chinese Garden in Jurong holds a lantern festival every year at this time with cultural shows, lion and dragon dances, calligraphy demonstrations and lantern processions for the children every evening. Special bus services are usually put on for this festival. Wear comfortable shoes and light clothing and be prepared for the crowds.

Navarathri

Navarathri, literally 'nine nights', honours the supreme goddess Devi in her three incarnations: Durga, Lakshmi and Saraswathi. The first three nights belong to Durga, who ranks among Hinduism's most powerful deities. She is the mother of all and represents, among other things, the triumph of good over evil. For the next three nights, devotees pray to Lakshmi, goddess of grace and wealth. They keep the last three nights for Saraswathi, who is revered as the goddess of learning and is thus popular with students. Those studying music, or any of the other fine arts, offer special prayers to her. It is customary to lay the tools of learning, including musical instruments, books and implements, in front of Saraswathi's picture. They remain untouched during her three days but on the next day are all taken up and made use of briefly because this day, the tenth, is believed to be especially good for new ventures.

In Singapore, Navarathri is also a chance to listen to the classical music of south India and to watch its classical dance. Many temples hold festivities, but the most elaborate are at the Sri Mariamman Temple in South Bridge Road. Musicians and dancers perform in the courtyard each night, usually between 7 and 10 pm. There are also performances at the Tank Road temple of Sri Thandayupathani and the Veeramakaliamman Temple in Serangoon Road. On the tenth day, a silver horse is carried through the streets from the Tank Road temple.

Thimithi

Devout Hindus walk across pits of glowing embers to honour the goddess Draupathi. Large crowds pack the Sri Mariamman Temple in South Bridge Road each year to see the fire-walking and to urge devotees on over the fiery four-metre (yard) stretch in the courtyard. As a prelude to the fire-walking, priests and devotees lead a chariot bearing the image of Sri Mariamman to other Hindu temples.

Onam

Like Ponggal (see page 185), Onam is a harvest festival, but it comes from Kerala on India's southwest coast. The festival falls between August and September and is celebrated by the Malayalees (from Kerala) over a period of 25 days. A bath and prayers are part of the morning ritual of Onam. Women

and children gather blossoms to decorate a pattern drawn on the ground in front of the home. Everyone practises vegetarianism on this day, and a vegetarian feast is offered first to a statue of Mahabali before the family sits down to lunch. Mahabali, a virtuous king of Kerala, returns at Onam to be with his people on a day of great singing, feasting and dancing. There are usually cultural activities, and in 1987 the Singapore Kerala Association set up Onam Village, had someone dress up as Mahabali and prepared a feast for the 'king' and his subjects. Contact the association at 44 Race Course Road or telephone 293-9195.

Festival of the Nine Emperor Gods

To the Hokkiens, the largest Chinese community in Singapore, the deities are venerated as *Kiu Ong Yah*, or Nine Emperor Gods, but apparently only in Singapore and Malaysia. Chinese street operas are held in their honour. There is an interesting parallel between this and the Hindu festival of Navarathri, which is also celebrated over the first nine nights of the ninth lunar month. Some years the dates of the two festivals coincide. *Kiu Ong Yah* are popular deities because people believe they can cure illness and confer wealth, luck and long life on those they favour. These potent deities are the sons of the Queen of Heaven, *Tien Hau*, who is also known as the Goddess of the North Star, *Tou Mu*. Just to complicate matters, this lady is also the Taoist Goddess of Mercy, or Kwan Yin. (By the way, she is from India.)

On the first nine days of the ninth lunar month, the nine are honoured in many Chinese temples, but you may need a strong stomach to watch some of the proceedings. At some temples, a medium may go into a trance, slash his tongue and smear his blood on to papers which devotees take away as amulets. Then there is the fire-walking. Only the devout who have abstained from meat and sex for a certain period can walk on the glowing coals unscathed. One of the best places in Singapore to see the celebrations is at the Kiu Ong Yah Temple on Upper Serangoon Road, at the eight-kilometre (five-mile) mark. You can also see the festival at the Leong Nam Buddhist Temple in Geylang Serai, at 19–E Jalan Pasar Baru.

Kusu Pilgrimage

For just one month of the year, Kusu Island is in the limelight. The ninth lunar month brings hordes of devotees to visit Kusu's Muslim shrine and Chinese temple and burnish the legend which tells of how a Malay and a Chinese were saved from drowning by a giant turtle that turned itself into Kusu Island. At the first stop, the Chinese temple near the jetty, pilgrims present offerings ranging from chicken curry to chrysanthemums and take away with them yellow ribbons and small bags of rice as 'insurance' for domestic peace and prosperity in the year ahead.

Then it is time to climb the 130 or so concrete steps to the *kramat*, or Malay hermit's shrine, at the top of the island's only hillock. The route is lined with wishing trees. Every branch bears at least one or two pink or yellow plastic bags, each containing a stone, which might stand for a hoped-for spouse or a wished-for son or daughter. At the top of the steps, the pilgrims offer more prayers at the shrine.

Some Kusu pilgrims set off for their pilgrimage while it is still dark, believing that it is especially auspicious to be there at first light to offer their prayers and joss sticks. A pilgrimage on the double ninth — the ninth day of the ninth month — is thought to be especially meritorious. Once a pilgrim, always a pilgrim, so each year the crowds can only grow larger. Getting to Kusu at all at this time means jostling with the throng of pilgrims, most of whom tote bags of fruit and rice, bottles of oil, bunches of chrysanthemums and marigolds and other offerings.

Deepavali

Serangoon Road, or Little India, is the place to be at Deepavali. This Festival of Lights (*deep* meaning light and *avali* garland) is the most important feast celebrated by Hindus. It celebrates the victory of light over dark, good over evil, when Lord Krishna vanquished the demon Narakasura, freed 16,000 virgins and then made honest women of them all by marrying the lot at one go. The lights are to guide Lakshmi, the Goddess of Prosperity, to one's home.

Deepavali is usually celebrated in October and November, and several weeks before the day, Serangoon Road is garlanded with lights and decorations. On the day itself, Hindus rise before first light, take an oil bath, don new clothes and visit the temple for prayers. Priests offer burning camphor and, after prayers, distribute holy ash and water, sandalwood paste, *kumkum* (vermilion powder) and flowers to devotees. Devotees bring trays of betel leaf, bananas, camphor and fresh flowers to the temple priests and exchange them for similar trays and a broken coconut, which is taken home for the family altar.

Some modern features, like the street light-up, raised eyebrows at first. Deepavali Thaathaa still does. Thaathaa (Tamil for 'grandfather'), modelled on the gift-giving Santa Claus, was created here in 1970 as a figure to whom Hindu children could relate and will in time, one supposes, become as accepted as electric lights. Beauty contests, though frowned on by the more religious, are also held at this time, and the Deepavali Queen quest aroused considerable controvesy in 1987, when it included a swimsuit parade for the first time.

Merlion Week

This carnival week in November is a warm-up act for Christmas. Just as the Merlion figure was created at the behest of Singapore tourism, so is Merlion Week. This does not mean, however, that it is not fun. Merlion Week is particularly enjoyable if you like powerboat racing, beauty parades, masked balls, fashion shows, food fairs and fireworks. Singapore crowns Miss Tourism during Merlion Week and hosts the International Singapore Powerboat Grand Prix in Marina Bay.

Christmas at the Equator

The Singapore Tourist Promotion Board knew they were on to a good thing when they decided to light up Orchard Road for the shopping season. The annual light-up contest, in which stores, shopping centres and hotels try their best to outshine one another, was conceived during the mid-1980s in the trough of an unprecedented slump in visitor arrivals. It was an immediate hit with Singaporeans and visitors alike, who thronged the Orchard malls taking in the sights and snapping innumerable photographs.

A choir from a local Christian congregation performing atop a specially built structure decorated with lights create the Singing Christmas Tree. This is usually on a vacant lot near the Mandarin Singapore on Orchard Road. Most hotels and shopping centres not only deck the halls but also hire choirs and carolling groups to perform. One group of singers recently made it to *The Guinness Book of World Records* for non-stop carolling. Most churches hold midnight services on Christmas Eve and some hold Christmas pageants as well. Carolling usually starts earlier.

Singapore Festival of Arts

This biennial festival—usually occurring in June—is a month-long feast of music, dance and drama during which local companies perform alongside visiting international companies. As with many other such festivals, a Fringe Festival runs concurrently. The Singapore Festival of Arts will next be held in 1994.

Books About Singapore

General

Clammer, John. *Singapore: Ideology, Society, Culture* (Singapore: Chopmen Enterprises, 1985)

Flower, Raymond. *Raffles: The Story of Singapore* (Singapore: Eastern Universities Press, 1984)

Hoe, Irene and Lloyd, R. Ian. *Singapore from the Air* (Singapore: Times Editions, 1985)

Landmark Books. *The Original Singapore Sling Book* (Singapore: Landmark Books, 1986)

Ministry of Communications and Information. *Singapore Facts and Pictures* (Singapore: Ministry of Communications and Information) Published annually.

Nair, C. V. A. Devan. *Not by Wages Alone: Selected Speeches and Writings of C. V. Devan Nair, 1959–1981* (Singapore: National Trades Union Congress, 1982)

Reith, G. M. ; revised by Makepeace, Walter. *1907 Handbook to Singapore* (Singapore: Oxford in Asia Paperbacks, 1985)

Saw Swee Hock and Bhathal, R. S., eds. *Singapore Towards the Year 2000* (Singapore: Singapore University Press, 1980)

The Place

Archives and Oral History Department of Singapore. *Chinatown: an Album of a Singapore Community* (Singapore: Times Books International, 1983)

Beamish, Jane and Ferguson, Jane. *A History of Singapore Architecture: The Making of a City* (Singapore: Graham Brash, 1985)

Berry, Linda. *Singapore's River: A Living Legacy* (Singapore: Eastern Universities Press, 1982)

Doggett, Marjorie. *Characters of Light: Early Buildings of Singapore* (Singapore: Times Books International, 1985)

Edwards, Norman and Keys, Peter. *Singapore: A Guide to Buildings, Streets, Places* (Singapore: Times Books International, 1988)

FEB International/Singapore Broadcasting Corporation. *Changing Landscapes: Geylang, Chinatown, Serangoon* (Singapore: FEP International/ Singapore Broadcasting Corporation, 1983)

Gretchen, M., Lloyd, R. Ian and Stewart, Ian C. *Pastel Portraits* (Singapore: Singapore Coordinating Committee, 1984)

Heinemann and National Archives. *Geylang Serai, Down Memory Lane* (Singapore: Heinemann & National Archives, 1986)

Hoe, Irene and Lloyd, R. Ian. *Chinatown, a Personal Portfolio* (Singapore: MPH, 1984)

Lee Kip Lin. *Emerald Hill* (Singapore: National Museum, 1984)
Lip, Evelyn. *Chinese Temples and Deities* (Singapore: Times Books International, 1986)
Times Books International. *Singapore Lifeline: The River and Its People* (Singapore: Times Books International, 1986)

The People

Cheo Kim Ban. *A Baba Wedding* (Singapore: Eastern Universities Press, 1983)
Chia, Felix. *The Babas* (Singapore: Times Books International, 1980)
Lee Siow Mong. *A Spectrum of Chinese Culture* (Petaling Jaya, Malaysia: Pelanduk Publication, 1986)
MPH. *Muslims in Singapore* (Singapore: MPH, 1984)
Nathan, Eze. *The History of Jews in Singapore 1830–1945* (Singapore: Herbilu Editorial & Marketing Services, 1986)
Saw Swee Hock and Wong, Aline K. *Youth in Singapore: Sexuality, Courtship and Family Values* (Singapore: Singapore University Press, 1981)
Siddique, Sharon and Purushotam, Nirmala. *Singapore's Little India* (Singapore: Institute of Southeast Asian Studies, 1982)
Sullivan, Margaret. *Can Survive, La: Cottage Industries in High-Rise Singapore* (Singapore: Graham Brash, 1985) A study of Singaporean craftsmen.
Winstedt, Richard O. *The Malays: A Cultural History* (London: Graham Brash, 1981)
Yen Ching Hwang. *A Social History of the Chinese in Singapore and Malaya, 1800–1911* (Singapore: Oxford University Press, 1986)

History

Archives and Oral History Department/Singapore News and Publications Ltd. *Pioneers of Singapore* (Singapore: Archives and Oral History Department, 1984)
Archives and Oral History Department/Singapore News and Publications Ltd. *Road to Nationhood: Singapore 1819–1980* (Singapore: Archives and Oral History Department/Singapore News and Publications Ltd, 1984)
Archives and Oral History Department/Singapore News and Publications Ltd. *The Japanese Occupation, 1942–1945* (Singapore: Archives and Oral History Department/Singapore News and Publications Ltd, 1985)
Buckley, Charles B. *An Anecdotal History of Old Times in Singapore* (Singapore: Oxford University Press, 1984)
Choo, Alexandra A. *Report on the Excavation of Fort Canning Hill Singapore* (Singapore: National Museum, 1986)
Harper, R .W. E. *Singapore Mutiny* (Singapore: Oxford University Press, 1984)

Hill, A. H., trans. *The Hikayat Abdullah: The Autobiography of Abdullah bin Kadir (1797–1854)* (Singapore: Oxford University Press, 1985)

Makepeace, Walter. *One Hundred Years of Singapore* (London: John Murray, 1923) This two-volume book is out of print but may be read in National Library's Southeast Asia collection).

Miksic, John. *Archaeological Research on the 'Forbidden Hill' of Singapore: Excavations at Fort Canning, 1984* (Singapore: National Museum, 1985)

Ministry of Culture. *Singapore, An Illustrated History, 1941–1984* (Singapore: Information Division, Ministry of Culture, Singapore 1984)

Montgomery, Brian. *Shenton of Singapore: Governor and Prisoner of War* (Singapore: Times Books International, 1984)

National Museum. *National Monuments of Singapore* (Singapore: National Museum, 1982)

Pearson, H. F. *Singapore: A Popular History* (Singapore: Times Books International, 1985)

Quahe, Yvonne. *We Remember* (Singapore: Landmark Books, 1986)

Sharp, Ilsa. *There is Only One Raffles: The Story of a Grand Hotel* (London: Published for Times Books International by Souvenir Press, 1981)

Song Ong Siang. *One Hundred Years History of the Chinese in Singapore* (Singapore: Oxford University Press, 1984)

Tan Kok Seng. *Son of Singapore: The Autobiography of a Coolie* (Singapore: University Education Press, 1972)

Turnbull, Constance M. *A History of Singapore, 1819–1975* (Kuala Lumpur: Oxford University Press, 1977)

Warren, James Francis. *Rickshaw Coolie* (Singapore: Oxford University Press, 1986)

Wise, Michael, ed. *Travellers' Tales of Old Singapore* (Singapore: Times Books International, 1985)

Wurtzburg, Charles. *Raffles of the Eastern Isles* (Singapore: Oxford University Press, 1984)

Natural History

Bhathal, R. S. *A Guide to Pond Life* (Singapore: Singapore Science Centre, 1981)

Briffett, Clive. *A Guide to the Common Birds of Singapore* (Singapore: Science Centre, 1986)

Ede, Amy and John. *Living with Plants: A Gardening Guide for Singapore and Malaysia* (Singapore: MPH, 1980)

Fleming, W. A. *Butterflies of West Malaysia and Singapore* (Kuala Lumpur: Longman, 1983)

Foo Tok Shiew. *A Guide to Common Garden Animals* (Singapore: Singapore Science Centre, 1987)

Foo Tok Shiew. *A Guide to the Wild Flowers of Singapore* (Singapore:
Singapore Science Centre, 1985)
Hails, Christopher and Jarvis, Frank. *Birds of Singapore* (Singapore: Times
Editions, 1987)
Nathan, Anne et al. *A Guide to Fruits and Seeds* (Singapore: Singapore
Science Centre, 1987)
Polunin, Ivan. *Plants and Flowers of Singapore* (Singapore: Times Editions,
1987)
Teoh Eng Soon. *A Joy Forever: Vanda Miss Joaquim, Singapore's National
Flower* (Singapore: Times Books International, 1982)
Wee Yeow Chin. *Common Ferns and Fern-Allies of Singapore* (Singapore:
Malayan Nature Society [Singapore Branch], 1984)

Society

Craig, JoAnn. *Culture Shock!* (Singapore: Times Books International, 1986)
Singapore International Chamber of Commerce. *Expatriate Living Costs in
Singapore* (Singapore: Singapore International Chamber of Commerce, 1986)
Toh Paik Choo. *Eh Goondu!* (Singapore: Eastern Universities Press, 1983)
Toh Paik Choo. *Lagi Goondu* (Singapore: Times Books International, 1986)
Tongue, R. K. *The English of Singapore and Malaysia* (Singapore: Eastern
University Press, 1979)
Wong, C. S. and Pinsler, Ronni. *An Illustrated Cycle of Chinese Festivities in
Malaysia and Singapore* (Singapore: MPH, 1987)

Government, Politics and Law

Asiapac Books and Educational Aids. *The Legal Status of Singapore Women
by Singapore Association of Women Lawyers* (Singapore: Asiapac Books and
Educational Aids, 1986)
Bloodworth, Dennis. *The Tiger and the Trojan Horse* (Singapore: Times
Books International, 1986)
Buchanan, Iain. *Singapore in Southeast Asia* (London: G Bell & Sons, 1972)
Chan Heng Chee. *David Marshall: A Sensation of Independence* (Singapore:
Oxford University Press, 1984)
Chan Heng Chee. *The Dynamics of One-Party Dominance: the PAP at the
Grassroots* (Singapore: Singapore University Press, 1976)
Clutterbuck, Richard. *Conflict and Violence in Singapore and Malaysia
1945–1983* (Singapore: Graham Brash, 1984)
Drysdale, John. *In the Service of the Nation* (Singapore: Federal Publications,
1985)
Drysdale, John. *Singapore: Struggle for Success* (Singapore: Times Books
International, 1984)
Fong Sip Chee. *The PAP Story: The Pioneering Years* (Singapore: Published

for the PAP Chai Chee Branch by Times Periodicals, 1980)
George, T. J. S. *Lee Kuan Yew's Singapore* (London: Andre Deutsch, 1973)
Josey, Alex. *Lee Kuan Yew: The Struggle for Singapore* (London: Angus & Robertson, 1980)
Ministry of Culture. *Biographical Notes of the President, Prime Minister and Ministers* (Singapore: Public Division, Ministry of Culture, 1977 [periodically updated])
People's Action Party. *People's Action Party 1954–1984: Petir 30th Anniversary Issue* (Singapore: Central Executive Committee, People's Action Party, 1984)
Rajaratnam, S. *The Prophetic and the Political* (Singapore: Graham Brash, 1987)
Thomas, Francis. *Memories of a Migrant* (Singapore: University Education Press, 1972)
Vasil, Raj K. *Governing Singapore* (Singapore: Eastern Universities Press, 1987)

The Economy

Lim Chong Yah. *Economic Restructuring in Singapore* (Singapore: Federal Publications, 1984)
Lim Chong Yah. *Policy Options for the Singapore Economy* (Singapore: McGraw-Hill, 1988)
Ministry of Trade and Industry. *Economic Survey of Singapore* (Singapore: Ministry of Trade and Industry) Quarterly and annual.
Ministry of Trade and Industry. *Singapore Economy, New Directions* (Singapore: Ministry of Trade and Industry, 1986)
Pillai, Philip N. *State Enterprise in Singapore* (Singapore: Singapore University Press, 1984)

Directories and Other Reference Works

Singapore Census of Population, 1980 (Singapore: Department of Statistics)
Singapore Street Directory (Singapore: Survey Department, 1988)
Who's Who in Malaysia and Singapore, 1983–1984 (Petaling Jaya, Malaysia: Who's Who Publications Sdn. Bhd, 1983) Singaporean personalities are found in vol 2.
Yearbook of Statistics (Singapore: Department of Statistics)

Singapore's Lee Kuan Yew

The impact that Lee Kuan Yew has had on his country can be conveyed in just four words. These words are the title of a book: *Lee Kuan Yew's Singapore*. The book, by T J S George, is highly critical (some would say prejudiced) which might explain its exclusion — along with other equally critical tomes — from the government yearbook's bibliography of works on Singapore.

But yes, this *is* Lee Kuan Yew's Singapore, a country dominated by the vision of the man who served as Prime Minister for 32 years. Possibly no other head of government has ever exercised so much influence over a country or had the satisfaction of seeing so many of his ideas translated into reality within his lifetime. Perhaps no other ever will.

While the entire country may be regarded as a kind of monument to his ideas, those ideas specifically exclude a proliferation of busts and statues of the man himself. Public monuments to Lee Kuan Yew - even if executed for private reasons with private means - are out. A bronze bust of Lee exists but resides out of sight somewhere in the National Museum's storehouses.

You will also have a tough time tracking down biographies of the man. One such attempt was first published in 1968. Written by his one-time press secretary, Alex Josey, who died recently, the two-volume book was reissued in a revised edition in 1971 but is not even in print now.

Simply titled *Lee Kuan Yew*, it is largely a summary of Lee's public speeches. However, the most absorbing part of the book is the opening pages of the first chapter, entitled 'Early Days', from which we learn that Lee always has scrupulously clean hands and neatly filed fingernails, seldom reads for distraction, makes friends slowly, watches his weight and is a firm believer in keeping fit.

'Every morning he does exercises, which include press-ups, skipping, and arm exercises with small weights. He has a very light breakfast, sips Chinese tea throughout the day, and makes dinner, also never heavy, his main meal. He enjoys a glass or two of wine in the evening,' wrote Josey.

Of Lee's pedigree, we learn that he is the eldest son of a retired employee of the Shell Company, Lee Chin Koon, who apparently still works in a watch and jewellery shop, and Chua Jim Neo, who died some years ago. Well-known for her Straits Chinese cooking, Chua was the author of a book of recipes titled *Mrs Lee's Cookbook*, which still sells well.

There is no authorized biography of Lee for the same reason that there are no public monuments: Lee abhors the cult of personality. Visitors will find no words engraved in marble extolling 'Our Glorious Leader' nor any inspirational thoughts from that leader embalmed in a political bible.

Paradoxically, no other democratically elected leader has so closely approached deification in the eyes of his people—particularly those old enough to remember what Singapore was like when Lee took over as Prime Minister on 5 June 1959. Lee was not yet 36 years old, but his People's Action Party had won 43 of 51 seats in the Legislative Assembly after weeks of campaigning.

He had married Kwa Geok Choo, a lawyer, nine years earlier. Both had been top scholars, having gained double firsts in law at Cambridge University. The eldest of their three children, Lee Hsien Loong, was just seven years old. Now often referred to as 'BG', in recognition of his rank as a brigadier-general in the reserves, Lee Hsien Loong is a cabinet minister.

As for how the elder Lee became a politician, he has said publicly that he did not enter politics. 'The Japanese brought politics to me,' he said, referring to the Japanese occupation of Singapore during World War II. Lee's nationalism was born out of a sense of outrage that foreigners could invade the country and order its people around. Still, Lee learned Japanese well enough to work as a translator for the official news agency. Despite his wartime experience, but also because of it, he is one of the few leaders in Asia (perhaps the only one) to urge his people to 'learn from the Japanese', a policy by which Singapore has clearly profited.

While he has on occasion spoken about himself and his family — usually to make a political point — Lee keeps his family life more private than do many world leaders. This keeps the gossip mills humming. However, Josey has written (but not in his biography): 'There is no secret Lee. Lee Kuan Yew is the same man offstage as he is onstage. Over the years he has become more secure and less aggressive. He has developed a sense of humour. He believes few Singaporeans can run the City-state as efficiently as he does . . . he likes his job. He rarely reads anything written about him. I doubt if he will write his memoirs. He prefers the judgement of history to the praise or criticism of contemporary writers.'

Practical Information

Hotels

Starting Above $250 per Night

ANA Hotel, Singapore
16 Nassim Hill, Singapore 1025. Tel: 732-122. Telex: RS33545. Fax: 732-222.

454 guest rooms and suites, business centre, health centre, conference facilities, disco, florist. A $20 million renovation programme was completed last year.

Goodwood Park Hotel
22 Scotts Road, Singapore 0922. Tel: 737-7411. Telex: RS24377. Fax: 732-8558.

127 single/double rooms and 108 suites. Chinese seafood, Sichuan, Shanghainese, Japanese restaurants, coffee shop, grill room, gourmet deli and bakery. Accepts Enroute, Carte Blanche, JAL and JCB cards.

Hilton International Singapore
581 Orchard Road, Singapore 0923. Tel: 737-2233. Telex: RS21491. Fax: 732-2917.

14 single rooms, 392 double rooms and 29 suites. Health centre, office and secretarial services, disco and flourist. A shopper's hotel. Givenchy floor has a dozen suites with a personalized concierge and valet service. Three no-smoking floors. Have high tea in the Music Room or champagne brunch on Sunday in the Orchard Cafe. Chinese and Continental restaurants.

Hyatt Regency Singapore
10-12 Scotts Road, Singapore 0922. Tel. 733-1188. Telex: RS24415. Fax: 732-1696.

317 single/double rooms, 431 suites. Tennis, squash and badminton courts. 24-hour business centre, fitness centre, banqueting and conference facilities. Cheery Italian restaurant. American restaurant has a jazz band in the evening, good cafe serving local and Western food, a wine and champagne bar, disco.

Mandarin Singapore
333 Orchard Road, Singapore 0923. Tel: 737-4411. Telex: RS21528. Fax: 732-2361.

1200 single/double rooms, 24 executive suites, three senior executive suites, 20 regency suites and five presidential suites. Central position on Orchard Road. Shopping arcade, health centre, nightclub, disco. Chinese, French, Japanese restaurants and grill room. 24-hour coffee shop: Chatterbox.

Marina Madarin, Singapore

6 Raffles Boulevard, Marina Square, Singapore 0103. Tel: 338-3388.
Telex: RS22299. Fax: 339-4977.

Deluxe rooms, 48 suites, 3 executive floors. Health centre, tennis and squash courts, conference and banqueting facilities, disco, office and secretarial services. Close to financial and commercial districts. Part of large complex. Close to the airport.

Le Meridien Singapore

100 Orchard Road, Singapore 0923. Tel: 733-8855. Telex: RS50163. Fax: 732-7886

413 rooms, 16 suites. Two rooms designed for handicapped guests. Private dining room for club guests. Lounge area for afternoon tea and cocktails, library, meeting room, office concierge and butler. Two French restaurants and a Hunanese restaurant. Charming garden. Good bakery. Accepts Carte Blanche and JCB.

The Oriental, Singapore

5 Raffles Avenue, Marina Square, Singapore 0103. Tel: 338-0066. Telex: RS29117. Fax: 339-9537.

418 single/double rooms and 100 suites. Squash and tennis courts, health centre, garden, jogging track, gift shop, office and secretarial services, conference and banqueting facilities. Part of a shopping and hotel complex. Close to business and financial districts. 15 minutes from the airport. Accepts Carte Blanche and JCB.

Pan Pacific Singapore Hotel

7 Raffles Boulevard, Marina Square, Singapore 0103. Tel: 338-8111.
Telex: RS388821. Fax: 339-1861.

763 single/double rooms and 37 suites. 24-hour butler service, private library, laundry, dry-cleaning valet services thrown in. Business centre (24-hours), ten food and beverage outlets including Chinese, Polynesian and Japanese restaurants, Continental grill room, deli. Disco and entertainment lounge, tennis courts, health centre, free in-house video.

Raffles Hotel

1-3 Beach Road, Singapore 0718. Tel: 337-8041. Telex: RS21586. Fax: 339-7650.

The *grande dame* of hotels in Singapore was restored recently and upgraded to an all-suites establishment. There are 12 food outlets, a business centre and health centre which operate 24 hours. The hotel even has its own theatre. Guests are ferried from the airport to the doorstep in vintage cars, part of the "back to the 1930s" ambience. 104 suites.

Shangri-La Singapore
22 Orange Grove Road, Singapore 1025. Tel: 737-3644. Telex: RS21505.
Fax: 733-72220/733-1029.

750 single/double rooms and 60 suites. A businessman's hotel with a 24-hour
business centre, three-hole pitch and putt for avid golfers, health centre, indoor pool,
squash and tennis courts, disco, shopping arcade. Excellent French restaurant: Latour,
(reservations essential). Also Japanese and Chinese restaurants, 24-hour coffee shop.
Accepts JCB.

Westin Stamford/Westin Plaza
2 Stamford Road, Singapore 0617. Tel: 338-8585. Telex: RS22206. Fax: 338-6862.

Westin Stamford: 591 single rooms, 578 double rooms and 80 suites. Health centre,
squash and tennis courts. Accepts JCB. Westin Plaza: 501 single rooms, 238 double
rooms and 47 suites. As above but with in-house video.

Both are part of the Raffles City complex, which also includes an office tower,
shopping centre, the Japanese department store Sogo, supermarket, post office, banks,
boutiques and Tourist Information Centre. Complex has a total of 17 restaurants and
lounges as well as a major convention centre in the hotel. Take in the sunset from the
Compass Rose lounge or the restaurant at the top (reached by express lift). Excellent
Italian restaurant: Prego, or eat Indonesian, *Nasi Padang* at the Rendezvous restaurant. The Raffles City atrium is becoming a frequent venue for music and other
performances.

Starting Below $250 per Night

Boulevard Hotel Singapore
200 Orchard Boulevard, Singapore 1024. Tel: 737-2911. Telex: RS21771.
Fax: 737-8449.

507 single/double rooms and 23 suites. Complimentary coffee and tea-making
facilities, good local food in coffee shop. American restaurant, Cantonese and
northern Indian restaurants. Accepts Enroute, Carte Blanche, JCB and JAL cards.

Crown Prince Hotel
270 Orchard Road, Singapore 0923. Tel: 732-1111. Telex: RS22819. Fax: 732-7018.

285 single/double rooms and 18 suites recently renovated. Well located for shopping.
Business centre, 24-hour room service, mini-bar, 24-hour complimentary in-house
video movies in room. Adjoining Esprit store. Excellent upscale Japanese restaurant,
Sushi Nogawa Kaiseki. The coffee shop is popular with locals. Sichuan restaurant.
Accepts JCB.

Excelsior Hotel
5 Coleman Street, Singapore 0617. Tel: 338-7733. Telex: RS20678. Fax: 339-3847.

113 single rooms, 147 double rooms and 12 suites. In historic colonial district, within easy walking distance of Fort Canning Park, a bus ride away from Chinatown. Close to city shopping. City Hall MRT station and Raffles City. Adjoining arcade has the country's best Indian vegetarian restaurant: Annalakshmi.

Glass Hotel
317 Outram Road, Singapore 0316. Tel: 733-0188. Telex: RS50141. Fax: 733-0989.

217 single rooms, 266 double rooms and 26 suites. Cabaret/nightclub. Close to Chinatown. As we go to press, under receivership but still functioning. Good but pricey Italian restaurant. Near the large Japanese department store, Isetan.

Hotel Grand Central
22 Cavenagh Road, Singapore 0922. Tel: 737-9944. Telex: RS24389. Fax: 733-3175.

349 single/double rooms and 12 suites. Shops, tour desk and travel agencies, gift shop, Japanese and Sichuan restaurants. Just off Orchard Road and across the road from Le Meridien Orchard.

Imperial Hotel Singapore
1 Jalan Rumbia, Singapore 0923. Tel: 737-1666. Telex: RS21654. Fax: 737-4761.

325 single rooms, 171 double rooms and 30 suites. Overlooks a Hindu temple. Close to Orchard Road, Liang Court Shopping Centre and antique shops on River Valley Road. Health centre, office and secretarial services, disco, conference and banqueting facilities, Sichuan, French and north Indian restaurants, jewellery and souvenir shops, drugstore, tailor.

King's Hotel
Havelock Road, Singapore 0316. Tel: 733-0011. Telex: RS21931. Fax: 732-5764.

118 single rooms, 198 double rooms and three suites. Next door to Isetan Department Store and Apollo Hotel, close to Chinatown. Photo-processing mini-lab, souvenir shop, office and secretarial services. Sichuan restaurant, 24-hour coffee shop, Japanese teppanyaki restaurant. Interesting piano bar, catering to Japanese men.

Omni Marco Polo Hotel Singapore
247 Tanglin Road, Singapore 1024. Tel: 474-7141. Telex: RS21476. Fax: 471-0521.

573 single/double rooms and 30 suites. In-house movies, disco, health centre, florist, conference rooms, office and secretarial services, bakery. Quality French food at La Brasserie. Also Continental cuisine, coffee shop, cocktail lounge with live music.

Ming Court Hotel Singapore
1 Tanglin Road, Singapore 1024. Tel: 737-1133. Telex: RS21488. Fax: 733-0242.

257 double rooms, 26 suites and 17 Tai Pan Club executive rooms. Located at end of main shopping area. Health centre, hairdresser, tailor, shops. Sidewalk café ideal for people-watching, the coffee shop has Malaysian cuisine, Japanese and Chinese restaurants. Accepts JCB.

Hotel Miramar
401 Havelock Road, Singapore 0316. Tel: 733-0222. Telex: RS24709.

335 single/double rooms and 11 suites. One of string of hotels on Havelock Road, close to Chinatown and the Singapore River. Health centre, tour desk, conference facilities, office and secretarial services.

Novotel Orchid Inn, Singapore
214 Dunearn Road, Singapore 1129. Tel: 250-3322. Telex: RS21756. Fax: 250-9292.

222 single rooms, 241 double rooms and 241 suites. Located in a prime residential area. The coffee shop and Sichuan restaurant (Dragon City) are well-patronized by locals. Also a French restaurant. Accepts JCB.

The Regent of Singapore
1 Cuscaden Road, Singapore 1024. Tel: 733-8888. Telex: RS37248. Fax: 732-8838.

230 single rooms, 128 double rooms and 65 suites. Pretty atrium, designer boutiques, exhibits of works by young local artists in lobby. Health centre, business centre, conference facilities. Cantonese and French restaurants, (the latter a branch of the Parisian Maxim's bakery. Within walking distance of Orchard Road.

Royal Holiday Inn Crowne Plaza
25 Scotts Road, Singapore 0922. Tel: 737-7966. Telex: RS21818. Fax: 737-6646.

34 single rooms, 329 twin rooms, 54 double rooms, 49 king leisure rooms, 19 studios, seven suites and one Presidential suite. Re-opened February 1990 after massive renovation. Strategically located within shopping/hotel/business/ entertainment district. Business centre, continental restaurant, Sichuan restaurant, 24-hour coffee shop, bar/lounge, personal safe in each room, swimming pool, banquet/convention facilities.

Tai-pan Ramada Hotel Singapore
101 Victoria Street, Singapore 0718. Tel: 336-0811. Telex: RS21151. Fax: 339-7019.

358 twin rooms, 115 double rooms and 11 suites. Also 16 apartments. Business centre, mini-bar, Sichuan restaurant, in-house movies, souvenir shop, tailor, complimentary shuttle bus (weekdays excluding public holidays) to business, entertainment and shopping districts.

York Hotel
21 Mount Elizabeth, Singapore 0922. Tel: 737-0511. Telex: RS21683. Fax: 732-1217.

315 single/double rooms and 85 suites. Adjacent to the Goodwood Park Hotel on Scotts Road. Health centre, complimentary tea and coffee-making facilities. 24-hour room service, florist, tailor, newsstand, bar with two resident bands. Serves local, Continental and Russian cuisine. Accepts Enroute, Carte Blanche, JCB, JAL.

Starting Below $100 per Night

Apollo Hotel Singapore
405 Havelock Road, Singapore 0316. Tel: 733-2081. Telex: RS21077. Fax: 733-1588.

232 single rooms, 63 double rooms and 22 suites. Conference facilities as well as office and secretarial service, nightclub/disco. Chinese, Indonesian and Japanese restaurants. Adjoining Japanese department store Isetan. At the time of writing, the hotel is being renovated. Features and prices may, therefore, be subject to change. Accepts JCB.

Harbour View Dai-Ichi Hotel Singapore
81 Anson Road, Singapore 0207. Tel: 224-1133. Telex: RS40163. Fax: 222-0749.

144 single/double Superior, 253 single/double Executive rooms, 21 suites and two *tatami* suites for sleeping Japanese style. Hotel in the business and financial district close to Chinatown and Tanjong Pagar MRT station. Business centre, conference rooms, Japanese restaurant, steak house, coffee shop, lounge, hair salon, boutique and souvenir shop.

Garden Hotel
14 Balmoral Road, Singapore 1025. Tel: 235-3344. Telex: RS50999. Fax: 235-9730.

143 twin rooms, 59 double rooms, seven suites and seven family rooms. In-house medical service, two swimming pools, gym and sauna, book and gift shop, florist, local and Western cuisine. Accepts Carte Blanche, Access, Barclays and Eurocard.

Ladyhill Hotel
1 Ladyhill Road, Singapore 1025. Tel: 737-2111. Telex: RS23157. Fax: 737-4606.

169 single/double rooms and one suite. Some rooms open directly onto pool area. Conference facilities, barbers, hairdresser, tailor, complimentary coffee and tea-making facilities, bar with resident band, 24-hour room service. Coffee shop with good local cuisine and friendly service. Also Swiss restaurant.

Peninsula Hotel
3 Coleman Street, Singapore 0617. Tel: 337-2200. Telex: RS21169. Fax: 339-3580.

301 single/double rooms and seven suites. Close to historic colonial district and city shopping. Mini-bar, hairdresser, shopping arcade, nightclub/disco, conference facilities, office and secretarial services. Coffee shop with good local cuisine.

RELC International House
30 Orange Grove Road, Singapore 1025. Tel: 737-9044. Telex: RS55598. Fax: 733-9976.

127 double rooms and 15 suites. Rates include American breakfast for two. Next door to plush Shangri-La Hotel. Conference and banqueting facilities, auditorum, IDD call facility, decent Sichuan restaurant, local and Western food in separate restaurant. No pool.

Hotel Bencoolen
47 Bencoolen Street, Singapore 0718. Tel: 337-0251.

61 single/double rooms and eight suites. In-house movies in room, IDD calls and telex facility, tour desk. MasterCard and Visa accepted.

New Seventh Storey Hotel
229 Rochor Road, Singapore 0718. Tel: 337-0251.

Four single rooms, 34 double rooms. The country's tallest hotel when it first opened. Close to Raffles Hotel, Arab Street and Kampong Glam. Fifteen minutes by car from airport, somewhat longer by bus (SBS service 390). No credit cards accepted.

Sloane Court Hotel
17 Balmoral Road, Singapore 1025. Tel: 235-3311/2/5. Telex: RS55058.

One single and 31 double rooms. Homey atmosphere. Rooms with private bathroom, telephone, and colour television. Office and secretarial services. No pool. Within a bus ride or 20-minute walk of Orchard Road area. Restaurant and pub serves Western cuisine. Visa, MasterCard and American Express accepted.

YMCA Singapore International House
1 Orchard Road, Singapore 0923. Tel: 337-3444. Telex: RS55325. Fax: 337-3140.

87 single/double rooms, six deluxe rooms, five superior rooms and 13 dormitories. Next to the National Museum, close to major shopping centres. Swimming pool, health centre, business centre, tour desk, games room, table tennis and billiards, courts for squash and badminton, drugstore, hair salon, conference facilities, IDD call facility, nightclub/disco, cafeteria serving local food, McDonald's outlet. Best value for the budget traveller.

Restaurants

Food from the provinces of China dominates the flavours of Singapore, because the Chinese community is the largest one here. There is no single national cuisine but a multitude of ethnic cuisines deriving from the country's multicultural origins and embracing the offerings of north and south India as well as Malay and Indonesian cooking. Nonya, or Peranakan, cooking is a unique cuisine developed after centuries of Chinese settlement in this region. Japanese, Thai, European and even Mexican food is easily available in fine restaurants everywhere. It is usually quite safe to eat and drink at open-air food centres, or what locals term 'hawker centres', but follow your instincts. Many food centres now use disposable crockery and cutlery.

Be warned that some places can be very expensive. Moreover, a restaurant that is otherwise inexpensive may have expensive dishes on the menu. Few restaurants display their menu outside, but you can ask to see one before you sit down. Some menus, even in what appear to be inexpensive Chinese restaurant, list no prices, and it is prudent to ask the price before ordering. This is especially true of seafood places, which are generally fairly pricey anyway and almost always have a large section of the menu marked simply 'market price'. Do the same at places like the Newton Food Centre (much frequented by tourists) to avoid a misunderstanding.

Chinese

Ban Seng Restaurant
79 New Bridge Road, Singapore 0105. Tel: 533–1471, 534–3637. Teochew.

Beng Thin Hoon Kee Restaurant
05–02 OCBC Centre, 65 Chulia Street, Singapore 0104. Tel: 533–0649. Hokkien.

Capital Restaurant
207 Cantonment Road. Tel: 221–3516. Credit cards accepted. Cantonese.

Cherry Garden Chinese Restaurant
The Oriental Singapore, 5 Raffles Avenue, Marina Square, Singapore 0103.
Tel: 338–0066. Sichuan.

Fook Yuen Seafood Restaurant
South Bridge Centre, 001–01, 95 South Bridge Road, Singapore 0105.
Tel: 532–7778. Also, Level 3, Paragon Shopping Centre, 290 Orchard Road,
Singapore 0923. Tel: 235–2211. Cantonese.

Jade Room Restaurant
Hotel Royal, 36 Newton Road, Singapore 1130. Tel: 254–8603. Open 11.30 am –
3 pm and 6.30 – 10.30 pm. Beijing.

Liang Kee
Block 1, Tew Chew Street 02–406, Singapore 0105. Tel: 534–1029. Teochew.

Min Jiang Sichuan Restaurant
Goodwood Park Hotel, 22 Scotts Road, Singapore 0923. Tel: 737–7411. Credit cards
accepted. Sichuan.

Mooi Chin Palace Restaurant
109 North Bridge Road, Funan Centre 01–05, Singapore 0617. Tel: 339–7766. Also,
Block 157, Ang Mo Kio, Avenue 4, 01–546, Singapore 2056. Tel: 459–7766.
Hainanese.

New Nam Thong Tea House
8-10A Smith Street, Singapore 0105. Tel: 223–2817. Breakfast daily 4 – 9.30 am.
Cantonese.

Ng Mui Song Eating House
268 River Valley Road, Singapore 0923. Tel: 235–6983. Open 6 am – noon daily and
6 pm – 1 am except Monday. Pork rib soup speciality. Teochew.

Sin Wah Coffee Shop
62 Joo Chiat Place, Singapore 1542. Tel: 344–0830. Open daily 8.30 am – 4.30 pm.
Nonya and Hokkien.

Spice Garden
Hotel Meridien, Level 3, 100 Orchard Road, Singapore 0923. Tel: 732–4122. Credit
cards accepted. Hunanese.

Tung Lok Shark's Fin Restaurant
177 River Valley Road, 04–07/09 Liang Court Complex, Singapore 0617.
Tel: 336–6022. Cantonese.

Local

Cafe Carousel
Boulevard Hotel, 40 Cuscaden Road, Singapore 1024. Tel: 737–2911. 24-hour coffee
house.

Silver Spoon Coffee House
6 Raffles Boulevard #03-242, Marina Square, Singapore. Tel: 337-8363/337-9450
Open 10–3 am.

Seafood

Jack's Seafood Garden
Automobile Association House, 336 River Valley Road, Singapore 0923.
Tel: 235–2336.

Kheng Luck Restaurant
Block 1204 UMDC Seafood Centre, East Coast Parkway, Singapore 1648.
Tel: 444–5911.

Long Beach Seafood Restaurant
610 Bedok Road (Bedok Rest House), Singapore 1646. Tel: 444–2922/445–8833.
Credit cards accepted.

Long Island Garden Seafood
220 Stadium Road (Kallang Park), Singapore 1439. Tel: 344–7722/344–2228. Credit
cards accepted.

Palm Beach Restaurant
National Stadium, Kallong Park, Singapore 1439. Tel: 344–1474

Indian

Hock Tien Keat Coffee Shop
54 Serangoon Road, Singapore 0821. Tel: 337–0010. Open 5.30 am – 9.30 pm.
Indian.

Moti Mahal
18 Murray Street, Singapore 0207. Tel: 221–4338. Credit cards accepted. North
Indian.

Muthu's Curry Restaurant
76/78 Race Course Road, Singapore 0821. Tel: 293–2389. South Indian.

The Tandoor
Holiday Inn Parkview, 11 Cavenagh Road, Singapore 0922. Tel: 733–8333: North Indian.

Indonesian, Malay, Nonya

Baba Café
25B Lorong Liput, Singapore 1027. Tel: 468–9859. Laksa Friday to Sunday. Closed Monday. Nonya.

Nonya and Baba Restaurant
262 River Valley Road, Singapore 0923. Tel: 734–1382/6. Nonya.

Rendezvous Restaurant
4/5 Bras Basah Road, Singapore 0718. Tel: 337–6619. Also, 02–19 Raffles City Shopping Centre, Stamford Road/North Bridge Road, Singapore 0617.
Tel: 339–7508. Indonesian.

Japanese

Keyaki Restaurant
Pan Pacific Hotel, Marina Square, 6 Raffles Boulevard, Singapore 0103.
Tel: 336–8111 ext. 4433.

Mitsubachi Singapore Coffee Shop
02–114 Lucky Plaza, 304 Orchard Road, Singapore 0922. Tel: 235–2772. Japanese coffee house.

Nanko Sushi
Daimaru Basement Supermarket, 177 River Valley Road, Singapore 0617.
Tel: 339–1111.

Senbazuru Japanese Restaurant
Level 6, New Otani Hotel, 177A River Valley Road, Singapore 0617. Tel: 338–3333.

Unkai Japanese Restaurant
Century Park Sheraton 02–00, Nassim Hill, Singapore 1025. Tel: 732–1222 ext. 1589. Credit cards accepted.

Korean

Kam Han Kguk Korean Restaurant
Golden Mile Complex 02–93, 5001 Beach Road, Singapore 0718. Tel: 296–2522. Credit cards accepted.

The Korean Restaurant
Specialists' Shopping Centre 05–32, Orchard Road, Singapore 0922. Tel: 235–0018. Credit cards accepted.

Polynesian

Tiki
Pan Pacific Hotel, 2nd Level Marina Square, 6 Raffles Boulevard, Singapore 0103.
Tel: 336–8111. Credit cards accepted.

Thai

Coco Steamboat Restaurant
Chinatown Plaza 02–10, 34 Craig Road, Singapore 0208. Tel: 221– 0883.

Parkway Thai Restaurant
Parkway Parade 02–08, 80 Marine Parade Road, Singapore 1544. Tel: 348–0783. Thai buffet lunch except Sundays and public holidays at $12.50++ ($6++ for children under 12). Also, Centrepoint 01–59/62, 176 Orchard Road, Singapore 0922.
Tel: 737–8080. Credit cards accepted.

Vegetarian

Annalakshmi Restaurant
Excelsior Hotel & Shopping Centre 02–10, 5 Coleman Street, Singapore 0617.
Tel: 339–9993. Open 8 am – 9.30 pm, except Thursday until 5 pm. Indian vegetarian.

Kingsland Vegetarian Restaurant
Block 34 Whampoa West 01-27, Singapore 1233. Tel: 298–2506. Also, People's Park Complex 03–43/46, Eu Tong Sen Street, Singapore 0105. Tel: 532–2651. Chinese vegetarian.

Western

Belvedere
Mandarin Hotel, 333 Orchard Road, Singapore 0923. Tel: 737–4411. French.

Compass Rose
70th Floor, Westin Stamford, 2 Stamford Road, Singapore 0617. Tel: 338–8585.
Continental.

El Felipe's Cantina
34 Lorong Mambong, Singapore 1027. Tel: 468–1520. Mexican.

La Brasserie
Omni Marco Polo Hotel Singapore, Tanglin Circus, Singapore 1024. Tel: 474–7141.
Open noon – 3 pm and 7 pm – midnight. Credit cards accepted. French.

Manhattan Grill
Boulevard Hotel, 40 Cuscaden Road, Singapore 1024. Tel: 737–2911.

Maxim's de Paris
Level 3, The Regent of Singapore, 1 Cuscaden Road, Singapore 1024.
Tel: 733–8888. Credit cards accepted. French.

Milano Pizza
Parkway Parade B1–18, 80 Marine Parade Road, Singapore 1543. Tel: 345–5303.
Italian.

Movenpick
B1–01 Scotts Shopping Centre, 6 Scotts Road, Singapore 0922. Tel: 235–8700. Credit
cards accepted. Also, B1–01 Standard Chartered Bank Building, 6 Battery Road,
Singapore 0104. Tel: 221–0340. Swiss.

Prego
3rd Floor Westin Stamford, 2 Stamford Road, Singapore 0617. Tel: 338–8585. Italian.

Restaurant
1819 Tuan Sing Towers B1, 30 Robinson Road, Singapore 0104. Tel: 223–4033.
Open 1 – 3 pm and 7 – 11 pm except Sundays and public holidays. Continental.

Restaurant Latour
Shangri-La Hotel, 22 Orange Grove Road, Singapore 1025. Tel: 737–3644. French.

Index

Practical information such as telephone numbers, opening hours and hotel and restaurant prices is notoriously subject to being outdated by changes or inflation. The author welcomes corrections and suggestions from guidebook users; please write to The Guidebook Company Ltd, The Penthouse, 20 Hollywood Road, Central, Hong Kong.